The Money Men

The Money Men

The Real Story of Fund-raising's Influence on Political Power in America

Jeffrey H. Birnbaum

CROWN

Published by Crown Publishers, New York, New York.
Member of the Crown Publishing Group.

Random House, Inc. New York, Toronto, London, Sydney, Auckland
www.randomhouse.com

CROWN is a trademark and the Crown colophon
is a registered trademark of Random House, Inc.

Printed in the United States of America

DESIGN BY SUSAN HOOD

Library of Congress Cataloging-in-Publication data is available.
ISBN 0-812-93119-X

10   9   8   7   6   5   4   3   2   1

First Edition

To my newest prize
Emily Birnbaum

And to the other Birnbaums as well
Esther, Deborah, Michael, and Julia

Contents

Author's Note

You can spend a lot of time reading the fine print of campaign-finance law, but if you really want to understand the culture, you need to know about chum.

Properly speaking, chum is chopped-up or live fish that hunters throw into the water in order to attract other fish. In the slang of campaign fund-raising, *chum* refers to the cheesy souvenirs that—believe it or not—never fail to attract big donors: cuff links embossed with the presidential seal and pen sets "signed" by the president or some other high-profile pol. You know: cheap giveaways from inside official Washington.

These are among the most coveted trophies in the money-raising world. One former White House aide who is now a big-name lobbyist still regrets that he never insisted that his old boss, President George Bush, give him one of the "good pairs" of presidential cuff links, which have bumpy—not flat—gold-colored seals. Former chairman of the House Committee on Ways and Means Dan Rostenkowski hadn't been so shy. He had a friend who wanted a good pair. So during one of his many meetings with Bush, the Illinois Democrat actually took the pair that the president himself had been wearing, leaving Bush with his cuffs flapping in the breeze.

This reveals one point that's usually missed about campaign money: Fund-raising is sometimes a function of pettiness and vanity, not greed and corruption, as is popularly believed.

There's a lot that's true—and important—about campaign fund-raising that nonetheless is overlooked. In fact, most people see no difference between one campaign-finance story and another. And who can blame them? The elements are always the same: a huge amount of money—more than ever before—pours into the coffers of Congressman A or Party B, corrupting not only our government but our entire way of life.

Of course nobody wants to read about *that*. It's so predictable and, worse, unpreventable. Why bother?

That's why I've written this book.

If you assume that campaign money is so distasteful that you don't want to hear any more about it, you're closing your mind to one of the most fundamental and most fascinating stories in American politics. It's okay to be outraged—more than okay. But it's wrong to be so disgusted that you don't want to read another word.

You miss all the good parts that way.

Take, for example, the real-life picture we should have of our elected officials. It's wrong to think of them sitting studiously through boring congressional hearings or making speeches to Rotary Club luncheons. Think of them, instead, in windowless offices grubbing for money almost every spare moment they get. Fund-raising is so essential to their reelections yet takes so much time that politicians have invented a virtual science of efficient solicitation.

Here's the typical scene: The lawmaker or would-be lawmaker sits at a desk surrounded by telephones. Aides seated nearby (there are usually two or three aides, but I've heard about instances involving as many as eight) dial up contributors and stay on the line until the would-be fund giver comes on. Then they put that person on hold until the lawmaker gets to their line. The politician is thus able to move seamlessly from one begging session to another, and groveling can go on nonstop.

So there's a picture for the ages: democracy on hold, literally.

Here's another one: Around a conference table in the suite of the Speaker of the House, just steps from the Capitol Rotunda, a dozen lobbyists and trade-association executives plot strategy with the highest-ranking lawmakers in Congress. This isn't an occasional meeting. It happens every week. On Thursday. At 11 A.M. It even has a title: the Thursday Group.

When Republicans took control of the House of Representatives in January 1995 after forty years in the minority, they reached out to their most loyal backers—in large measure their *financial* backers—and rewarded them with seats at that table. And they, in turn, used that position to help House Republicans pass Newt Gingrich's Contract with America, which was, in effect, their wish list, ranging from limits on corporate lawsuits (a favorite of the U.S. Chamber of Commerce) to an increase in tax breaks for stay-at-home moms (beloved by the Christian Coalition).

The point is that money men are *players*. They aren't dark figures lurking in the background, plotting political intrigue. They are central to the drama. They make a difference in the way laws are made and implemented. Without them, the politicians wouldn't *be* politicians. And they insist on, and invariably get, politicians' attention. That's the way it works.

When new members of Congress come to Washington, they don't know anybody except the few fellow lawmakers who came out to stump for them and the handful of money men who, in effect, financed their campaigns. This small circle is the most pervasive influence on any lawmaker throughout his or her career.

Think of it as the Them-That-Brought-You-to-the-Party syndrome. Add to these few people an eventual network of former staffers (who also end up raising money, by the way) and you have the makings of almost any circle of power in the nation's capital.

And therein lies an irrevocable condition of legislation: Few voters know anything about what goes on in Washington other than what appears in the headlines. But the relatively small group of industries, labor unions, and wealthy individuals who have interests in the capital know *everything*. And more often than not, these same people insert themselves into the inner circles of lawmakers, usually as money men.

This means that all those scare stories about vote buying are only partly true. A rich interest group can't just show up and buy legislation. In fact, late-arriving funds in any policy battle are worthless unless they're part of a much larger and longer-term scenario of access and insider activity. The real money men are the ones who are there early, stay late, and are more than just people who write checks.

They are people such as Steve Hart, a lobbyist and major Republican money man, who routinely sat in on high-level strategy meetings of GOP lawmakers and their staffs, in part because he also served as lawyer to their fund-raising committees. They are people such as Dirk Van Dongen, president of the dowdy National Association of Wholesaler-Distributors, who helped organize the Thursday Group and also once raised two million dollars for a gala at the 1996 Republican national convention in San Diego. They are John Sweeney, the president of the AFL-CIO, who is responsible for the election or reelection of more Democrats to Congress than anyone else.

These are money men who bring more than money. They are advisers. They are activists. They are vote getters and vote counters. They are friends to the powerful. They are kingmakers. And they are crowned princes of the Potomac. They are part and parcel of the culture that pervades our nation's capital. They are people few of us know, but we all should if we care what happens to the laws of our land.

This book isn't an exhaustive documenting of the ins and outs of campaign fund-raising. It is more of an introduction to an important world that most of us think we know but really don't. It also is *my* rendition of that world and doesn't purport to be the last word or the "right" answer about anything. It is the culmination of what I have learned—or I think I have learned—after many years on the beat.

I have been covering money and politics in one way or another ever since I came to Washington in 1982 as a reporter for *The Wall Street Journal.* I was first immersed in the topic in 1984 when I was given one of the *Journal*'s most coveted beats, tax legislation. That sounds boring, but for *The Wall Street Journal* it was exciting and absolutely essential because tax law sits at a volatile nexus of government and business—in other words, it is the home turf of money politics.

As a result, the tax-law beat and ones much like it had been entrusted over the years by the *Journal* to some able and now well-known reporters—Bob Novak, now of CNN and the Chicago *Sun-Times;* Paul Duke, later of *Washington Week in Review;* Mike Miller, now of the *Los Angeles Times;* Bob Merry, now of *Congressional Quarterly;* and Al Hunt, still of the *Journal,* who hired me for the job. I have always felt privileged to be a member of such an elite club.

I was even more fortunate because I was assigned to cover what turned out to be the most sweeping rewrite of the tax code since the inception of the income tax, the Tax Reform Act of 1986. That was the Super Bowl of lobbying and the most intensive education in the ways of the money men that anyone could ever want.

With Alan Murray, I went on to write my first book, *Showdown at Gucci Gulch,* which is the inside story of that tax bill. But I didn't stop thinking or writing about the influence of money. I continued to cover Congress and national politics. And I always learned more about either topic by hanging out in the halls with lobbyists or chatting up old friends at fund-raising receptions. Money men know, and it was my job to find out.

As my next book project, I took a close-up look at lobbyists, following several of them around for two years. *The Lobbyists* was their story, real names and all. Later, as a senior political correspondent for *Time* magazine, I covered factional politics that ranged from the gun lobby to trial lawyers. I also detailed the dealings of the Thursday Group.

When later I was named bureau chief of *Time*'s sister publication *Fortune,* I was encouraged to design several stories that focused on power and money. One set of stories sprang from an annual survey of Washington insiders that we did to rank the most influential lobbying groups in town. It's called the Power 25. I also wrote about the presidential money chase leading to the 2000 presidential election, including the new trick on the scene, Internet giving. Those articles compelled me to keep in near-constant contact with a handful of the nation's top political fund-raisers, which in turn made *Fortune* among the first publications to foresee the George W. Bush financial juggernaut.

Senator John McCain's rousing successes that stemmed from attacks on money men aced the need for a new book. Campaign contributions are a big political issue, and that's ample reason to learn more about them. So, after all these years of work in the vineyards, I thought I would try my hand at filling that need. To that end, I make you two promises.

First, I will strive to speak in laymen's language. I have learned that the rest of the country is so alienated from Washington that the only way to tell what I know is to write as if I were the bureau chief of a foreign capital. Second, I will try to steer clear of the kinds of information you expect to read. The real story is so much more compelling.

Jeff Birnbaum
Washington, D.C.

The Money Men

1

Why You Should Care

Almost everyone who works in official Washington eventually has what can be described as the Moment: that instant when they finally realize that money plays too big a role in politics, way too big. Not that it's a surprise. No one can possibly be happy with a system that compels politicians to spend a third of their time begging for contributions. Yet it's still a shock to see the bazaar up close. It's one thing to know and another to see with your own eyes. It makes a difference.

One of my friends experienced his Moment in the mid-1980s when he worked as a press secretary for a southern congressman. At the time, the lawmaker was a hot commodity: He was undecided on whether to vote to fund construction of the B-1 bomber. The Reagan administration, frantic for support, wanted his backing very badly, so White House aides were eager to bargain. In a meeting one day, my friend witnessed the deal as it was struck. The congressman pledged to vote to fund the aircraft in exchange for a VIP tour of the White House for twenty or thirty of his largest and most loyal campaign contributors. The congressman didn't ask for a new dam or a new road or a new grant to help his neediest constituents. Instead, he traded his greatest power, his vote on the House floor, to please the handful of people who *really* matter to him: the money men who were so key to his reelection.

Campaign cash, and lots of it, buys advertisements that, in turn, lure voters to the polls. The more money, the more votes. It's that simple and that venal. Money talks, at least on TV and radio. And the candidate who can put more of his or her ads onto the public airwaves (and local cable channels) has the better chance of winning. Period.

That's why lawmakers and executive-branch appointees assist their moneyed constituents whenever they think they can get away with it. They can't always, of course, and big donors are sometimes losers in the game of legislation. Still, it is the rare lawmaker who doesn't keep handy—or at least keep in mind—the list of his or her best financial friends. When they call, they are listened to. And conversely, when the lawmakers call them, the donors jump. (Lawmakers often *demand* contributions, which to the givers seem more like shakedowns.) In any case, it's a symbiotic—or, more accurately, a parasitic—relationship that absorbs too much of our leaders' attention. It also is part of a deeply ingrained system that's as difficult to fix as it is horrific to behold.

But behold it we must. On the threshold of a presidential election, the time is right to focus on this important corner of public policy. We all know vaguely that something is wrong in Washington, especially with its money culture. I hope to show how the money chase works and, in some cases, how we think it works but doesn't really. Only then can we think clearly about how we can—and cannot—change it for the better.

Washington is awash in campaign cash. It has flooded over the gunwales of the ship of state and threatens to sink the entire vessel. Political donations determine the course and speed of many government actions that—though we often forget—will deeply affect our daily lives. The deluge of dollars pouring into lobbying and elections is one of the main reasons Americans are turned off by Washington and its arcane ways.

Like so much of what goes on in the nation's capital, fundraising is widely misunderstood. Yes, political giving in its many forms is hugely important. And yes, all of us would be better off if a lot of political giving had never seeped into the system. Yet not all donations are offered for nefarious purposes, nor do they always lead to nefarious ends. In fact, the individuals or groups that give the most don't always win. The relationship between contributions and government action is much more complicated than mere quids and quos.

One thing is clear. Political giving is raging like wildfire. George W. Bush shattered all records in his run for president. Indeed, the combination of a surging stock market and huge political stakes have made 2000 the Year of the Firehose. Campaign cash is gushing everywhere now, but the situation has been developing for many years. In one out of six congressional races in 1998 at least one of the candidates spent one million dollars. That was ninety-four candidates in seventy-six congressional districts. Just a decade earlier, only ten House candidates reached the million-dollar mark. The last presidential election cycle cost just over two billion dollars, a record. This time, expect the first three-billion-dollar campaign.

Election experts used to think that fewer than one hundred thousand people would give one thousand dollars to a presidential candidate during any election. Few believe that anymore. According to Wayne Berman, a Republican fund-raiser in New York and Washington, "because of the incredible prosperity America is experiencing, people who used to give two hundred and fifty dollars come up with one thousand dollars. New and younger people are stepping up as well. Who knows what the limit is?" Berman's friend Peter Terpeluk is even more exuberant. "There's a money wave the likes of which we've not seen in Republican presidential politics," he said.

Money, money everywhere. But not all of it carries the same weight. And not all of it goes to candidates. The laws and rules that govern political fund-raising are many and peculiar. They also are largely ignored. As we move more deeply into the subject, the distinctions between the kind and size of campaign gifts will become clearer. But here is the short version.

At the federal level, the most that any person can donate to a candidate is one thousand dollars per election. Political-action committees (PACs), which are amalgams of individuals, can give five thousand dollars. But that's just the start. Individuals, labor unions, and corporations can give as much as they want to political parties. That's the so-called soft money or, more appropriately, sewer money. This money, in effect, is used to make a mockery of the limits on direct giving to candidates. Think of it as legal cheating. And there are a lot of other ways to give huge gifts as well.

In other words, a thousand dollars doesn't buy much for the donor anymore. Not a photo with the candidate. Not a thank-you note. It barely gets folks into a chip-'n'-dip reception. Congressman Tom DeLay of Texas, the most powerful member of the House of Representatives, encouraged former staffers to raise twenty-five million dollars from a relatively small number of wealthy individuals to counterbalance the even larger amounts that will be pouring into congressional races from the AFL-CIO. The bulk of both of these financing schemes will come in hundred-thousand-dollar dollops. The notion, spawned after the Watergate scandal in the 1970s, that campaign finances should be limited and fully disclosed has been, in effect, completely undermined.

"It doesn't take much imagination to deliver as big a check as you're capable of writing," says Larry Makinson, executive director of the nonpartisan Center for Responsive Politics. "Even if you don't know where to send it, somebody can tell you the name of the committee."

We live, then, in a new era: the Greed Era. The candidate or interest group with the largest treasury has a massive advantage. As a candidate, the fuller your bank account, the higher your chance of victory in political skirmishes. But, like the cold war, these aren't one-sided battles. Everybody who comes to compete brings a bundle of cash. The more one side antes up, the more the other side raises in response. This is true in elections and in fights in Congress over legislation. There's an arms race in political-money land, escalating all the time.

Here's what that means: The country's first presidential primary is held not in New Hampshire but on K Street in Washington (the lobbyists' main drag), on Wall Street in New York City, and on Michigan Avenue in Chicago. The presidential wanna-bes of both parties don't just court run-of-the-mill voters; they spend at least as much time wooing the wealthy few who make megabucks along those famous thoroughfares. Winning their support is the true first contest of the election season. The presidential candidates who are able to collect the magic sum of fifteen million dollars by the time of the New Hampshire primary are the only ones who have any chance of attaining their party's nomination. And the only way to raise that much is to charm the money men.

The number of people who give is quite small. In 1968, only 8 percent of the adult population gave contributions in any amount to any candidate or party—local, state, or federal. By 1992, the figure had dropped to 4 percent, according to the Center for Responsive Politics. In 1992, almost 80 percent of all the funds contributed to congressional campaigns came from PACs (the great majority of which were corporate PACs), from individuals contributing two hundred dollars or more (who constituted less than one third of 1 percent of the total population), or from wealthy candidates themselves. Overall, business accounted for approximately half the total, out-contributing labor by seven to one.

Although small, this elite world is seeing dynamic change. A new generation is taking hold as we move into a new century. Top fund-raisers estimate that at least a third of the contributors to the presidential campaign of George W. Bush were completely new to the process. Even larger numbers were brought in by John McCain and by Bill Bradley on the Democratic side. The Lew Wassermans of Hollywood and the Robert Mosbachers of Houston are beginning to fade from the scene, and younger go-getters, in their thirties and forties, are taking their places. There is a changing of the guard all over the country. General Motors's Max Fisher, the grand old man of Detroit Republican donor chasing, has handed the reins to Heinz Prechter, a maker of sunroofs. Berman and Terpeluk were disciples of Mosbacher. Ever a competitive lot, fund-raisers fight for preeminence with each other— nowhere more so among Democrats than in Los Angeles, where David Geffen of DreamWorks SKG, businessman Eli Broad, and Ron Burkle of Yucaipa Companies battle to be number one.

Why? What makes people want to give or, more important, raise political contributions? The reasons are much more diverse than most people think. Some raise funds at the highest level to get a job in the next administration. Nearly a quarter of the top fund-raisers in the 1996 Clinton campaign became ambassadors during the second Clinton administration. Some raise to gain status in their communities. After all, being the big man's guy in town makes that person a big man himself. Other fund-raisers are Washington groupies or idealists or so rich that they can dabble in anything that amuses them, such as politics. And, yes, some raise funds for coarsely self-interested reasons, especially professional lobbyists.

But money raising is not just about one thing.

At the same time, we have more cause than ever to care about the influence of money on politics. The reason is that our system of government is slowly falling apart. Fewer and fewer people vote, yet more and more money is drenching the electoral and legislative process. Ergo, the exclusive crew of financial contributors have more and more clout in the capital.

Put more sharply, the most significant fact about fund-raising has nothing to do with money. Rather, it is this: Most Americans know little and care less about the substance of most decisions made in Washington. National policy making has become little more than light entertainment on cable-television channels. The only time people really notice the federal government is when it does something to anger them or when serious problems afflict the nation. Even in times of crisis, citizens pay attention to the Beltway gang for only a brief while. At least, that's been the recent pattern.

Ever since the cold war ended with the collapse of the Soviet Union in the late 1980s and the bulls began their long run on Wall Street in the early 1990s, Washington hasn't played as much of a role in Americans' daily lives. With no life-threatening enemy to protect us from and no economic downturn to recover from, the U.S. government has struggled to justify its existence, at least on major matters.

The result has been a distinct and disturbing disconnection between the government and the people it's supposed to serve. Government's actions have been more like those of a soap opera than those of a real representative democracy. Its language has become focused on process, not results. The only relationships that seem to matter in official Washington are incestuous ones that maintain power for the people who already have it.

The alienation is enormous. At the height of the debate over the impeachment of President Clinton at the end of 1998, a Fox News/Opinion Dynamics poll asked whether people believed that their daily lives would be affected if Clinton was forced to leave office. Fewer than a third of those polled said yes. Two thirds said the change would matter not at all or only a little.

The federal government, in other words, is suffering from a serious lack of respect. The Pew Research Center for the People and the Press found in late 1998 that a hair-raising 68 percent of Americans were frustrated with or outright angry at Washington. A quarter century earlier, by contrast, 70 percent of Americans said they had at least a fair amount of confidence in the U.S. government to handle domestic problems.

Rather than get mad and try to change the system—to make it work for them—most Americans have given up. They don't vote. Less than half of eligible Americans, sometimes far less than half, even bother going to the polling booth. The 1996 presidential election had the lowest turnout in nearly seventy years for a presidential ballot—only 49 percent. In 1998, voter turnout was so small that in some districts candidates for the House of Representatives were elected with fewer than one in five of the possible votes. True, 72 million people voted in 1998. But 116 million people who could have voted didn't. That 38 percent was the lowest turnout rate since 1942. Though 7.5 million more Americans were eligible to vote—and at least 5.5 million of them did register—than in 1994, the number of citizens voting fell by more than 2.5 million, according to the Committee for the Study of the American Electorate. The outlook is for continued declines, especially in nonpresidential election years.

Americans also are woefully ill informed about their government. A breathtaking number of people stopped recently on a midwestern street by a television-news crew couldn't explain the difference between the House and the Senate. One woman stated with confidence that the Starr report on the Lewinsky affair was authored by Ringo Starr. According to a survey not long ago, 40 percent of Americans can't even name the vice president.

These aren't small problems. Lack of knowledge about Washington doesn't stop Washington from doing what it does. Neither does ignoring the place. In fact, neglect only makes things worse for the average American. Here's why: Everybody has an opinion, but increasingly only zealots vote. And that's the nub of the problem with campaign fund-raising: Most people don't care and don't know about Washington, but the people who do care and do know run the show. And that is especially true for the moneyed interests.

Lawmakers give all sorts of reasons for why they cast votes as they do on controversial matters. "It was the right thing to do" is their favorite, and more often than the cynics suspect it can even be true. Most people think congresspeople decide how to vote based on national polls, gauging the direction of public opinion and going that way as quickly as they can. In reality, there are relatively few votes on which a lawmaker will ever buck his or her party. Many other votes are dictated by local or regional needs. For instance, the senator from Kansas will always vote pro-wheat. Idahoans are predictably pro-potato.

But on those few issues where lawmakers actually have a choice, a poll of sorts *is* taken, but not the big, national polls most of us associate with the term *poll.* What really matters on such votes is careful nose counting of select activists. Thanks to low voter turnout, a meticulous assessment of, say, the support of organized labor by a Democrat or of small-business leaders by a Republican may prove pivotal. Any lawmaker who can persuade and mobilize the groups that are his or her loyalists has a fighting chance at surviving almost any controversial vote.

In any district or state, there is a solid phalanx of voters for each party who can be counted on to vote in any election. The winner, then, is the candidate who can attract the voters who are on the margins. In the alternative, candidates can work to flush out folks who don't normally vote. That was the key to victory for Jesse Ventura in his surprise election as governor of Minnesota in 1998.

In either case, money is central. Ventura didn't have more money than his opponents, but he had enough to get himself heard. It would be wrong to state flatly that campaign cash determines the outcome of elections. At the same time, it would be naive to suggest that money doesn't have a major role. In the entire House of Representatives, there are only a few dozen truly competitive races in any election year. (Of the 435 seats up for grabs in the 1998 election, less than forty were ever in doubt.) The incumbents so hugely outraised their potential opponents that there was never a chance for most challengers to get into the race.

So here's the picture. Very few elections are contests. Most lawmakers can take their reelections for granted, thanks to the advantage of incumbency, which includes huge fund-raising abilities. In those elections that are competitive, fewer and fewer people decide the winner. Indeed, the mobilization of blocs of voters often determines the outcome. In other words, groups that have the resources to organize voters or who can, through campaign contributions, buy political advertising that has the same effect, have a disproportionate say in who runs the nation's capital.*

To penetrate the fund-raising world, to understand the sway it holds, you must stop thinking big. Instead, think small. Very small. A small audience and a huge amount of campaign—or lobbying—cash. That's the formula that makes the labors of the money men so intriguing, and dangerous.

Despite the public's lethargy, elections do have consequences because what the government does can be ignored only at one's peril. It makes a difference who the president is and what he or

---

*Naturally, these money men are also the people or interests most deeply affected by government decisions. Hence the problem.

she believes. It makes a difference who runs Congress and in what way. When times are flush, a government's actions may seem less consequential, but they never really are. Everywhere you turn, Uncle Sam is sticking his nose in our business.

This is obvious on big-ticket items. When Congress hikes or cuts taxes, when a new highway or bridge is built, or when the president launches a missile attack, we know about it and tend to care, especially if we're personally caught in the action. No ambiguity there.

But most of what Washington does isn't so overt. In fact, it appears most of the time as if Washington is gradually pulling back from its formerly monumental impact on the average person's life. Whenever you look, you hear about another industry being deregulated. The drumbeat for tax cuts is growing ever louder. And few people advocate *more* government programs anymore. But this is an illusion. Behind the veil, strings are still attached. Looser controls on commerce and budget surpluses have only emboldened the bureaucracy. "The number of rules and their costs keep increasing," Pietro Nivola, a regulatory expert at the left-leaning Brookings Institution, told *Fortune*. "And that is the wave of the future."

Pushing the trend are legions of bureaucrats that remain mostly unknown to the public but that have a lot of power. The people in charge of Congress and the White House exercise considerable control over these largely unseen regulators. And there are lots of them. In the Clinton administration, there were the headline-grabbing heads of giant cabinet departments, such as Carol Browner of the Environmental Protection Agency, Bruce Babbitt of the U.S. Department of the Interior, and the people in key posts at the Occupational Safety and Health Administration (OSHA) and the Federal Communications Commission. Who sits in these important chairs is determined by who wins elections. This is even more true below this very visible level. Many of the most searing decisions are made by people almost no one has heard of who work for these top names. For instance, most Americans never knew Terry Medley. But the forty-six-year-old administrator of the Animal and Plant Health Inspection Service in the U.S. Department of Agriculture held the future of fruits and vegetables in his hands. Without fanfare, he had overseen the development of regulations dealing with genetically altered plants for a decade, and since the United States is essentially setting international standards as well, he became a thorn in the side of agribusinesses all over the world. Or take Michael Davis of the Army Corps of Engineers. Only farmers and real-estate developers knew much about the forty-one-year-old deputy assistant secretary for policy and legislation. But in their arena, Davis was huge. He was the man behind Permit 26, which reduced the size of a wetland plot that came under the corps' scrutiny to three acres from ten and thus vastly increased his office's heft. The home builders' lobby called the new regulation "a stake through the heart of the development community."

And where do these bureaucrats and regulators come from? They are appointed by the president and confirmed by the Senate. In other words, they are the products of elections—elections that by and large the money men pay close attention to and control disproportionately.

Money politics leads to perverse results in government policy. Here's one: Contrary to what you might suspect, the last thing that many politicians really want is to win, at least when it comes to legislation. Take the deficit issue. After decades of budget deficits, the federal government now predicts annual surpluses. No party wanted to end the deficit more than the GOP. "The Republicans have won the deficit issue!" GOP pollster Frank Luntz exulted at the first indication of the taming of the deficit. "What could be better?"

Losing the deficit issue, that's what. Elected officials often dread seeing their most cherished goals actually become law. When that happens, they have nothing new to promise and no way to distinguish themselves from their opponents. And, more significant, they have no way to instigate their givers to pull their wallets out. Republican pollster Tony Fabrizio terms this phenomenon "victory disease" and worries that his party has a bad case. Now that the Democrats have agreed to balance the budget, cut taxes, and restrain federal spending—all longtime GOP slogans—what can Republicans criticize? The Republican Party hasn't been so bereft in victory since the cold war ended. "I'm not convinced we as a party are prepared for this vacuum," Fabrizio lamented to *Fortune.*

The biggest beneficiaries of the Republican victory have turned out to be Democrats and their fund-raising. From now on, most budgetary battles will be waged on turf friendly to them. Congress will no longer be consumed with finding ways to cut government spending—Republican territory—and will focus instead on how to allocate the revenue it has. As it happens, the programs Americans like best—education, health care, environmental protection—have all been staked out by Democrats and are central to their desire for federal activism.

On the other hand, if the economy stops roaring ahead at its breakneck pace of late, it's also possible the deficit will come back. One way or the other, declares Republican consultant Mike Murphy—almost wistfully—"the deficit will be back!" At least that's what Republicans hope.

Here's a bold statement and, for the most part, a true one: The Federal Election Commission is the most ineffective agency in Washington. On purpose. No lawmaker worth his voting card wants a powerful regulator overseeing his election. So Congress and a long series of presidents have arranged not to have one. If you want to know why our system of campaign finance has gotten so out of hand, look no further.

The agency has been impotent since it first started in 1975. The reason is simple: It can't muster a majority on any issue that matters. The agency is one of the few independent regulators whose governing commission is divided equally along party lines. It has three members appointed by the Democrats and three members appointed by the Republicans. That means that any significant controversy is never resolved. All actions are blocked by three-three ties.

Lots of important decisions have been derailed, according to the Center for Responsive Politics. The commission is supposed to audit the campaigns of presidential candidates who accept public funding. That's most of them, and it's a very big job. During the audit of President Clinton's 1992 campaign, FEC auditors found that the campaign had used a questionable accounting method to secure more than three million dollars in public funds as a way to repay debts incurred during the primaries. The commission's three GOP members agreed with the auditors and wanted the Clinton campaign to refund to the Treasury the full three million. The three Democrats on the commission united against any repayment and said the dubious accounting system was justified. In the end, the stalemate resulted in no repayment, though the commissioners did recommend that the law be "clarified" to prevent similar problems in the future. In the meantime, the Clinton campaign got a windfall.

The FEC, in fact, has made a mockery of Washington regulating. It's been illegal for corporations to donate money to federal candidates since 1907. It's been illegal for labor unions to do so since 1947. And since 1974, it's been illegal for an individual to contribute more than one thousand dollars to a candidate. Yet thanks to the FEC, these laws are violated in spirit almost every day. In an otherwise obscure ruling in 1978, the FEC opened the door to unlimited soft-money giving by allowing corporations, labor unions, and individuals to donate to the national parties. Ten years later, the Dukakis and Bush presidential campaigns took advantage of the loophole and began the trend that has put the fund-raising system under its darkest cloud.

It's easy to find fault with the way the United States funds its elections. Too much money sloshes around, creating the temptation for fraud, thievery, and outright corruption. Politicians spend too much time shaking down moneyed interests for cash, time that would better be spent thinking about the vast majority of people who never contribute a dime. Even the staunchest defenders of the status quo believe that the system can be improved.

What isn't so obvious, and what's harder to know, is how the system actually works. Beyond the general wisdom, or rather, the cartoonish expectation of election fund-raising, is a very real, very active world that has been a part of the American scene as long as there's been an America. Like it or not, money and politics mix and always will, no matter what the best-intentioned reformers prefer. Nobody in elective office is pure when it comes to campaign finance.

To understand what's wrong with political fund-raising one must first know what it is. In other words, one must be conversant with what's normal, accepted, and routine. Only then can one see, by contrast, where the problem lies. In addition, some of the most awful things about routine behavior aren't apparent without looking more closely than usual at the system as it stands.

My credo, and the credo of my wonderful colleagues, who share this acquired journalistic taste, is to follow the money. Find out whose financial interest is on the line in any congressional dustup and the "why" behind the "what happened" comes quickly into focus.

The longer I look, though, the more misconceptions I see about this peculiar world. One is fundamental. Politics is about large promises and incremental action. Lawmakers are forever pledging to end poverty or welfare or taxes or you name it. But they can never do any of those things. Our Democratic processes are set up to prevent rash acts by balancing competing interests. Fund-raising to support politics is very much the same. We always hear about how terrible fund-raising is. It's corruption incarnate, a blight on the body politic. In fact, most political donations come as surely as the sun rises and sets. Many politicians have little trouble raising money and have more of it than they need.

Nor is it true that run-of-the-mill contributions are inevitably bad. A thousand dollars is a lot of money to most people. And relatively few people ever give the legal maximum to candidates. Ninety-six percent of Americans don't give a penny to any politician or political party in Washington. Thousand-dollar contributions come from one tenth of 1 percent of the population. But enough people are givers at the thousand-dollar level or near to it to mitigate the corrupting effect of a single contribution of that size. I have never heard of a lawmaker selling a vote for so little money. The desperate grab for cash has made even the maximum contribution insignificant on the influence meter.

The rapid growth of giving over the Internet also has widened the circle of people who make political donations. The election of 2000 started what could become a revolution in campaign finance. Thousands of new contributors were enticed by the ease of Internet giving, and millions of their dollars poured into the coffers of candidates, particularly at the presidential level. The kings of this trend were the insurgent candidates, Democrat Bradley and Republican McCain. McCain in particular received a rush of contributions via cyberspace after his landslide victory in the New Hampshire primary. Since Internet giving was still in its infancy, McCain continued to rely mostly on money men to fatten his treasury. At the same time, the cyberdonations amounted to millions of dollars, though the average Internet gift to McCain was just over one hundred dollars.

Indeed, it is apparent that tracking such modest contributions can be a leading indicator of popular support for a candidate. When George W. Bush announced in mid-1999 that he had raised thirty-seven million dollars in increments of a thousand dollars or less and that only one third of that money came from his home state of Texas, what we learned was that he was widely accepted by Republicans across the nation as the man to beat for the nomination. More important than the actual amount that Bush collected, in fact, was the number of people who shelled out for his campaign: an astounding and politically impressive seventy-five thousand at that stage alone. By year end, it was 171,000.

The potential for wrongdoing comes in what happens above and outside this routine system. The real powers in politics are not necessarily the people with big wallets but the ones with large Rolodexes. Given the huge demand for thousand-dollar checks, no candidate can simply reach out for donors one at a time. The candidate, rather, usually relies on well-connected volunteers to solicit large numbers of their friends and associates. These check gatherers are the most influential people in the money chase. The Bush campaign called its top gatherers Pioneers. They each committed to raise one hundred thousand dollars—in other words, to contact at least a hundred of their friends and associates and persuade them each to give the Bush campaign a thousand dollars. That's hard work and one reason why that kind of funds is called "hard money."

If you want to look for people who qualify as "special interests" with clout in the halls of the Capitol, look to the major solicitors of thousand-dollar checks for the candidate who wins an election. Bush's more than 150 Pioneers will likely include a disproportionate number of ambassadors should the governor be elected president.

Then there are the soft-money givers. No one can make a good case that six- or seven-figure contributions to the political parties do not convey undue influence. They do. Money buys access, and lots of money buys lots of access. That's why the money is spent in the first place. The national parties, as well as individual candidates for office, literally sell face time with themselves and their most prominent associates for established amounts of campaign contributions.

The most precious commodity in Washington isn't money (as it is in most every other major city in America). It is the time of elected officials and of senior executive-branch appointees. Even the newest of congressmen, let alone senior lawmakers, have every minute of their day consumed by meetings, speeches, and gatherings of all sorts. Because of their importance, money men get a greater share of that time than any other citizen. And as a result, the worldviews of our national decision makers are inevitably skewed. Hang out with millionaires, and you begin to think like millionaires. Who knows what our governmental leaders might otherwise think and do if they didn't have to pander to the people who pad their political pockets?

What they wind up doing is sometimes bad enough. Bernard Schwartz was one of the biggest soft-money givers to the Democratic Party. He dumped hundreds of thousands of dollars into the coffers of the Democratic National Committee. As one perk of his generosity, he got to ride with the president in Air Force One. Schwartz contended that his fealty to the Democrats was the result of deep conviction and philosophical sympathy. His donations, he said, had nothing to do with the fact that the company he chaired, Loral Space and Communications, made satellite technology that could be exported only with the U.S. government's okay. Even if that was true, the appearance of impropriety is too great to ignore. That goes double since we have learned that the Clinton administration permitted Loral to sell highly controversial technology to China, technology that might have helped the Chinese in targeting their nuclear missiles. The notion that one transaction (the soft-money gifts) had nothing to do with the other (the technology sale) is preposterous.

What isn't in dispute anymore is that *something* must be done. Scandal after scandal has rocked the nation's capital. From overnights in the Lincoln Bedroom to illegal foreign contributions from Asia and elsewhere, it is obvious that what was once a hunger for money by politicians has become a form of gluttony. Corporations, labor unions, narrow interest groups, and wealthy individuals are buying their way into our government at a pace that threatens to destroy the democracy that we all hold so dear.

Proof of this comes not just from the tried and true reformers such as Common Cause. In recent years, participants in the money chase have themselves turned into zealots for reform. Jerry Kohlberg, for one, was once a major donor to Democrats. But the more fund-raising dinners he sat through, the more he felt a distaste for what his dollars wrought. So Kohlberg became a convert and is spending more than a million dollars a year to persuade his fellow givers to rebel. "Nobody likes the system," Kohlberg concludes, "not the politicians, not the voters, and not the business leaders who supposedly win out."

But that doesn't mean it will change. *Reform* sounds wonderful, but the word means something different to different people. Democrats, for instance, are much more interested in stopping soft money than Republicans are. Why? In 1998, Republicans raised nearly 50 percent more soft money than the Democrats did. Remember that lawmakers care most about getting re-elected. Then think again about the chances of changing the system that elected them in the first place. Don't hold your breath.

Also, don't give up. The money men cannot be given free rein forever. Read on to see how and why they get away with as much as they do.

2

A History of Legal Bribery

Americans are crazed by the influence of money in politics. The outrage is so rampant that even a probusiness research group called the Committee for Economic Development produced a hand-wringing study entitled *Investing in the People's Business: A Business Proposal for Campaign Finance Reform.* Its introduction is breathless in its condemnation of the current system: "The American public believes that our campaign finance system is broken. The vast majority of citizens feel that money threatens the basic fairness and integrity of our political system."

So there! Take that Mr. Business-As-Usual. The very corporate (read: special) interests that are supposed to benefit from the sheer volume of money in politics are out there shaking their fists in anger at the corruption of it all.

Well . . . journalists have a saying about events like this. There's no such thing as a new story, only new reporters. And that's the case with electoral fund-raising. There has never been a day, as long as there's been a republic in America, that critics haven't railed against the dastardly influence of special interests in Washington (or other major U.S. capitals), so awash in campaign cash are they all.

Even George Washington was accused of irregularities. In his 1757 race for a seat in the Virginia House of Burgesses, Washington is said to have distributed the equivalent of more than a quart and a half of rum, wine, beer, and hard cider to each person in his district. That wasn't too difficult: The entire district had fewer than four hundred citizens. Still, it was the principle of the thing.

Mark Twain wrote satirically about fund-raising. Muckraking journalists wrote seriously about it. Indeed, the entire twentieth century was punctuated by politicians who rode the special-interest hobbyhorse right into the White House—from Woodrow Wilson to Jimmy Carter. And for good reason. The money men had, and have, a lot of swat.

So let's take a moment to reflect on this. One of America's most enduring myths is that big, bad rich people and ugly, heartless corporations control our government, and in many ways ourselves, all for their own selfish ends. We the people are the unwitting victims of this cruel manipulation. Until, of course, we fight back courageously and, against the odds, win. The underdog beats the nasty overseer. What could be more American?

This deeply held worry-and-redemption theory is in part what has motivated the populist movements that have recurred at regular intervals throughout our history. A scandal breaks and then a savior, in the form of a man of the people, rises up. He then flushes out the old regime, encrusted, as it always is said to be, by establishmentarian self-dealers, and brings in the new, bright, shining heroic leaders who will work to restore true democracy and fairness for us all.

The less melodramatic shorthand of this pattern in politics is the nearly annual call for "change" by whatever candidate wants to upset the incumbent class.

The problem is that, like all myths, this is an appealing simplification that doesn't describe the world as it really is. Its first and foremost shortcoming is its notion of control. Washington is filled with control freaks: people who believe they are smart and able enough to be in charge and, in fact, actually think they do control their worlds. In fact, Washington, more than almost any other place in the United States, is a city in which *no one* is in charge.

Official Washington was designed to be dysfunctional by the founding fathers. The system of checks and balances among the three branches of government and the extra step in the legislative branch that forces all legislation to pass both the House and the Senate were meant to ensure that most initiatives fail. Only the most overwhelmingly acceptable proposals for change succeed. Hence the adage that it is far easier to stop something in Washington than it is to make it happen.

That's even truer at the ground level of nearly every dispute in town. The facile idea that big money always wins is confounded constantly by the fact that it doesn't. A typical Washington dustup pits one exquisitely financed interest group, which is itself often a small subset of some other interest group, against another extremely well financed interest group. The winner in such contests is rarely preordained and sometimes hard to pinpoint. As in life, Washington is characterized by small defeats and incremental victories—if you're lucky.

"The days are over when some big interest came to town, snapped its fingers, and made something happen," Senator Ron Wyden, Democrat of Oregon, has said. "Washington is decentralized, it's diffuse. People want to hear persuasive arguments. I tell groups when they come to me, 'Tell me an argument that would persuade people at a town meeting in Oregon.' That's what makes a difference."

Nevertheless, the American people believe in the myth of control. And, true or not, that belief makes change in control a political necessity every once in a while. The history of campaign fund-raising is marked—or, rather, scarred—by this desire. Periodic scandals have reminded citizens of the myth of ugly powers in control. As a result, the ever-growing importance of money in politics has been interrupted temporarily by intervals of "reform." The irony is that each of the reform efforts has invariably led to other scandals.

When America was small, so was the extent of the legal bribery that we have come to think of as campaign contributions. In its infancy, the United States was thinly populated, and only property-owning white men could vote. Of the four million people who were citizens in 1776, a mere eight hundred thousand—one out of every five adults—could cast a ballot, according to an excellent history compiled by the Center for Responsive Politics. In addition, elections were simple enterprises: A few public speeches and some handbills were about all they entailed. The first professional campaign managers, always a massive cost, didn't appear on the scene until 1828.

But as the number of voters expanded, so did the cost of campaigns. The 1838 mayoral race in New York City was the first major race in which outright vote buying was reliably recorded. The going rate was said to be twenty-two dollars per uncommitted vote, and in those days, that wasn't cheap.

As the country got larger, so did government, and so did the determination of politicians to win elections. Bigger government meant more clout for them. At the same time, the larger government got, the more corporations and other moneyed interests had at stake. The Civil War made that abundantly clear and was, in effect, a turning point in the development of the whole influence cycle in Washington. The federal government began spending vast sums to finance the war, taking on billions of dollars of debt in the process. That fact ramped up the commercial importance of both the city and its government, a situation that has never been reversed since, and probably never will be.

In a letter on November 21, 1864, Abraham Lincoln wrote: "As a result of the war, corporations have become enthroned, and an era of corruption in high places will follow. The money power of the country will endeavor to prolong its rule by preying upon the prejudices of the people until all wealth is concentrated in a few hands and the Republic is destroyed."

The accusation, of course, is hyperbolic. But Lincoln was on to something. Then as now, the captains of industry were also the princes of campaign finance. Major players in those days included the Du Ponts, the Vanderbilts, the Astors, Jay Gould, and Cyrus McCormick. According to historian Richard Hofstadter, during the post–Civil War period "capitalists seeking land grants, tariffs, bounties, favorable currency policies, freedom from regulatory legislation and economic reform, supplied campaign funds, fees, and bribes, and plied politicians with investment opportunities."

In the years that followed, two scandals erupted that still serve as templates for the outrages of today. The first involves the personal fortunes of lawmakers in Washington. The second involved campaign financing, which is a different form of corruption.

About fifty lawmakers lined their pockets with stock provided by Crédit Mobilier, a company formed to build the first transcontinental railway. The corporation needed a hand from Congress, and it lent a hand to them in the form of free stock. When the payoffs later came to light in the 1870s, Ulysses S. Grant's second administration was irrevocably tainted (even though Grant had nothing to do with the scam), and the public got its first major-league taste of high-level corruption in the nation's capital. In some ways, voters have never viewed the capital in the same way again.

The other scandal involved the so-called Whiskey Ring, which skimmed off liquor-tax revenues to benefit first one party, then both of them. Significantly, the pilfering of the levy didn't enrich anyone personally. Rather, the money was used to finance reelection efforts. More and more money was needed at the end of the 1800s to elect candidates to federal office. And as pressure grew for funds, means had to be found.

Here's the point: straight-out bribery, such as in the Crédit Mobilier scandal, is the way most people envision the corruption of Washington. They see lawmakers and high-level presidential appointees getting rich off the public trust. In fact, those situations are rare—at least in comparison to the everyday, almost routine, and somewhat more subtle form of corruption that is at the heart of campaign finance.

In short, because elections are expensive and getting more expensive all the time, candidates have to lean on private donors to foot the enormous bills. Taxpayers, except in the case of the presidential election (and then only reluctantly), aren't willing to pay politicians to run for office. Voters are annoyed enough that there are politicians at all. The notion that they might be willing to finance elections with tax dollars is all but out of the question.

So politicos have no choice but to be Willie Suttons of the hustings. Unless they reach into their own pockets for the dough, they need to raise lots of money for their campaigns and, therefore, must go to where it is. As with Sutton, banks are one place. They don't rob them, of course, but the candidates do ask persistently for donations. In response, the financial-service companies (that's what we call banks and their affiliates these days) are happy to oblige and become major contributors. So are many other industries that are heavily or even moderately regulated by the federal government: railroads, insurance companies, labor unions, drug firms, aerospace manufacturers—the list goes on and on. Such companies, unions, and wealthy individuals that have stakes in the actions of Washington have ample reasons to give amply to people running for office. And they do!

That isn't outright bribery. The officials in question aren't being enriched by the funds. But it is subtle and, yes, legal bribery. The system encourages and protects this kind of giving. In many ways, in fact, donating to politicians is a way to participate in our coveted form of democracy. But then again, there's something just not quite right about lawmakers and future lawmakers being absolutely dependent for their elections on the very same interests that they are supposed to keep in check as officers of our government. But we have digressed.

As money politics took root, it expanded to the big cities. Corrupt political machines sprouted all over the country in the late 1800s and early 1900s. There was Boss Tweed's Tammany Hall in New York City, "Bathhouse John" Coughlin's in Chicago, "Doc" Ames's in Minneapolis, Colonel Butler's in St. Louis, the "Old Regulars" in New Orleans, and Boies Penrose's in Pennsylvania. Payoff money was central to each operation. Samuel Gompers, founder of the American Federation of Labor (AFL), once approached Senator Penrose and urged him to support anti–child labor legislation. Penrose famously replied, "But Sam, you know as damn well as I do that I can't stand for a bill like that. Why those fellows this bill is aimed at—those mill owners—are good for two hundred thousand dollars a year to the party. You can't afford to monkey with business that friendly."

It was also about this time that the forces for reform began to rear their heads. In 1867, Congress passed the Naval Appropriations Bill, which was the first federal attempt to regulate campaign finance. It prohibited officers and employees of the U.S. government from soliciting money from workers in naval yards. Then, in 1883, came the Civil Service Reform Act, which extended the naval ban to all federal civil-service employees. In the era of the bosses, federal workers had been expected to make campaign contributions in exchange for the right to keep their jobs.

Why? The industrial revolution had brought money politicking to the forefront. Writing in 1973, historian George Thayer called the half century following the election of 1876 "the golden age of boodle" and noted colorfully that "Standard Oil did everything to the Pennsylvania legislature except refine it." He added: "Never has the American political process been so corrupt. No office was too high to purchase, no man too pure to bribe, no principle too sacred to destroy, no law too fundamental to break."

Modern campaign fund-raising can be traced to the presidential election of 1896 and one Marcus Alonzo Hanna, a wealthy Ohio businessman and chairman of the Republican National Committee. On behalf of William McKinley, Hanna raised and spent between six and seven million dollars, then a record. McKinley's opponent, William Jennings Bryan, was able to raise only $650,000. Guess who won? Hanna accomplished this remarkable feat of fund gathering in part by, in effect, demanding that businesses donate to the Republican Party. Each company paid according to its "stake in the general prosperity." This was the first recorded shakedown by a politician of the supposed powers that be. It was not to be the last.

Hanna, on McKinley's behalf, also introduced the rudiments of the modern-day political campaign. He issued the first regular press releases, hired hundreds of trained stump speakers, erected billboards by the score, and distributed millions of posters, buttons, and fliers. All of which cost money, lots of it. The year before the McKinley victory, Hanna remarked: "There are two things that are important in politics. The first is money, and I can't remember what the second one is."

Stories of this kind were known to the public, and another bout of reform began in earnest soon after the election. In 1905, President Teddy Roosevelt, ever the crusading maverick, proposed that "all contributions by corporations to any political committee or for any political purpose should be forbidden by law." Roosevelt also called for public financing of federal candidates through their political parties. Two years later, under the Tillman Act, corporations and national banks were prohibited from making direct donations to candidates for federal office—a ban that since has been largely circumvented.

The one element of reform that was initiated around then and that has remained effective through the years was disclosure of campaign contributions. In 1910, the Federal Corrupt Practices Act set up disclosure requirements for candidates for the House. The next year, Senate candidates were brought into the fold.

Still, reform quickly fell behind the accelerating pace of money gathering for political ends. The disclosure laws, for example, weren't vigorously enforced. Nonetheless, these laws, which were revised in 1925, remained the basis for campaign regulation until 1971.

While the statutes remained stagnant, government got larger and more prominent with the First World War and the beginnings of the New Deal. In addition, many more people became active in politics with the approval of the Seventeenth Amendment, which instituted direct popular elections of senators, and the Nineteenth Amendment, which gave women the right to vote. Elections were rapidly becoming big business, and the need for money continued to climb.

Organized labor entered the federal-election fray in a major way in 1936. John L. Lewis, head of the Congress of Industrial Organizations (CIO), delivered a contribution of $250,000 to

President Franklin Roosevelt. Roosevelt initially rejected the donation because he feared associating too closely with unions. But by the election, FDR's fund-raisers had drained the labor group of more than half a million dollars. No one's money is unwelcome in the heat of a campaign.

Labor also provided an innovation that would prove to be the launching pad for both reform *and* abuse. In 1944, the CIO raised money to reelect Roosevelt through something it called a political-action committee (PAC). The money came from voluntary contributions from union members, rather than from union dues. This was important because the Smith-Connally Act banned unions from donating money from their treasuries directly to candidates in the same way that corporations had been barred from making direct contributions years earlier. But this kind of voluntary contribution was okayed under a separate law, and so off to the races were unions and their PACs.

Thus was established what I will call the water theory of campaign giving. Campaign contributions and the desire to make them are a persistent and permanent part of the world we live in. No matter how earnestly reformers want the money to stop, it just keeps coming. Government is too massive, too significant a portion of the lives of too many people who can open their wallets as a tool of persuasion. Think of the contributions as water flowing like a river. Reformers might throw some stones into the river, creating a dam or two, but the water will always seek its own level and get around the obstacles somehow. That's the way it is with campaign funds; they will always find a way, somehow.

After World War II, especially in the late 1950s and 1960s, politicians got even more reason to collect whatever the powers that be wanted to give: The costs of electioneering skyrocketed. Radio and television advertising proved to be effective lures for votes, but they were so expensive that they radically changed the way campaigns were both run and paid for. Between 1956 and 1968, spending for all U.S. campaigns nearly doubled, from $155 million to $300 million, while outlays for broadcast media increased sixfold, from $10 million to $60 million.

Despite this astronomical increase, the major sources of campaign funds remained pretty much the same: corporations, labor unions, and wealthy individuals, generally connected to business and finance. According to the Center for Responsive Politics, during the 1950s and 1960s "each of the major parties had its stable of reliable super-donors—the Mellons, Rockefellers, and Whitneys on the Republican side and the Laskers, Kennedys, and Harrimans pitching in for the Democrats. Meanwhile, most Americans, then as now, made no campaign contributions at all."

As a precursor to the major reforms of the 1970s, and mostly as a reaction to the ever-rising costs of campaigning, Congress passed legislation in 1971—the Federal Election Campaign Act (FECA)—that replaced the Corrupt Practices Act with a comprehensive system of laws and regulations. Among other things, it required full and timely disclosure of campaign contributions and donors, set limits on media advertising, and established limits on contributions from candidates and their families. In a significant boost to PACs, however, it also permitted unions as well as corporations to solicit contributions from members, employees, and stockholders.

The next eruption of scandal and reform came, famously, with Watergate and its many allied misadventures. Many remember the illegal cash that paid the burglars of the Democratic National Committee offices in the Watergate complex. But there was much more chicanery than that. Richard Nixon benefited from gigantic and often improper donations from, among others, Robert Vesco ($200,000 cash, delivered in an attaché case), Howard Hughes (a $100,000 contribution via a safe-deposit box belonging to Nixon's friend Bebe Rebozo), Clement Stone ($73,000 reported, $2 million unreported), and, according to a 1974 Senate Select Committee, "at least 13 corporations" and their "foreign subsidiaries" (which made over $780,000 in "illegal corporate contributions").

Wild, yes? No wonder there was a spate of new laws. The truly ambitious attempts to revamp the law began with the FECA Amendments of 1974, which were sweeping and were intended to discourage any other president from rampaging as wantonly as Nixon had. The amendments, for instance, provided the option for full public financing of presidential elections. Candidates who took taxpayer money, called matching funds, to augment their campaigns had to abide by limits on their spending during both the general and primary elections. And to help enforce it all, the Federal Election Commission was established as the watchdog of campaign fund-raising.

The most familiar reforms from this period were the contribution limits that remain in force to this day. An individual can give no more than one thousand dollars to a candidate for each election. PACs can give up to five thousand dollars per candidate, per election. In the aggregate, individuals can donate no more than twenty-five thousand dollars to candidates a year. PACs have no such limitation. When you hear Republicans argue that the limits on giving are too low, it's because they have remained at the same rate, despite inflation, since the 1970s.

Almost as quickly as reform fervor took hold, it abated. The much-lauded new laws were challenged as infringements of the First Amendment. Civil libertarians, among others, protested that the government had no right to say how much a citizen can spend to make his or her voice heard. And in 1976, in its landmark decision in *Buckley v. Valeo,* the Supreme Court agreed. Money, according to the Court, was tantamount to speech in these days of high-cost media. The Constitution insists that speech has to be unbridled. In other words, candidates must be allowed free speech even at a time when such a right was often very expensive. The Court thus struck down the limits on candidate expenditures, unless the candidate deals away his right to unfettered spending by accepting public financing. And with that, one of the most cherished goals of reformers was dealt a mortal blow.

In a small concession to the reformers, however, the high court said it was all right to continue to require disclosure of donations and to establish reasonable limits on the amount an individual can contribute to candidates. These were prudent barriers to corruption. But it wasn't okay to cap the amount that an office seeker can spend to persuade people of his or her point of view. Here, then, is one of the most confounding dilemmas of campaign finance: The largest obstacle to reform is the First Amendment.

A central goal of campaign-finance reform is to level the playing field among interests that vie for support and attention. Reformers ask, in effect, "Why should we allow Interest X to get so much more powerful and persuasive than other interests simply because it has more money?" Good question. But if the only way to knock Interest X from its perch is to take away the advantages that its money brings, government must necessarily restrict its access to public discourse. But the *Buckley* decision says that can't be done. As much as we don't want to hear it, money equals speech. And that has put a damper on almost every attempt to address the problem.

Expenditure limits, the court ruled in *Buckley,* "represent substantial . . . restraints on the quantity and diversity of political speech [because] virtually every means of communicating ideas in today's mass society requires the expenditure of money." And while a few types of donations can be capped, the high court added, efforts by groups that operate independent of candidates and by any group that wants to make its case on an issue can't be infringed.

So much for starry-eyed hopes of restraining the power in charge. Even worse, from the reformers' perspective, was the additional assertion by the Court that candidates can spend as much of their own money as they want on their own campaigns. This gives a huge edge to personally wealthy people who want to run for Congress or the presidency. And worst of all, the high court also ruled that groups or individuals could spend whatever they please to defend or oppose a candidate as long as those expenditures weren't coordinated with the candidates or their committees. These so-called independent expenditures created an enormous loophole that all but invalidates the remaining campaign-finance laws.

In another instance, reform turned directly into scandal—or at least into more of a mess than had existed before "progress" was achieved. While PACs had existed for a long time prior to this round of reforms, no one had ever been certain of their legality. The 1974 law altered that: PACs were declared legit. Individuals became able to donate up to five thousand dollars to the PAC of their choice, and that was considered a great step forward.

Why? As envisioned by the "citizens' lobby," Common Cause, PACs were supposed to be a way to keep an eye and probably a brake on special-interest giving. The extensive disclosure re-quirements imposed on PACs were supposed to chill the efforts, especially among profit-grubbing corporations, to contribute their way to prominence in Washington. Moreover, interests that otherwise wouldn't be heard could amalgamate lots of small checks from less-than-affluent citizens and give them a voice for once.

It didn't work out that way. PACs were embraced by all manner of "public interest" forces, from environmentalists to educators. But they were exploited with even more zest by those same heartless corporations that Common Cause and other reformers wanted to squeeze out of the picture. Company executives were able to contribute more than small checks to their company's PACs, and that money could be dispensed by other executives on behalf of the corporation. Presto! PACs, particularly corporate PACs, zoomed after 1974, all promoting corporate interests.

From 1974 to 1982, the number of PACs organized by businesses and labor unions more than quadrupled, from 608 to 2,601. By 1992, the number of PACs was 4,195. Most of the initial rise, to the chagrin of the reformers, was in corporate PACs. Today 43 percent of all PACs are corporate; only 8 percent are labor. PAC reform, in fact, is a sterling example of what Nelson Polsby and Aaron Wildavsky call "misplaced idealism." As they explain in their classic text, *Presidential Elections,* PACs were created in order to reduce the role of money. Instead, they turned out to be just one of the many vehicles to increase it. PACs, in other words, are where the water theory meets the law of unintended consequences.

Here's how the Center for Responsive Politics summarizes reform's failure:

> The "Watergate reforms" of the 1970s succeeded in ending the days of unregulated, free-wheeling, under-the-table campaign finance at the federal level and instituted for the first time a system of reporting and disclosure that at least provides accurate information regarding the sources and uses of much of the money in federal elections. At the same time, however, these reforms only served to sanitize, rationalize, and legitimize the same old system of privately-financed federal elections dominated by wealthy

individual and corporate contributors. This system is still in place today.

B*uckley* didn't destroy *everything* that reformers wanted. The Supreme Court upheld voluntary public financing of presidential elections, and that was considered a great advance. After all, taking public funds required the candidates to limit their spending. But, as ever, when one hand gives, another takes something away. So-called soft money has made a mockery of public financing at the presidential level. It and its many allied forms of legal cheating have rendered the entire effort to control and regulate campaign fund-raising a farce.

What is soft money? And what are the other nasty loopholes? It's not easy to explain. And that's the way Washington likes it. Campaign finance is purposefully arcane and jargon filled. That way only the insiders and experts can make any sense of the scheme and control the way it operates and how it changes. In addition, the more complex and bizarre the rules, the more profit that can be made by these same insiders in overseeing and maintaining the system. It is thus in many different corners of the law, and in many different places in life.

In any case, think of the following section of this book as a kind of layperson's glossary of loopholes. It is the explanation that the experts know but don't like to tell everyone else. (In fairness, I should say that the Center for Responsive Politics has its own version of this explanation, which it aptly calls "A Bag of Tricks," on its website, www.opensecrets.org. I used it and several other sources to help me hack through the thicket.)

Soft money is a term meant to contrast with *hard money*. That doesn't help much, of course, since neither term describes anything very well. Here's my best shot anyway. Hard money is what most people envision when they think of campaign contributions. It's the money a person or a PAC gives to a federal candidate or to a political party for use in federal elections.

Hard money is strictly limited by the law. Soft money isn't, and that's putting it lightly. Soft money isn't capped either in amount or by source. Soft money supposedly doesn't go directly to candidates and therefore isn't regulated by federal laws. (That's a big lie, but that's another story.) In any case, the way soft money works is this: labor unions, corporations, and wealthy individuals can contribute however much they want to "nonfederal accounts" at the national parties. These accounts pay for state elections and "party building" operations, such as voter education and registration drives.

These are not small donations. Companies and individuals have donated upward of two million dollars to the parties over the years. That's why a better term for soft money is sewer money, so despicable is this obvious grab for access and influence.

How could this have happened? The Federal Election Commission, which has turned out to be a paper tiger of a regulator, opened the way for soft-money trickery in 1978 when it permitted the Kansas Republican State Committee to use union and corporate donations to finance federal as well as state elections. Whenever a federal election came at the same time a local one, a party's nonfederal accounts could be tapped to pay for generic bumper stickers and yard signs that say "Vote Republican" or "Vote Democratic." The obvious advantage of pushing off some of the costs of campaigning to these easier-to-fill soft-money coffers inspired the parties to start collecting big money big-time. By 1991, the FEC had to require the parties to disclose their soft-money donors, so popular a tool of fund-raising had the loophole already become.

Even though by law some hard money had to be mixed in with

the soft money for many "party-building" functions, soft money quickly became the focus of national-party fund-raising. During the 1992 election cycle, the two major parties raised a total of $89 million in soft money. In 1996, the parties together raised $263.5 million. The next time around, Katie, bar the door.

As tough as it may be to imagine, the soft-money loophole has been widened several times over the past twenty years. The widest gap is called issue-advocacy advertising. It may sound innocuous, but it isn't. It is the *Buckley* decision gone haywire.

In *Buckley v. Valeo,* the Supreme Court ruled that federal restrictions could apply only to "communications that in express terms advocate the election or defeat of a clearly identified candidate for federal office." In other words, unless a commercial or advertisement expressly says to elect someone or to defeat someone or to cast a ballot one way or the other, then it isn't political and thus can't be restricted. Ridiculous as it may seem, this means that a commercial that praises a candidate or bad-mouths his opponent cannot be subjected to any federal regulation as long as it avoids certain "magic words," including *elect, defeat,* and *support.*

As a result, all manner of legal cheating has been justified under the banner of issue advocacy. The most notorious example is the millions spent by the Clinton-Gore operation (via the Democratic National Committee) in 1996. While hapless Bob Dole was spending hard money to win the primaries—and thus was out of cash when he finally won enough delegates to clinch the nomination—Bill Clinton was drafting commercials to sing his own praises, paying for them with soft money donated to the Democratic National Committee.

These were called issue ads because they never came out and said, "Vote for Clinton." But they did everything short of that. In one ad, called "Defend," the narrator intoned, "For millions of working families, President Clinton cut taxes. The president defended our values, protected Medicare, and now, a tax cut of fifteen hundred dollars a year for the first two years of college. The president's plan protects our values." Who could possibly argue that this wasn't intended to reelect the president? No one. But under the legal cheating of issue advocacy, ample soft money footed the bill.

Bob Dole finally got around to the same trick, but he was late in the game. Still, he tried. Using mostly corporate funds given to the Republican National Committee, Dole allies ran an ad that concluded, "Talk is cheap. Double talk is expensive. Tell Mr. Clinton to support the balanced-budget Amendment." Sounds like a campaign commercial to me. Later in 1996, the Dole forces ran an even more campaignlike spot: a straight biography of the Kansan, complete with flattering photographs and footage. Perfectly fine under the porous campaign-finance system.

Interests aren't patient with politics. Nor do they trust either the parties or their favored candidates to do the right things. Remember, Washingtonians are control freaks. So lobbyists have loopholes. They, too, can spend freely on elections, despite the laws that were passed to prevent that from happening.

First off, lobbying groups, like the national parties, can air issue ads. And they do—millions and millions of dollars' worth of them. They routinely skip the national parties and place ads in districts in which their preferred candidate is in danger of losing (or of winning only narrowly). Usually these types of commercials attack the opponent with very pointed policy arguments that come right up to, but never cross the line of, open advocacy. In 1996, for instance, the AFL-CIO spent thirty-five million dollars trashing the House Republicans' Contract with America plan, keying on Medicare cuts, as a way to elect Democrats to the

House. The U.S. Chamber of Commerce fought back with a lower-budget flight of ads that claimed "labor bosses" were trying to steal the election. Other groups ranging from the Sierra Club (read: a pro-Democrat group) to the Christian Coalition (read: a pro-Republican group) also engaged in thinly veiled partisanship through issue-ad campaigns.

The Christian Coalition didn't bother with commercials. It put its issue advocacy right into the hands of its followers. For the last several election cycles, on the Sunday before the Tuesday elections, Christian Coalition members have handed out tens of millions of "voter guides" right in church parking lots and pews. The Chesapeake, Virginia, lobbying organization pretended for years that these were "educational" and "nonpartisan." That was baloney. They were pleas to vote for the GOP candidate in congressional elections, which, as per the law, stopped short of outright asking for a vote. Still, the Coalition slanted the policy positions of the candidates in ways clearly designed to promote the Republicans. Eventually, even the limp Federal Election Commission moved to put a stop to that.

Though distasteful, all these contortions to appear impartial are understandable. When a faction wants to make its case, it needs to elect its own people to Congress. And if that takes a little sleight of hand, what's so terrible?

But election rules are so riddled with exceptions that, believe it or not, these same groups can back a candidate openly—even call explicitly for his or her election—and spend the moon in doing so as well. How? What about all those "magic words"? Well, the answer is that there's another term in our glossary of shame that sanctions such direct support; it's *independent expenditures.*

The Supreme Court cleared the way for any group, usually through its PAC, to work for the election or defeat of an office seeker as long as the group doesn't coordinate its efforts with the candidate it supports. Such expenditures don't tend to be as massive as soft money–fueled issue-advocacy ads. But they are also more straightforward and, thus, more effective. Starting in the mid-1980s, lobbying groups shelled out large dollars to boost their favorite candidates.

The spending often proved pivotal. In 1986, the American Medical Association PAC expended $100,000 of its $1.5 million in independent expenditures to overtly support Democrat David Skaggs for Congress from Colorado. After being down in the polls by twenty points earlier in the year, Skaggs went on to win narrowly, with 51.5 percent of the vote. Skaggs spent $500,000 of his own money. Clearly, the doctors' independent spending was important.

The AMA is far from alone in this practice. Over the years, the National Rifle Association, the National Association of Realtors, the National Right to Life Committee, and the National Abortion and Reproductive Rights Action League (NARAL) have all stepped into election contests to root for their preferred candidates.

But that's not nearly the end of the story. Another increasingly popular way to exceed the fund-raising limits is called bundling. On paper, a PAC can give a candidate only five thousand dollars. In practice, PACs and their organizations can give hundreds of thousands of dollars. They do this by acting as conduits for individual checks all made out to the same candidate, or by coordinating the donation of lots of checks to a candidate at around the same time.

Sending along checks in bundles in these ways can make quite an impression. A Delaware-based bank called MBNA America, through its employees and PAC, bundled more than $868,000 in 1994, including $143,339 to the state's senior senator, William Roth, and $88,450 to the state's lone congressperson,

Mike Castle. That same year, Amway, the direct-sales giant, delivered $144,970 in a bundle to Congresswoman Sue Myrick, Republican of North Carolina.

The absolute masters of bundling are lobbying groups. EMILY's List, an organization that supports female candidates who are prochoice on abortion, donates millions of dollars each election cycle through bundled checks. By this method (to be examined in more detail later), the group has become the nation's largest political-action committee. The Association of Trial Lawyers of America is also into this game. It actually honors its members who send checks of designated amounts to designated candidates at the designated time—all with the blessing of the Federal Election Commission.

So now we know the terminology (at least some of it, more later) and a little bit of the history, too. It's clear that ferocity in fundraising isn't new and that there are so many ways to get around the current campaign-finance laws that the statutes barely exist at all. But in some ways that's a little too abstract and distant to relate to personally.

When I'm on assignment for *Fortune,* talking to people around the country, they voice very passionate reactions to money politics. They hate it. They feel deeply injured by the whole mess in Washington. They understand in a general way (though not in any detail) how deeply enmeshed in the legislative process wealthy interests are, and they guess (though don't really know) that they are less well off as a result. And they wish it weren't so. The money men, they can see, are part and parcel of those crazy Beltway shenanigans that can be referred to only with a dismissive shake of the head and an epithet tossed at no one in particular.

Yes, they feel that something is bitterly, inexcusably, and maybe unalterably wrong. Things have gotten so out of whack in

Washington that even a benumbed veteran like me can see the disaster in waiting in sharp relief. John McCain went a long way by harnessing the issue.

I got an inkling of this feeling almost from the day I started to cover the capital nearly eighteen years ago. It's difficult to describe how completely lost and overwhelmed a newcomer to the city can be. The official part of town is so elaborate and layered. And every one of those layers seemed to have its own culture and ceremony, even its own language. As is readily apparent to anyone who has been in Washington for any stretch, English isn't spoken there. Dialects of English are. My simple layperson's tongue was barely passable when I first came to town.

One of my early stories for *The Wall Street Journal* brought home the importance of money and connections in such an atmosphere. I wrote a profile of Ridgewell's, at the time the premier caterer in the Washington area. What astounded me was the number of parties that took place almost every night of the week *at the Capitol of the United States.* That's right, in odd nooks and corners of the people's house, and in many other party rooms in the office buildings of Congress nearby, all manner of interests and factions, from wheat growers to venture capitalists, feted lawmakers with canapés and campaign cash (delivered later, no doubt).

Surely these party goers from outside Washington were suffering the same culture shock as I. But with a little money—or rather, with a whole bunch of money—it was obvious that the language barrier was mostly lifted. Shrimp and duck pâté were potent levelers.

When I started to cover tax legislation a little later, the excesses of that first revelation began to dawn on me. Lobbyists were enmeshed in every detail of the tax-writing process. They also were the object of jealousy of a large part of the congressional staff. Even lawmakers wished they could be lobbyists, so easy were their lifestyles compared to theirs and so thick were their wallets.

I watched generation upon generation of loyal staffers and diligent solons "leave the Hill" to "go downtown." Translation: stop legislating in order to lobby for legislation on behalf of the largest, most high-paying interests in the land.

Suffice it to say that "lobbyist envy" is a malady when it afflicts the lawmakers whom we elect to represent *us*.

By the end of the 1980s, I had no doubt that the temptations of the affluent world of the money men were undercutting even the most powerful lawmakers in Congress. In 1989, Speaker Jim Wright was caught in a scandal that included selling books to lobbying groups in order to evade limits on outside income. He resigned in disgrace. That same year, Tony Coelho, the third-ranking Democrat in the House, also quit over a special bond deal that a Democratic fund-raiser had put the chronically cash-short Coelho into as a favor. A third member of the Democratic leadership also disappeared after questions were raised about a mortgage on his mother's house.

Every time I turned around, another top Democrat was under siege over his finances and was under threat of losing his job. I remember clearly at one point staking out one of them (which meant I was standing with other reporters outside an office waiting for something to happen) when I started to feel disoriented. I looked to my left, and I looked to my right, and for the life of me I couldn't remember which scandal I was covering.

Certainly it was time to go home. But I couldn't. The bad news kept coming, and it was my job to report on it. That's been the story ever since. Every year is different in Washington, but it has been the rare year in which some major figure isn't caught in a terrible uproar over finances, personal or electoral.

The last two decades have been rife with episodes of excess. The mid-eighties brought the Keating Five. Charles Keating, who had operated the failed Lincoln Savings and Loan, managed through loopholes in the law to contribute more than $1.3 million to five U.S. senators, including McCain of Arizona, now, of course, one of the most fervent campaign-finance reformers in Congress. Keating gave $850,000 to three tax-exempt voter-registration projects as a way to help Senator Alan Cranston, Democrat of California, and, in return, to help himself and his flailing business. In 1988, Keating said, "One question . . . had to do with whether my financial support in any way influenced several political figures to take up my cause. I want to say in the most forceful way I can: I certainly hope so!"

The mid-nineties entrapped Newt Gingrich, then the Speaker of the House. The ambitious Gingrich had been the chief stalker of Jim Wright, and his relentless criticism of the Speaker had been a major reason for his downfall. But Gingrich didn't see the seeds of his own troubles in Wright's example. He should have. To engineer his rise to power, he took over and expanded a group called GOPAC, which at heart was a farm team for Republicans. Its original mission was to find and train young Republicans to run for office at the state and local levels. These local lawmakers would later step up to the big time of Congress, the group hoped, with the help of GOPAC all along the way.

In Gingrich's hands, GOPAC became a money machine. He charmed a band of superrich conservatives and persuaded them to donate giant sums to GOPAC under the promise of anonymity. After all, GOPAC wasn't a "political organization" but rather an educational one, and donations did not have to be disclosed. In fact, contributions were often tax deductible, which political donations are not.

Despite such a designation, the organization gradually changed in reality from an educational group to an extremely well financed vehicle for electing Republicans to the House *and* promoting the ideas of Newt Gingrich. Even the enforcers of the ridiculously flouted campaign-finance law could see through this scam. But Gingrich was never charged by the House Ethics Committee with violating anything with regard to GOPAC directly. Rather, he was chided by the House over a technically inaccurate statement he made in relation to one of the far-flung entities that worked closely with the Gingrich group. In other words, he had his wrist slapped over a technicality. At the same time, everyone who read between the lines understood that his political greed had done him in.

No one, though, went as far as Bill Clinton. In 1995 and 1996 he presided over more than 103 coffees at the White House, staged specifically to attract big donors for his then-troubled reelection campaign. He didn't stop there. According to *The New York Times,* Clinton allowed and perhaps encouraged top Democratic Party finance officials to reward at least twenty wealthy donors for their large contributions by inviting them to stay overnight in the Lincoln Bedroom. The *Times* reported that the sleep overs regularly occurred within days or weeks of the date on which the guests or their companies sent hundred-thousand-dollar checks to the Democratic National Committee. The going rate for attending the coffees, insiders say, was fifty thousand dollars.

Clinton, we all now know, is a man of voracious appetites. But perhaps his most insatiable desire was for campaign cash. His hunger for winning meant he and his people would take money from almost anywhere, including, as it turned out, illegal Chinese sources. His reelection effort, in retrospect, was among the most venal exercises in presidential campaign history. Clinton's grab for funds, both hard money and soft, spelled the end of what little integrity remained in the system of public financing for presidential elections.

That leaves only anarchy for the presidential race in 2000. George W. Bush's decision to eschew matching funds freed him from much federal regulation. He feared that the self-financed

Steve Forbes could unleash his millions and derail his juggernaut. But by raising more money than any other candidate ever, he also put the final nail in the coffin of the post-Watergate reforms. If there is ever to be any restraint on the money men again, the next few years will tell the tale.

Washington, as we've seen, has always been in the market for campaign funds. What's different now is that the attention has become an obsession. Fund-raising is nonstop with lawmakers, whether they face a tough election or not. And that's relatively new. Just ask Jim Slattery. He's now "downtown" (read: a lobbyist), but for a dozen years he was a well-regarded Democratic member of the House from Kansas.

A failed bid for governor of his state kicked him "off the Hill" in 1994—and, on balance, he wasn't terribly distressed. Making more money is rarely a crisis, even for a dedicated pol. But despite his cushy circumstances, Slattery couldn't help but complain one day in a K Street eatery. Fund-raising, he asserted, had gotten too nutty for him. "My phone keeps ringing off the hook," he said in 1999, which wasn't even an election year. "Members are calling me constantly asking for two hundred and fifty–dollar checks." That's breathtaking. Members of Congress are taking the time to shake down a former colleague for a pittance.

Sure, fund-raising isn't new. But surely the world of political finances deserves much closer inspection.

3

Fund-raisers Aren't Who You Think

Bags of cash.

That's what many people envision when they think of political fund-raising. And it wasn't so long ago that they were often right (although I hear from old-timers on Capitol Hill that it wasn't bags of cash—it was envelopes).

But it isn't the same anymore. I know it's not fashionable to say so, but the days of flagrant corruption are long gone. It would be a lot easier for reformers, and a lot juicier for storytellers like me, if lawmakers could be bought and sold like dime-store candy. Oh, for the days of Pendleton's Gambling House in the latter 1800s, when members of Congress would either win big or lose just enough to encourage or to shame them into casting the right vote!

Unfortunately, searchers for the higher path must look much deeper and farther to find what's really wrong with the system these days. The long march of scandal over the last 150 years has transformed Washington into a veritable swamp of restraint and propriety. The rules and regulations are so strict that lawmakers can barely go to lunch anymore without worrying about an ethics investigation.

That isn't to say that everything is on the level. Elections are still expensive and growing more so every year. And the money has to come from somewhere, though *not* for the most part from the taxpayer. So while the capital has become a much more ethical place, it isn't pristine, not by a long shot. And the people at the heart of its intricate web of relationships are the money men.

Who are they? They aren't who you think they are. For one thing, they aren't all stinking rich. They also aren't all interested in bending politics to their own narrow-minded, self-interested views. Some just want to contribute to the party of their choice. And some do so, well, for the parties. Literally. I guess that gives a whole new meaning to the term *party animal.*

Oddly, the most extraordinarily important, indispensable people in the fund-raising process are *not* the ones who have oodles of dollars to donate. That honor belongs to a group we should call the Solicitors: the politically active individuals who know lots of other people who are willing to donate a thousand dollars each to the candidates they back.

That bears repeating. In the quirky world of campaign fund-raising, the most vital people aren't the check writers but the check *raisers.* These people are rarely the names you see in newspaper accounts about money men. Why? Because it's spectacular to read about million-dollar gifts to the GOP by, say, those nasty tobacco companies or by the deeply conservative DeVos family (one of the two that controls Amway, the Michigan-based direct-sales giant). And the cigarette makers and the DeVoses *do* have clout in the capital, but they're not as keenly important to the system as the more workaday folks who *collect* millions of political dollars, a thousand bucks at a time.

Politicians understand that it's harder to raise those thousand-dollar checks than merely to write one big one. They also know that the smaller contributions are more useful as well, since they can be used to help candidates directly; the big gifts can pay for only indirect support, generally through the political parties. That's why proven solicitors are in high demand.

Democrats, for instance, love a baby-faced forty-three-year-old home builder named Terry McAuliffe. He's the most prolific fund-raiser in the history of the party. He raised all of Bill Clinton's reelection loot in record time in 1996 and, in the 1980s, was instrumental in reviving the Democratic Party in Congress with a shower of cash in the face of the rout led by Ronald Reagan. He trained an entire generation of young, energetic Democrats in the art of solicitation.

As a result, any Democrat with aspirations to run for president in 2000 was eager to be McAuliffe's best friend. Vice President Al Gore braved one of the decade's worst snowstorms to fly back from Chicago to attend McAuliffe's fortieth birthday party. The grip-and-grin photo wall of McAuliffe's Washington office featured a photo signed by "Al" that said, "You really are the greatest!"

But House Democratic Leader Richard Gephardt had already done Gore one better. A few years earlier, Gephardt (who over the years has actually become a real chum of McAuliffe's) drove to West Virginia, bought a golden retriever, kept it in his home for a month so he could housebreak it, and delivered it to the McAuliffe family home in a box with a bow on Christmas Day.

Republicans went through the same ritual with their own set of solicitors. Steve Forbes (who raised money despite his personal wealth) wooed Washington hostess and potent fund-raiser Julie Finley by sending her a three-pound box of Godiva chocolates after he did *her* a favor by speaking to a group she headed. An emissary of Congressman John Kasich beseeched insurance lobbyist Brenda Becker to join the Kasich presidential campaign as she dashed, appropriately enough, between appointments on Capitol Hill. And several major candidates visited Woody Johnson, the well-connected chairman of New York's Johnson Co. One who was late in coming was Lamar Alexander, but, Johnson noted wryly, "he's one of the few."

Think of this type of visitation as the pilgrimage candidates must make to the great men and great women among the solicitors if they want to have any chance of being elected. Former Senator Bob Dole remembers the day he "went to Lew Eisenberg"—the moneybags chairman of Granite Capital International Group in New York—as an important step on his road to the 1996 GOP nomination. Any serious candidate had to endure the same hat-in-hand trek in 1999 in anticipation of the 2000 election. None of the serious candidates could afford not to see Mr. Eisenberg—literally. And so he and the other solicitors never lacked for dinner invitations.

Likewise, Vice President Gore was careful to please the right people, and not just McAuliffe. For instance, while it was President Clinton who named Tom Leonard, a Philadelphia money raiser, to the board of Fannie Mae, which is one of Washington's plummest appointments, it was the vice president who took credit for the nomination by calling Leonard with the good news. Not surprisingly, Leonard later became a solicitor in the Gore for President drive.

So if you thought presidential candidates spent all their time in Iowa and New Hampshire, fuhgeddaboutit! Those trips are mere stopovers between meetings with the relative handful of people who really count: the solicitors.

A full-blown presidential primary campaign costs upward of twenty million dollars. That means the top candidates have no choice but to find at least twenty thousand givers. The only feasible way to do that is to woo and win fund-raisers who have enough time and enthusiasm to cajole their friends and associates into supporting the candidate of their choice. Lamar Alexander's top solicitor, Ted Welch, for example, explicitly and very early on identified 750 people who he thought would be willing to raise twenty-five thousand dollars for Alexander. He kept the sacred names in a book known simply as The List.

Converting that list to dollars obviously didn't turn out to be easy. Certainly not for Alexander, who stumbled early in 1999. But it isn't easy for anyone. The reason: there are a finite number of thousand-dollar contributors. Presidential finance expert Stan Huckaby estimated there are only fifty thousand of them in the entire Republican Party. The Democrats probably have a like number. In other words, there are about one hundred thousand thousand-dollar givers, or one hundred million dollars of top-dollar contributions, available overall. That calculation was rendered obsolete by the incredible George W. Bush fund-raising operation, but the fundamental thinking is still sound.

For the 2000 election, there were at least a dozen candidates who were each trying to sweep together twenty million dollars. Even when you toss in several million dollars from smaller donors, demand clearly outstripped supply. It was a sellers' market and always will be. And the real sellers in this case were the check *raisers*. The same situation held for all manner of candidates for federal office, not just for president.

Moreover, there aren't that many people who qualify as real, live solicitors. First off, such people can live only in certain places. Some 80 percent of the money raised for presidential contests comes from the ten largest states. Even within those states, there are only certain cities, mainly the largest ones, where any serious amount of money can be raised. That means, in effect, that the solicitors have to be situated in the right cities in the right states. Anyone who knows anything about those other places, the money-men backwaters, is nice to have around but not essential.

As its way to tell the story of the presidential contest in 2000, *Fortune* magazine set out to identify the nation's most sought-after solicitors. At first blush, that would seem to be a hugely ambitious project. In fact, the solicitors' job is so specialized and the number of people who are good at it is so small that fingering the right people turned out not to be so daunting a task. In any city, only a handful of people in either party have the ability or the energy to gather a few dozen thousand-dollar checks for the candidate of their choice. And most of the serious solicitors know each other.

As a result, *Fortune* compiled the first-ever guide to the top presidential fund-raisers. The list was organized by city and by region. Geographically speaking, there weren't too many surprises. The hot spots included Boston, Los Angeles, Chicago, and New York. But a few places were oversubscribed. Chief among these was Washington, D.C. Lobbyists are among the most active solicitors; their business often depends on their ability to gather funds for the people in power or soon to be in power. Silicon Valley, with its concentration of stock-rich high-tech entrepreneurs, also merited mention, which probably would not have been the case four years previously.

The professions of the solicitors ranged widely. Several were lawyers. Many others were in real estate, a profession that can afford time for politics. An equally large number of solicitors were in financial services, an industry that is heavily regulated in Washington but that also lends itself to leisure time. There was a smattering of oil-and-gas guys as well. But the list almost completely lacked people of sedentary wealth. The solicitors for the most part were high-income working stiffs. It turns out that solicitors need to have extensive, active business contacts as well as motivation beyond mere ideology to press those contacts for so much cash.

You've probably never heard of Wayne Berman, Peter Terpeluk, Beth Dozoretz, or Alan Solomont. But you should. Certainly anyone who wants to be president or a member of Congress has. They are among the key people to see in the powerful world of political solicitors. In the run-up to Campaign 2000, candidates breakfasted, lunched, and generally schmoozed these folks—and top fund gatherers like them—for months. Whoever these people blessed were the candidates who had the best chances to become our next president. The ones they rejected didn't have any chance at all.

Candidates had no choice but to beg hard for the allegiance of these specialized fund-raisers. In the twenty years that the current presidential-election system has been in place, the candidate who has raised the most money within the system has won his party's nomination. It is as simple and as venal as that.

At the same time, having lots of money hasn't always been a good indicator of electoral prospects. Just ask Senator Phil Gramm. Before the 1996 primaries, the Texas Republican had plenty of loot; it just didn't buy him votes. The money was able to make Gramm heard. It didn't—and, in fact, couldn't—force people to like the message or the messenger.

Nevertheless, the selections made by the solicitors can be a fairly accurate gauge of broader public opinion, if read carefully. GOP consultant John Grotta has calculated that nominees tend to be not just those people who raise the most money but those with the largest number of small contributors from the greatest number of states. If a candidate gets wide geographic support from, say, hundred-dollar or two-hundred-dollar donors, chances are the electorate at large will back him or her, too. Much of Senator Gramm's money, for instance, was relatively big-dollar and came narrowly from his home state of Texas and a couple other places. When solicitors are able to range widely and gather funds from everywhere in the nation, they know—and the rest of us can guess—that they have a winner.

Just how grateful to these solicitors is a future president? According to a confidential memo obtained by *Fortune,* the Clinton-Gore campaign in 1996 had eighty-one individuals who each raised more than fifty-three thousand dollars. Of those, twenty—or nearly 25 percent—became ambassadors or received some other choice job offer from the Clinton administration. In addition, all but twenty-eight of them were treated to at least one of those infamous White House coffees, which were meant as either an inducement to give or a reward for a sizable pledge of, I'm told, at least fifty thousand dollars.

Finding givers can be tough slogging. "Anyone who says they enjoy fund-raising has to have their head examined," said Debbie Dingell, a Democratic fund-raiser and wife of Michigan congressman John Dingell. "I hate it. I hate it more and more," she said. "I want to help, but it's distasteful to ask people for money. Your friends don't return your calls."

But the money does come—and more lately than ever. There are more reasons for this, though, than preconceptions on the subject generally allow. People who are losing the fund-raising race usually snarl about the dangerous dominance of "special interests" and sneer about "the best Congress (or White House) that money can buy." There's enough truth in that characterization to make it sell to the public. But solicitors raise money for a wide variety of reasons. The most significant one is that they believe that their candidate will win, plain and simple. Some people gather checks to promote their ideology, not just their own "special interest." And others do it for fun. Yes, fun.

How else can we explain such oddities in the political market-place as Lamar Alexander? Here was a guy who had a chance to catch fire in early 1996 when Bob Dole was proving to be a pill as a national candidate. But the former Tennessee governor and U.S. secretary of education proved to be even duller than Dole. Mr. Electricity he wasn't. Attending a speech by Alexander was like watching peas boil. He lost his audience and any chance of becoming president.

Everybody thought so, except for Alexander, of course, and, perhaps more important, Ted Welch. Welch, a Nashville real-estate magnate with a yen for politics, had been an Alexander partisan for many years and believed—truly believed—that the very smart and quite able Alexander would make an excellent president. As a result, Welch became Alexander's chief solicitor and stumped across the country with the candidate to ask people for money. Even Alexander's "Little Plaid Book," which was supposed to be a lighthearted compilation of clever and funny nuggets of wisdom from the candidate, cited Welch. "When raising money," it quoted him as saying, "don't forget to ask for the money." Fair enough.

The dapper and determined Welch was among the elite of GOP fund-raisers. He was once the top man in Washington for the national party and broke records chairing fund-raising dinners there. He was also considered a fund-raisers' fund-raiser: He was as generous with his own money as he asked others to be with theirs. And—here's a shocker—he never wanted anything from the candidate or from the party other than electoral success. He was a dedicated Republican, and in the case of Alexander, a dedicated backer. But he didn't use his skills to enrich or empower himself or his business. That made him a much-beloved figure even among the solicitors pounding the pavement for other candidates.

"He's the best" is what his colleagues invariably said of Welch. They knew that as soon as Alexander's campaign cratered, the sixty-four-year-old Welch would be out raising money for whomever the Republicans chose as their standard-bearer. Indeed, months before Alexander dropped out of the race in the summer of 1999, George W. Bush backers were peppering Welch with phone calls and other entreaties.

So for years, when the question was asked incredulously, Why would anyone give money to Lamar? the real answer was two words: Ted Welch. After all, Alexander came out of nowhere and returned there just as quickly. But alongside Ted Welch, Alexander had become an accomplished fund-raiser, learning from a master. He and Welch flew to the homes of donors around the nation and performed a political song and dance. Alexander sang the song—about electability and political moderation. Welch closed the deal. He would instruct—that's right, instruct—the potential donor where to give and how much. The duo never failed to ask for the money, and they often got it. Whether it was for Alexander's precampaign PACs—called Campaign for a New American Century and We the Parents—or for the presidential race itself, Alexander said proudly, "We are rarely rejected."

One other reason Alexander and Welch met with such early success is that they understood deeply that donors never liked to be bothered too much. Another bit of wisdom in Alexander's "Little Plaid Book" was this: "Hold at least one $100-a-plate fundraising dinner, where, for $200, the donor can stay home."

As soon as Alexander's campaign sank after his disappointing, sixth-place finish in the Ames, Iowa, straw poll in August 1999, Welch received calls from three of the remaining Republican candidates. They all wanted him to join their team of solicitors. "You can never have too many fund-raisers," Welch said with a laugh. And there are few as well equipped to raise funds as Ted Welch.

Not every solicitor is as altruistic as Welch. Let's face it, interests want a friend in the White House and lots of friends in Congress. That's why the ranks of Democratic gatherers are heavy with trial lawyers and labor leaders. Republican raisers are often real-estate developers and oil-company executives. And some fund-raisers play both sides, just in case. Examples include Carl Lindner of American Financial, the company that owns Chiquita, and Ron Perelman, the cigar-chomping head of Revlon. Florida's Sugar Crystals Corporation is headed by the Fanjul brothers: Pepe, the Republican, and Alfie, the Democrat. Sweet deal, no?

At the same time, conspiracy theorists will be disappointed to learn that the vast majority of check raisers don't seek any specific quid pro quo from the politicos they raise money for. What many of them crave is status and minor celebrity in the nation's capital. They hunger to be close to the powers that be. The nastiest battles between fund-raisers are always over who gets to sit next to the president or to the presidential wanna-be. It may seem absurd to the uninitiated, but to these people top pols are the rock stars of the Beltway.

No matter their motivation, money gatherers have several traits in common. Most of them have already made at least one fortune and dabble in politics because they get a kick out of it. Few would turn down the appointment to the Court of St. James if offered it, of course. And some, especially the professional lobbyists, are happy to mix politics with business development.

But at the highest levels, fund-raisers get involved for the sport of it. They are determined to beat the other team. And, more frequently than you would guess among adults, they even want to outraise the other people on their own team. Getting credit for achieving the largest number on the fund-raisers' tote board is the aspiration of even the most laid-back member of this exclusive, very sharp-elbowed club.

The best of the solicitors labor for years to locate the most reliable and responsive givers and then are loath to share their hard-earned quarries. The list is all. "I guard my database," said Georgette Mosbacher, a New York cosmetics executive and one of the country's most prominent female fund-raisers. The candidates she has backed have sometimes asked her to lend them her list. But she tells them, "I never do that." There is too much danger of "poaching" by other fund-raisers. And there's the worry of "database burnout." Mosbacher, like any major fund-raiser, is careful not to overtax the people who have learned to trust her political judgment.

And the asking can get heavy at times. In one week during the current election cycle, Mosbacher was asked to raise funds for three in-state and six out-of-state office seekers. She also had already fielded calls from a half-dozen presidential hopefuls. But ultimately she narrowed the field, tossed overboard a handful of the requesters that week, and decided to raise money for only one presidential wanna-be, Senator John McCain of Arizona. Her donors didn't need any more badgering, she explained, especially from people who were largely strangers to her.

In the run-up to the 2000 election, there were a few shortcuts to success for any candidate for federal office. If you were a Republican, you could cozy up to two groups that few people outside of the inner circles of politics had ever heard of: the Republican Leadership Council and the Republican Governors Association. They were both places where big bucks could be raised by whoever matched the basic requirements.

The Republican Leadership Council was conceived in the wake of the 1996 presidential election, which for GOP money men was better known as the "Dole disaster." Its existence could be attributed to two facts about Republican money men. First, fund-raisers want more than anything else to win, and they *hate* to lose. (This is true of Democratic money men as well.) Second, GOP fund-raisers are more part of the country-club set than of the true-believer, Christian-conservative brand of Republicanism.

The Republican Leadership Council was a collection of the party's most prodigious fund-raisers who wanted to produce winning candidates by buying respect for GOP-style centrism. The heavy-hitting founders of the group included the above-mentioned Lew Eisenberg of the Granite Capital International Group, John Moran of Rutherford-Moran Oil, and Henry Kravis of the investment-banking firm Kohlberg Kravis Roberts.

These guys, like most of the party's major check raisers, were conservative on fiscal issues and tolerant on social matters, especially abortion. This stood in sharp contrast to a sizable chunk of the party's rank and file, which insisted on strict social conservatism, including a prolife stance on abortion. In other words, the money folks in the Republican Party were not Christian fundamentalists by any stretch. In fact, as the RLC proved, they were all but at war with the righteous right of their own party.

One of the necessary traits of a winning candidate for president in the Republican Party was the ability to unite these two disparate factions. George W. Bush accomplished that feat and hence bore the title of nominee presumptive almost from the start of the election season.

He also secretly won the hearts of the RLC, which helped keep him far ahead of the pack financially. Some of the RLC's funds came from a PAC, but the big bucks were funneled more discreetly at private fund-raisers hosted by clusters of RLCers. No office seeker, especially for president, could want deeper-pocketed friends.

The Republican Governors Association was also a stepping-stone on the road to high-velocity fund-raising. In 1998, when presidential fund-raising for 2000 got started, Republican governors represented nearly 75 percent of all U.S. citizens, or thirty-two states, including eight of the nine most populous. More to the point, Republicans controlled the fund-raising apparatuses in the nation's most productive fund-raising venues from Pennsylvania to Michigan and from Texas to California. That's why GOP presidential hopefuls spent so much time talking to governors from such contribution-laden places as Illinois, New Jersey, and New York. If the governors were impressed, so would be their loyal money gatherers. That was another key to George W. Bush's blastoff; he was a member in good standing of that influential crew and had the support of many of them right from the start.

From the earliest days, in fact, the race for the White House was much easier to read when viewed through the prism of campaign finance. An early understanding that Bush was going to conquer both the Republican Governors Association *and* the Republican Leadership Council would have been enough to all but declare him the winner of the ever-more-essential money chase.

Maybe these weren't the party bosses of old, but they did come close.

Indeed, campaign fund-raising provided an excellent lens through which to handicap any presidential contest. As far back as 1998, for instance, several Democrats appeared to be jockeying to challenge Al Gore. In the GOP, the 2000 election looked like it might attract two thousand combatants. But in fact, the only candidates who had a prayer were the ones who had histories or were working hard to develop histories with the money gatherers.

That whittled the field of Democrats to four: Gore, of course; Congressman Richard Gephardt of Missouri, who had worked for years with the fund-raising arm of the House Democrats called the Democratic Congressional Campaign Committee; former senator Bill Bradley, who had raised tons of dough as a member of the Senate Finance Committee; and Senator Bob Kerrey of Nebraska, who had chaired the Senate Democrats' fund-raising committee since 1995, an arduous task he would never have taken on unless he had national aspirations. Senator John Kerry of Massachusetts might also have been a contender, but only if his millionaire wife, Teresa, bankrolled him.

You could have winnowed the Republicans the same way. Texas governor Bush was the early favorite not just because of his familiar name but because Texas is a huge fund-raising state, and the members of his father's national network of fund-raisers were known to be eager to pitch in as well. Revenge for the elder Bush's defeat in 1992 was all the inspiration many old Bush cronies needed. John McCain had a head start because he could raise tons of money from corporate interests as chairman of the Senate Commerce Committee. In addition, Steve Forbes was surely seen as a serious contender largely because of his own money. House Speaker Newt Gingrich was a first-rate, national-level fund-raiser and so couldn't be dismissed out of hand. (As it turned out, he disqualified himself by resigning from Congress after the drubbing House Republicans took in 1998.)

Other Republican candidates situated themselves so they could mingle with the major givers. Lamar Alexander worked with the Eagles program of the Republican Party, which was its club for fifteen-thousand-dollar-a-year contributors. Dan Quayle was the honorary chairman of the Chairman's Advisory Board, which was a slightly less generous group of givers, at five thousand dollars each annually.

But the lesson was clear. Anyone who wanted to be taken seriously by the voters as a presidential candidate had to be taken seriously by the solicitors first, even campaign-finance reformers like Bradley and McCain.

That wasn't an easy task. Candidates had to hustle to stay current with high-level fund-raisers. Donors and their solicitors changed constantly. What's more, the top tier of fund-raisers were in the midst of a generational shift during the 2000 election, just as in so much of America at the time. Some of the icons of the fund-raising business were fading into retirement and their disciples stepping up.

The summer of 1998 was the kick-the-tires phase of the presidential contest. The candidates and fund-raisers were feeling each other out. The most sought-after givers and gatherers spread their money around during that period, and the candidates happily took it—mostly for their "leadership PACs," a euphemism for prepresidential funds. These early contributions allowed the fund-raisers to hedge their bets until they could see how the race shook out. The money provided the candidates with the wherewithal to travel the country, test their messages, and make friends who would later come in handy when the presidential election got under way in earnest in 1999.

To be fair, some of the courting was done by the fund-raisers, not the candidates. Sure, the candidates needed dough, but the gatherers wanted a winner. And when they thought they had found one, they could be as ardent as moonstruck teens. Governor Bush was so hot a prospect almost from the start that a five-thousand-dollar-a-seat fund-raising dinner in Washington in mid-1998 to benefit Bush's reelection as Texas governor was oversubscribed before the invitations went out. The meal had to be moved from a private home to the more spacious Four Seasons Hotel to accommodate the overflow.

Early in the race, Gore also had more than enough people to help him raise funds, especially from the money-raising centers. After all, he *was* the presumptive nominee. The vice president's PAC, Leadership '98, in effect held tryouts for fund-raisers around the country. Gore envoys, led by lobbyist and close Gore adviser Peter Knight, organized steering committees to raise money in major cities. The most aggressive fund-raisers for the PAC were recruited for the real event in 2000.

But not many people clamored to give often and early to Gore's presidential bid when the time came. There was a decided lack of enthusiasm for Gore among Democratic solicitors. People who paid attention to the money chase knew that augured ill and not just for the narrow issue of money raising. They knew that the trend was also the harbinger of broader political problems to come.

In 1997, the Joyce Foundation of Chicago paid four well-regarded academics to survey contributors to determine the who and the why of campaign giving. Not surprisingly, the donors surveyed were people of means. Who else would contribute to a politician? The annual family income of 20 percent of the donors to congressional campaigns was over five hundred thousand dollars. Eighty-one percent of the contributors earned more than one hundred thousand dollars, making them a rarefied breed indeed. In 1996, less than one tenth of the population reported incomes of one hundred thousand dollars or more.

In addition, nine out of ten of the donors were white, four fifths were male, and more than four fifths were forty-five years of age or older—pretty much a detailed description of rich people in the United States. One half identified themselves as conservative, and less than one third called themselves liberal. Sixty-two percent gave to more than one candidate in 1996. Serial donators these.

Their reasons for giving varied. Nineteen percent said they were motivated by general ideology or partisanship. Sixteen percent were focused on promoting some very specific issue. An example of this kind of person was a young female environmentalist who told the Joyce scholars: "If we don't stop despoiling the air and water, there will be no political system to worry about in the future." This individual gave to candidates of both parties, so long as they agreed with her environmental activism.

Interestingly, 16 percent of the contributors admitted that they gave as a way to enhance their personal contact—and the personal contacts of their friends—with the candidate. These are people who crave a personal relationship with members of Congress. The Joyce study quotes one donor, in this case a small businessman, saying, "I don't contribute to somebody I don't know." This individual also said he enjoyed socializing with politicians and the status that comes with it.

Twenty percent of the respondents said they made donations because they wanted to have the best person in Congress to help the folks back home. At the same time, only 14 percent conceded that they contributed to the candidate who they thought would win the race and thus grant them access once in office. That seems low to me.

The most remarkable display of candor came when the donors were asked whether office holders ever pressured them for donations. In the Joyce Foundation study, four fifths of the respondents said that office holders regularly pressured them for contributions.

Better, though, to listen to the solicitors themselves. They can tell their own stories far more persuasively than any study—or I—can.

Let's start with Mark Weiner, a Democratic fund-raiser from Rhode Island whose company, Financial Innovations, makes, among other things, buttons and other tchotchkes for Democratic candidates. "Most fund-raisers are good people who do it because they like the result of it," he said. "There is no greater thrill than watching the candidate you backed get up there at the White House. It's a tremendous feeling to see someone you worked for win."

But for Weiner, as for so many big-time fund-raisers, the rush of feeling wasn't abstract or experienced from afar. If you raise enough money, you are welcome close-up and personal with the candidate you backed. That's who those VIPs in the cozy little receptions before and sometimes after candidate rallies always are. Said Weiner: "It was great to be in Arkansas on election night, an indescribable feeling." No doubt that feeling was enhanced because he and his solicitor pals were treated to a view of Bill Clinton that night in Little Rock that not everyone was privileged to have.

But doesn't Weiner want something more than a close-up view? "I've never asked Bill Clinton for anything, except once," he confessed, "when my daughter wanted to see his dog. And we didn't get to because he was on his way out."

You read that right. Weiner didn't want anything of substance from Clinton other than a small, social favor—and maybe a story to tell his friends about the encounter. Although he didn't get the favor, he did get the story. And that was enough.

Believe it or not, having a story to tell is a lot of what fund-raisers want most. They have an almost childlike desire to show off and be "cool" by virtue of their mere proximity to power and celebrity. Mitchell Kertzman, a software entrepreneur, and Alan Solomont, a nationally known political fund-raiser from Boston, once made a detour on a visit to the White House during the Clinton years. They sneaked away to see the White House press room in the bowels of the West Wing.

The place is nothing to write home about. It's cramped and cluttered and the opposite of glamorous. But write—or, rather, phone—home is what Kertzman and Solomont did. Giddy with excitement, they each grabbed a telephone and called their wives. They still love to tell the tale. It's a perk of campaign fund-raising.

Solicitors also like to be sought. Just ask Georgette Mosbacher, a senior McCain fund-raiser. "They court me a lot because they want access to my Rolodex," she said of candidates for elective office and of other solicitors. "My list produces a lot," she added, referring to the amount of campaign contributions. "They know that."

Mosbacher notes with disdain that one reason her fellow solicitors want her list is that it contains many corporate chief executives who are friends of hers but potential clients to them. The more access to a candidate lobbyists show they have, the more lobbying business they can drum up, she explained.

So why does Mosbacher raise money? She's a devoted Republican. She's good at raising money. Also, I can't help but think, she likes all the attention. "There isn't a day that goes by I don't get a phone call that someone [running for office] is coming to town," she let me know.

And her list isn't the only reason for her popularity. She also is in demand because of her diligence. When she commits to raising money, she really raises it. She may have been a socialite, but she has the reputation as someone who is willing to do the hard work that fund-raising invariably entails.

"It's never fun to raise money, never," she said. "You do it because you believe in something. It takes calls and phone calls back. I have to convince others that the candidate is someone worthy of giving money to."

In other words, fund-raising is sales, and the best fund-raisers are also first-rate salespeople. And Mosbacher is a saleswoman. "I have gotten to a point where I just don't hear a 'no' and talk right through it," she said. "I'll go pick up a check personally if I have to. I have no shame. If I make a commitment to something, I follow through."

That kind of devotion isn't handed out haphazardly, though. "I'm particular about who I support and who I raise money for," said Peter Berlandi, a Boston Republican who eventually decided to raise money for George W. Bush. "Your credibility is on the line."

Berlandi, who headed Custom House Street Associates, explained that he had been "in sales" almost his whole life and that he liked raising money. "If you believe in your commodity," he added, "it's easy to sell."

For years he believed in former Massachusetts governor William Weld and said, "It made me proud to raise money for him. I looked at it as a sales business; if somebody said no, I never took it personally."

Besides, money is what makes campaigns go. Other than the candidate, greenbacks are the only other indispensable item. "In order to run effective political campaigns, you need money—for the advertising, the bumper stickers, it's all essential," Berlandi said.

"A lot of candidates run away from raising money. For some reason they think it's dirty," he added. "But that's the way it's done. You don't have a business without sales, and you don't have a campaign without money."

In exchange for the service of providing funds, Berlandi continued, the candidate has an obligation to listen to the fund-raisers' views. "People who give money also have ideas about issues," he said frankly. For him, at least, giving money had to be a two-way street. "If I don't have input in a campaign," he explained, "I won't be a guy who just raises money."

Moral: While it's true that fund-raisers don't control the political tactics or the policy positions taken by a candidate, no one should be fooled into thinking that their advice has no bearing at all. Solicitors are people whom the candidate has no choice but to listen to.

Why *no* choice? Because there's one area in which solicitors clearly make a difference, and it's that phase of a campaign that can be called the first cut. Long before voters hear about a candidate, particularly for president, fund-raisers and solicitors are called in to peruse the merchandise. If they like what they see, they vote with their dollars and their time. If they don't like what they see, they stand back, and, more often than not, the candidate never has a chance to make himself or herself known to the public.

"The system works as a filter," said Howard Leach, one of the Republicans' most important solicitors, who lives in San Francisco. To make a run for president, he explained, "You have got to have a very, very broad base and tremendous support." And that starts with the approval of the fund-raiser class.

These days the selection is done in rooms all across America. Many, many rooms. Too many, in fact, for anyone to allege a conspiracy. *Fortune*'s guide to solicitors listed more than 130 of them around the country and only scratched the surface of activists who raised tons of money for the 2000 election. Still, the money men have a large say, far larger than their numbers would otherwise grant them.

The money men enjoy the burden. Lodwrick Cook, a longtime GOP money man from Los Angeles and chairman of Global Crossing, thought the process produced better officeholders. Forcing candidates to go out and ask for financial support, he said, "is a good testing ground. It's a challenge, and it's a good idea to see how they meet that challenge."

A candidate needs more than salesmanship to raise political cash, Cook explained. He or she also must demonstrate an ability to put together an organization, which isn't a bad trait to possess, especially if the candidate is running for president. "The job is big enough and tough enough that a candidate has to organize a team and know how to run it," Cook said. "That's a toughening process." And one that any candidate needs to show he or she can weather.

The solicitors have to go through some hazing as well. The local real-estate mogul or the county's top securities trader doesn't just wake up one morning and decide he's going to be the hub of the wheel for Congressman X or Senator Y. It takes time to develop a reputation as someone whom donors can trust. Yes, trust. Because what solicitors really do is dispense political advice. Contributors must trust that their friend the solicitor won't try to persuade them to contribute to a dolt or a loser.

"People give for two reasons," said Philadelphia money man David Girard-diCarlo, a lawyer, "the candidate and also the person who's doing the asking." Of donors, he added, "They have to have confidence in you. If they don't, you won't get the money. You have to demonstrate over time that you can deliver."

What does he mean by *deliver*? Partly, he means scoping out correctly which candidate is going to win. But he also means delivering the candidate to the givers. Being a solicitor "can mean, occasionally, getting them access, an audience," Girard-diCarlo said. "They [the donors] need to know that if you make a phone call on their behalf you have an opportunity to have a fair audience."

That's right. Fund-raisers require access. "If you can't do that, you have a tough time raising money in this business," Girard-diCarlo explained. "You have to be a player with the candidate. If you're going to raise substantial dollars, you have to have some visibility with that candidate. It's really not that complicated."

And then he quickly added, "I don't see anything wrong with that."

Reformers and a lot of other people *do* see something wrong with that. But that's the way it is. Moneyed constituents possess higher status than constituents who merely vote.

Girard-diCarlo was even higher in the pecking order than most other solicitors. He was a top money man for Republican governor Tom Ridge of Pennsylvania, who in turn was one of the biggest backers of the presidential aspirations of George W. Bush. So when potential donors received a call from Girard-diCarlo, they were really getting a request from two people: Bush and the sitting governor. Girard-diCarlo raised hundreds of thousands of dollars without much fuss.

"I'm quite confident I can raise a fairly significant amount of money both here and across the country," Girard-diCarlo said, demonstrating a typical money-man swagger. He claimed he could easily raise fifty thousand dollars a day and added, "If you can't raise a half million to a million dollars easily and quickly, you're not in the right game." Apparently, he was.

Bill Brandt, Jr., president of Development Specialists in Chicago, was in the right game as well. He said he hosted a major fund-raising event for Democrats every two months or so. He had raised funds for each of the last several presidential races, and as a result his phone simply didn't stop ringing with requests for money. After an election is over, he said, there is maybe a week and a half of downtime before people started calling about the next election. Not that he minded, really. He was glad to raise money for the cause.

"I'm a Democrat and a pragmatic Democrat," he said, "and the goal is to win." Still, he claimed that he didn't enjoy fund-raising. He said, in fact, that, like Debbie Dingell, asking for campaign contributions was a good way to lose friends. "Your friends don't return your calls because they never know when it's about money."

On the other hand, Brandt's access to the folks at the top of the federal government made him plenty popular as well. He said most Americans don't have a clue about how to deal with Washington. So he got lots of calls out of the blue from people who need to know whom to talk to in order to get things done in the nation's capital.

But he said that wasn't why he got involved. He was a money man because if he wasn't, who knows what direction politics might take? He was dismayed at the way issues were debated in Washington (i.e., not at all) and that elections were often decided largely by turnout, which more often than not was despicably low. Money was needed to create more voter turnout, he said, and he would much prefer to turn out Democratic voters.

Also, he admitted, he was frankly flattered that some of the nation's leading elected officials ask for his opinion. Such was a benefit of raising big dollars. "They ask and they listen to what you have to say," he said proudly. "It may not lead to anything in particular, but at least they ask, and your voice gets heard." Besides, he added with a little laugh, "every so often you can tell them they're full of beans."

But not all such access attained by money men is so innocent or disinterested. Philip Corboy was a trial lawyer in Chicago. Giving money to Democrats, he said, was a way to ensure that trial lawyers could continue to operate free from limitations that

Republicans often wanted to impose on his profession. Of fund-raising, he said, "I put it down as rent for the lifestyle, the philosophy I follow. There is a cost to being successful in the business I'm in. And part of it is looking out for the interest of the people I represent by spending money on the people by whom they are represented. I contribute to people running for office who think the way I do."

But even for Corboy, soliciting funds wasn't all business. Getting to hang out with the big names, such as Senator Ted Kennedy, was a thrill worthy of a few hours of labor on the telephone. Not long ago, Corboy recalled, Kennedy had been in town and had referred to Corboy as "the Michael Jordan of trial attorneys." Afterward, Kennedy sent the lawyer a thank-you letter for a donation and addressed it "Dear Michael."

"Being called Michael Jordan by Senator Kennedy is the chocolate sundae," Corboy confessed. In fact, a lot of fund-raising is done by people who have few worries about finding their next meal but are always on the lookout for a new kind of sundae.

A caveat: Internet fund-raising became a noteworthy adjunct to the more traditional means during the 2000 election. Millions of dollars were raised this way. John McCain's maverick campaign in particular appealed to the independent-minded users of the World Wide Web, and he harvested millions of dollars without any prodding from the candidate or his solicitors.

Everyone believes that cybergiving will continue to grow, perhaps substantially. But very few people expect that the personal touch will ever go out of style or, for that matter, ever cease to be the primary means of raising campaign cash. Even as McCain hauled in millions of dollars via the Internet and staged the first real Internet fund-raiser, he continued to depend on money men, including the very lobbyists he attacked on the hustings.

On the campaign trail, there was no group of people McCain

derided more often than Washington lobbyists. To wild applause on the night he won the New Hampshire primary, he declared: "I asked you to help me break the Washington iron triangle of big money, lobbyists, and legislation that for too long has put special interests above the national interest."

But in the nation's capital, McCain's solicitors included a who's who of those very same lobbyists—most of whom had pleaded for their corporate clients before the congressional committee that McCain headed, the Senate Commerce Committee. In early 2000, a McCain fund-raising event in Washington, D.C., was organized by a "Victory Committee" of nearly four dozen people, two thirds of whom were lobbyists for railroads, airlines, and aerospace, telecommunications, and high-tech companies. Virtually all of them lobbied the commerce panel.

McCain dismissed any notion that he might be swayed by the lobbyists' efforts on his behalf. But it was striking how many of McCain's most active fund-raisers in Washington also worked for companies that cared a great deal about his committee's work. The Victory Committee included lobbyists for at least two railroads (CSX and Union Pacific) as well as a top executive for the Association of American Railroads. The committee also included people who lobbied for Microsoft and America Online, SBC Communications and BellSouth, News Corporation and GTE, Lockheed Martin and Honeywell, the National Cable Television Association and the National Association of Broadcasters. Also listed were lobbyists with interests as diverse as the National Soft Drink Association, the National Association of Wholesaler-Distributors, the Cellular Telecommunications Industry Association, the Information Technology Industry Council, and the holding company of Arizona's utility, Arizona Public Service.

Two lobbyists listed on the event's invitation merited a special mention above the Victory Committee as part of the prestigious National Campaign Steering Committee. They were Vin Weber, a former lawmaker whose lobbying firm represented AT&T and Microsoft, and Ken Duberstein, a former White House aide whose lobbying firm worked for CSX, General Motors, the National Cable Television Association, United Airlines, and Time Warner.

How could McCain make good on his promise to "launch a national crusade to take our government back from the special interests and return it to the people"? The Washington fund-raiser certainly made you wonder. The event also made clear that the day when money men would no longer play a vital role in fund-raising was many years away. Indeed, judging from the McCain event, that day probably would never come as long as wealthy interests worried about Washington.

4

Buying into the System

F und-raising is marketing. The most effective solicitors
are little more than political salesmen. Their job is to gin
up enthusiasm for a candidate or a cause and to inspire people to open their checkbooks. Over the years, their methods of
inspiration have gotten quite elaborate and sophisticated.

The incentives range from friendly persuasion to outright in-
timidation. The heavy-handed stuff is far less common, though
probably better known. Even people who watch Washington casually know that Tom DeLay, the third-ranking Republican in
the House, is nicknamed "The Hammer" partly because of the
way he put the arm on lobbyists to contribute to GOP causes.
Lobbyists say privately that DeLay and his people often made
clear that they either contribute to Republican candidates or find
themselves in legislative Siberia—unable to make their cases to
the Republicans who held sway in Congress.

What isn't as well known is the more subtle but also more in-
sidious threat that has become routine among donors to the national parties. Both the Republican and the Democratic parties

have established what they call donor programs, which have institutionalized the amount of face time that givers are entitled to get with the most important lawmakers in the land. The parties even have a specific price list for the amount of access the donors can purchase.

Money for favors isn't supposed to be so blatant. When advocates of the present system try to justify the way things are, they assert that legislation *isn't* bought outright with campaign cash. After all, that would be bribery. They concede, instead, that giving money to a politician or a party may make that person or party more willing to hear the donor's point of view. Just maybe.

But that's a ruse. Washington is precise and buttoned-down. When the mode of dress is listed as "informal," don't be fooled into thinking that you should dress casually. *Informal* in Washington means "not formal." The dress for the evening, then, should be read as, "Don't wear a tuxedo, but a jacket and a tie is a must." The same rigidity applies with a vengeance to the etiquette of fund-raising.

Political donors can ante up by simply mailing in a check or clicking an Internet icon and leaving it at that. But that's rare. Most fund-raising is done on a schedule and under a well-defined structure. For instance, when House Democrats realized in 1999 that they could wring more dollars from corporate executives, they didn't send out a mass mailing. They set up a carefully designed donor program and hosted a lunch with reporters to get out the word.

In a private room upstairs in the National Democratic Club on Capitol Hill, under portraits of Democratic presidents past, Ellen Tauscher, the congresswoman from California and the new head of Democratic Business Forum, detailed for assembled reporters what ten thousand dollars could buy.

Once a month, Tauscher said, anybody who gives that amount to the Democratic Congressional Campaign Committee would be entitled to participate in a conference call with one of the House's most senior Democratic lawmakers. One month it might be Minority Leader Dick Gephardt. Another month it might be Charlie Rangel, the ranking Democrat on the powerful House Ways and Means Committee. But rest assured, she said, the people on the phone would be only the top guys.

In addition, Business Forum members would be entitled to attend a meeting in person, either in Washington or elsewhere, with a similar set of bigwigs. Those also will occur once a month or so. No need to remain a telephone call away. Such donors can thus personally bend the ears of the Democrats who have the most to say about everything from taxes to commercial regulation.

And why would executives want to pay for such access? Aren't members of the minority party—the Democrats in this case— pretty useless in modern-day Washington? The majority controls both the substance and timing of legislation. So why bother with Democrats?

Basically, Tauscher said, smart businesspeople think ahead. Democrats might well be the majority party in the House after the 2000 elections. She didn't put it that way, though. She asserted that in fact they *would* be. Donors, then, would be wise to think of the contribution—and the get-to-know-you time they can buy—as a combination investment and hedge. With control of the House up for grabs in 2000 (so narrow was the GOP majority at the moment), Minority Leader Gephardt might well become Speaker Gephardt in 2001. And Charlie Rangel could soon be chairman of the Ways and Means Committee, the most pivotal figure in all tax and trade matters.

From that perspective, making friends with Gephardt or Rangel or any other senior Democrat would seem like a good thing to do for an executive with Washington interests. And ten thousand dollars doesn't seem like a lot to pay for the privilege.

Then again, the executives might wonder, why should they try to suck up to House Democrats? Aren't they just a bunch of old-style liberals who would cut off corporate types at the slightest provocation? Wouldn't giving money to Gephardt's crew be aiding the enemy?

Here's where target marketing comes in. Ellen Tauscher isn't your average Democrat. In her twenties, she owned a seat on the New York Stock Exchange. She went on to start her own high-tech company and, at the time of press briefing, was as solidly probusiness as any member of Congress. "I have signed both sides of a paycheck," she said proudly, "the back *and* the front." Referring to business executives, she added, "I speak their language." She also espoused their preferred policies on issues from free trade to tax cuts.

That's why the Democrats cleverly made her the front person for their new money-raising operation. The not-so-nuanced message of the Business Forum program was that executives better pay up or be left out.

Rhode Island congressman Patrick Kennedy, the son of Senator Ted Kennedy, was in charge of the Democratic Congressional Campaign Committee. At the same lunch, he made clear that executives would be wise in the extreme not to ignore this plea from Tauscher. "If they want to see their views reflected, they have to be part of the team," he said, in a not-so-thinly veiled threat. He added, "This is an opportunity for the business community to make the probusiness part of our caucus strong."

Tauscher's presence was a way to make the executives feel better about giving. Said Kennedy, "There are going to be some people who would be more motivated to dig deeper" when they see an attractive advocate for their positions doing the asking.

The Business Forum was far from the only formalized shake-down that the national parties had to offer. In fact, the forum was designed as a complement to the program that the House Democrats already had up and operating under the name the Chairman's Council. The chairman, in this case, was John Dingell, the ranking Democrat on and former chair of the House Commerce Committee.

Dingell's influence was the market that Washington-based lobbyists wanted to target. They were the kinds of people who needed access to Dingell and his lesser colleagues in order to do their business. For the chance to see Dingell under the Chairman's Council program, they happily ponied up $2,500 annually of personal funds, $5,000 in PAC funds, or $10,000 in corporate or soft-money funds. The benefits included quarterly receptions and dinners with key Democrats in Congress, break-fast briefings with political leaders, and receptions prior to the annual Democratic Congressional Dinner with John Dingell himself.

Tauscher's Democratic Business Forum, in contrast, was de-signed to reach beyond the Beltway to attract actual business ex-ecutives. Tauscher was a two-term lawmaker, and her clout in the capital was nowhere near Dingell's. He was the most senior lawmaker in the entire House. Lobbyists would pay to see him. But real-world business executives, especially those in fast-rising Silicon Valley near Tauscher's district outside San Francisco, would be willing to put money toward a Democratic Party that was more like her. At least that was the Democrats' hope.

What's amazing about this is that it isn't unusual. Both the Republican and Democratic national committees, as well as each party's House and Senate campaign committees, have menus of donor programs that pledge increasing levels of access to party big shots in return for increasing levels of contribution. The programs make explicit a long-understood principle of American governance: Money buys access, and more money buys more access.

Fortune published the first comprehensive listings of the parties' major donor programs. The best known of these is the Republican National Committee's Team 100. The four-year membership program begins with a contribution of one hundred thousand dollars. To remain a member, a Team 100er has to give twenty-five thousand dollars in each of the next three years. In return, members are invited to national and regional meetings in "exclusive" locations, as well as to international business missions, the Republican National Convention, and RNC gala events. They also are offered what promotional materials call a "special" relationship with party leaders, who regularly attend Team 100 meetings.

In other words, Team 100 members get to have a sit-down meal with the nation's top Republicans at regular intervals each year. Not many people get to do that!

Team 100 folks also get to tag along for the events of the two other major donor programs at the RNC. The first is the Republican Eagles. Eagles pay fifteen thousand dollars in order to attend four national meetings in Washington and several golf and tennis tournaments with key lawmakers. They also get the services of so-called regional directors, who can help them with their Washington needs—whatever that might mean. The other program is the Majority Fund, which, for fifteen thousand dollars, entitles its members to attend quarterly dinners with key GOP legislators, monthly meetings of other sorts of high government officials, and regular issues briefings on matters of current interest.

Elaborate, no?

Well, it gets more complicated. The Republican National

Committee isn't the only GOP entity grasping for cash. The House and the Senate Republicans each have their own fund-raising operations. Just as Ellen Tauscher raised money for House Democrats, Republican members of each chamber of Congress also concentrate on raising money for their colleagues. The National Republican Congressional Committee, for instance, hauls in the dough for House Republican candidates through its own donor programs.

For example, the NRCC's Congressional Forum, for twenty-five thousand dollars in soft money or fifteen thousand dollars in PAC or personal funds, clears the way for donors to dine with the Speaker of the House and other GOP leaders, to attend monthly dinners with committee chairmen, and to receive VIP treatment at NRCC events, including the annual NRCC golf tournament. For ten thousand dollars in corporate funds or five thousand dollars in PAC or individual funds, a person can join the House Council. This provides breakfast with key House members (no dinner for a mere ten grand), as well as invitations to a few other NRCC confabs.

Senate Republicans have their own set of attractions. The National Republican Senatorial Committee has its Chairman's Foundation, which is limited to an exclusive sixty members. For twenty-five thousand dollars a year, each member is entitled to four or five dinners with senior GOP senators, as well as the benefits of the slightly less expensive Senatorial Trust program.

The Senatorial Trust provides quarterly meetings with senators in Washington as well as the ability to chat with senators when they venture outside the Beltway a couple times a month. The cost: ten thousand dollars in personal funds only. This is a program that isn't for PACs but is directed at executives who want personal contact with their lawmakers—just as in Ellen Tauscher's Business Forum. But the PACs aren't neglected. Senate Republicans also offer the Republican Senate Council, which, for fifteen thousand dollars in PAC funds, provides lunch and dinner with senators, a fall retreat with senators and their staffs, and golf and tennis with key senators.

No one is left behind. The Presidential Roundtable is for five-thousand-dollar givers and the Inner Circle is for thousand-dollar givers. There's even a program that caters to couples. For fifteen thousand dollars, a couple can become an Inner Circle Life Member, which entitles two people, presumably married, to attend Inner Circle events until death do they part. The events include two meetings a year in Washington and a third out in the provinces. How romantic.

The Democrats are not to be outdone. The Democratic National Committee also featured a hundred-thousand-dollar program. (In fact, both parties have been in the hunt for hundred-grand givers since 1988.) The Jefferson Trust entitled big-giving Democrats to weekend retreats with party leaders, dinners with the president or vice president, issue briefings, and regular faxes detailing the party's line of the day.

The Major Supporter program is for fifty-thousand-dollar donors and features small events with the president and the veep and "very high attention" from the staff of the Democratic National Committee. This is an echo of the regional directors, tasked to pay attention to the major donors a few blocks away at the Republican National Committee.

Ellen Tauscher also wasn't the only Democrat who was trying to woo business leaders. The Democratic National Committee had its Democratic Business Council. For fifteen thousand dollars from PACs or corporations or ten thousand from individuals, the Business Council program provided a special retreat, periodic briefings with heavy-hitter Democrats, and an event of some sort with the president. It also was something of a fraternity of (usually) youngish business executives who philosophically were in tune more with the Democrats than with the Republicans.

The Senate Democrats had their own intricate web of programs. They ranged from the Majority Trust (twenty thousand dollars annually in PAC funds or fifty thousand in corporate funds) to the Leadership Circle (ten thousand dollars annually for individuals, fifteen thousand for PACs, or thirty thousand in corporate funds) to the Roundtable (five thousand dollars annually in PAC funds or fifteen thousand in corporate funds). The benefits rose with the price tag. The Majority Trust featured a Super Bowl weekend and other retreats. The Leadership Circle entitled members to three weekend retreats. And the Roundtable had only an "issues conference" each autumn. How dull.

Both Republicans and Democrats were expert in gathering dollars from small donors as well. Oddly enough, the Republicans were better at corralling small-check contributions through the mail and telemarketing techniques. To make up for that, Democrats were especially clever about staging events to attract the same kind of dedicated, though less affluent donors.

The first was the Saxophone Club. President Clinton was well known as a high-school saxophonist, and he still liked to toot away as an adult, including once, famously, on a late-night talk show. For $250, young Democrats could get a saxophone pin to wear on their lapels, get policy briefings, and attend parties that featured musical entertainment.

Hillary Clinton got into the act with a donor program for women called the Women's Leadership Forum. For $125 a year, women, often young, got political briefings and partisan faxes, a quarterly newsletter, and, most important, an annual conference that featured speeches by both Hillary Clinton and Tipper Gore. Both the Saxophone Club and the Women's Leadership Forum raised lots of money, but they also raised the level of enthusiasm among rank-and-file Democrats. That's important, too.

As established and rigid as these programs appeared, they were not the final word in money raising by the parties. Not nearly. Each election cycle presented a new set of circumstances and, in that way, a new opportunity for target marketing. In 1998, for instance, the Democratic party added Unity '98, a soft-money program that swapped gifts as large as one hundred thousand dollars for small meetings with the president in Washington and big cities around the nation, including Miami, Palm Beach, Chicago, New York, Los Angeles, Boston, and St. Louis. Proceeds were divided among the various Democratic factions—the DNC, the DCCC, and the Democratic Senatorial Campaign Committee (DSCC).

Republicans took a different tack. The party's solicitors found themselves pounding would-be benefactors so incessantly that they decided the best way to raise lots of money was to dun the most generous givers just once and then promise to leave them alone. The program was called the season pass. It cost a quarter-million dollars.

Unfortunately, money demands being what they are, the season pass didn't last the whole election season. The Republican Party broke its promise and went back to these big givers for more anyway. Officials asked for more money toward the end of the 1998 cycle, when they thought there was a chance, thanks to the Monica Lewinsky scandal, for the Republicans to make big gains in the House. But given the loss of House seats that year, the donors were none too pleased.

In any case, the 2000 election presented a different situation. The stakes were higher and the desire to win finally was almost overwhelming. Therefore, efforts to sell a season pass grew exponentially. As in years gone by, the pass cost $250,000 a year. But in 1999, efforts were stepped up to convince the holders to sign up for two straight years. *The New York Times* erroneously but memorably called this program Team One Million.

This was hardly the end of the grubbing for bucks. Also in 1999, the GOP created a new program called Media 2000. Contributions of at least one hundred thousand dollars were solicited specifically to pay for issue advertising.

No one would doubt that these ads were really campaign ads. What's more, there was never any question from the beginning that the fund was set up because so many George W. Bush backers wanted to donate much, much more than the thousand dollars they were restricted to giving under the regular campaign-finance system.

Media 2000 was really Bush $100,000.

Democrats weren't far behind in their money-raising strategy. In 1999, the Democratic National Committee created Leadership 2000. Its entry fee was $350,000, either raised or donated by prominent contributors. And it, too, was designed to pay for issue ads presumably to bolster the candidacy of Vice President Gore. Two of Gore's top fund-raisers, Alan Solomont and Dan Dutko, were the original people in charge of this farsighted soft-money program.

The parties provide many ways for different sorts of people and interests to buy access to their most prominent leaders. Markets are carefully targeted, and maximum contributions are gathered at every opportunity. But how does this actually work at ground level? What does a contributor think about when choosing a donor program? How does someone buy his way into the system?

On behalf of *Fortune,* I asked Nick Franklin, the man who controlled the political purse strings for a large California-based health-maintenance organization called PacifiCare Health Systems. Franklin wasn't your typical corporate executive. He earned his spurs not in marketing, manufacturing, or finance but in the rough-and-tumble of campaigns and elections.

Prior to becoming a senior vice president of PacifiCare, Franklin chaired the Democratic Party of New Mexico, ran unsuccessfully for the U.S. Senate, and worked as a private lobbyist. He said he would rather spend his evenings watching the latest cable-TV shouting match from Washington than review his company's balance sheet. "I'm a news junkie," he admitted.

In many companies, that wouldn't qualify Franklin to do much more than bloviate at the watercooler. But at PacifiCare, he was a star. The federal government was the ten-billion-dollar company's largest customer (through Medicare), as well as its biggest regulator, which made Uncle Sam a key player in PacifiCare's financial health. In addition, the entire HMO industry was under constant attack by the Clinton administration for failing to serve its patients well.

So out of self-preservation, PacifiCare invested heavily in the legislative process—all told, about two million dollars a year. It contributed generously to candidates, to their parties, and to a growing number of groups whose purpose was to bend the public-policy debate in its direction. In effect, Franklin served as manager of the company's political portfolio.

Some corporations are embarrassed to admit they have Nick Franklins, so distasteful to consumers is the purchase (or attempted purchase) of governmental favors. Yet they do. They must! Businesses hate federal regulation, but they have to deal with it. They need experts like Nick Franklin to guide the way. The menu of places to put Washington-directed dollars has grown hugely in recent years and so has the amount of money flowing into the system. Any company that fails to keep pace can find itself at a competitive disadvantage.

What follows is a rare look at how one company decided how to allocate its limited resources among these almost unlimited options. It isn't a pretty picture.

As a political professional, Franklin's duty is to insist that "money doesn't buy votes." And in fact, Capitol Hill is a much more ethical place than it was when Franklin began working there thirty years ago. "The Capitol Police were patronage jobs," Franklin recalls. "I remember some of the guys couldn't pass the shooting test; they gave 'em guns, but they didn't give 'em bullets." Nowadays, everyone shoots with live ammo, including the lobbyists. Influence peddling is a serious business, and the primary weapon is money.

What it buys, though, is access, which comes close to buying votes, but not quite. PacifiCare, an average-sized dispenser of cash in the capital, played the game cleverly. Like almost every corporation with issues before the government, it had that boring old standby, a PAC, which makes contributions directly to candidates for Congress. About 250 PacifiCare employees filled the kitty, and two representatives of management decided where the money went: "Nick and me," said Pat Simmons Douglass, PacifiCare's director of government relations.

In the 1997–1998 election cycle, PacifiCare's PAC shelled out roughly one hundred thousand dollars to more than fifty candidates, 70 percent to Republicans, who were friendly to the embattled HMO industry, and 30 percent to Democrats, who weren't as friendly but nonetheless possessed the important right to vote.

At one time, PAC giving was the beginning and the end of the Washington story for corporations. No longer. Peter Kennerdell of the Public Affairs Council, a Washington-based society for government-relations executives, estimates that PAC contributions represented only between 1 and 10 percent of the amount that corporations pay out for politics these days. Most of the rest comes straight from corporate coffers and goes to a variety of efforts that fall under the hazy and unseemly sounding headings of lobbying and soft money.

PacifiCare joined the soft-money bandwagon. In 1998, it contributed roughly one hundred thousand dollars to a variety of
party committees. In return for its money, PacifiCare was guaranteed regularly scheduled face time with the nation's most powerful lawmakers—something only the best-heeled of our society
can afford. It became a member of the NRCC's Congressional
Forum; it joined the DCCC's Speakers' Club; and for a specially
negotiated mix of ten thousand dollars each of soft and hard
money, it became part of the DSCC's Leadership Circle.

The method worked. At a dinner reception in Washington
that was part of the House Republicans' Congressional Forum,
Pat Douglass got to chat with Congresswoman Sue Kelly of New
York. Kelly was there as a member of the House's Small Business
Committee, whose chairman and GOP members were scattered
among the lobbyists that night, just as the soft-money program
had promised they would be. Happily for Douglass, Kelly was
also a member of the House's health-care task force, which was at
that very moment drafting legislation that would have changed
the federal rules governing HMOs. The brief conversation that
evening led to a more intensive discussion the next day in Kelly's
Capitol Hill office. "I don't think we convinced her," Douglass
recalled. "But she was very interested and wanted to know about
the way we run our HMO." No corporate pleader could hope for
more.

The guiding principle behind investments with both soft and
hard dollars was this, according to Franklin: "no cattle calls."
Fund-raising dinners are often ballroom-scale affairs in which
the benefactors are blurs in a crowd to their targets. With finite
resources, Franklin and Douglass couldn't afford such anonymity. So rule one was: Give soft money only through donor
programs that permitted regular contact with the people whose
opinions the company needed to know and shape. Rule two:

Bring hard-dollar checks in person and, when possible, only to relatively intimate fund-raising events. PacifiCare passed up larger-scale meetings it was entitled to attend to concentrate on the ones that were smaller and more likely to leave an impression on the guest of honor.

At the same time, there are lots of places to spend money in politics these days. And corporations will invest almost anywhere that can help them attract an audience of key lawmakers and decision makers—including, believe it or not, think tanks. PacifiCare was among many companies that buy themselves a steady stream of sympathetic meetings with lawmakers by giving to the Democratic Leadership Council, an advocacy group for probusiness Democrats, and its affiliated think tank, the Progressive Policy Institute. For a ten-thousand-dollar payment to each group, Franklin and his people were guaranteed to have the ears of senior Democrats who aren't toadies of organized labor, such as senators Joe Lieberman of Connecticut and John Breaux of Louisiana.

But there was a limit to the effectiveness of personal contact. Friendly persuasion often wasn't enough, especially for PacifiCare, which didn't have a Washington office and couldn't take advantage of all the meetings it was entitled to attend. (It hired lobbyists by the month, but more on that later.) That's why it and other corporations poured money into all manner of new and extremely nontraditional election-time enterprises. They paraded under various banners: issue advertising, express advocacy, independent expenditures. But they all fell into the same general category: tricks up the political sleeve.

The fastest growing of these was issue advertising. Businesses were no longer content to hand funds to candidates or their parties and then sit back to watch them do what they may. Instead, they were increasingly going on the offensive themselves, both over the airwaves and in newspapers. Faced with the prospect of an anti-HMO onslaught led by President Clinton, PacifiCare spent twenty-five thousand dollars to join a specially formed pressure group called the Health Benefits Coalition. In turn, the coalition, which boasted a thousand business members, bought advertising in carefully selected markets and labeled the president's Patients' Bill of Rights as a big-government bungle that would increase health costs.

You might remember some of the ads. The nastiest was a radio commercial that featured a fellow who mimicked Senator Ted Kennedy. The Massachusetts Democrat fumbled around at an operating table, creating what turned out to be "Frankenstein's monster." Not long after the ad ran, polls around the country began to reflect the view that maybe Clinton shouldn't push so hard for more federal controls.

That was the air war. PacifiCare also prepared to fight a subterranean battle. For fifty thousand dollars, it retained a "grassroots" lobbying company called Direct Impact. The northern Virginia firm developed and maintained a list of PacifiCare patients (arranged by congressional district) who were fans of their health-care coverage and were willing to call or write their congresspeople whenever PacifiCare asked them to. (Other health-care companies had done the same spadework with Direct Impact and were also ready to strike when the need arose.)

As in any conflict, however, nothing can substitute for having people on the ground. And PacifiCare had collected as many D.C. ground troops as it could afford. It paid its main trade association, the American Association of Health Plans, nine hundred thousand dollars a year, which was about midrange for a corporation its size. A lot of HMO-industry lobbying was coordinated there. In lieu of a Washington office, the company also retained two big-name lobbying firms, the Dutko Group and the Wexler Group. To Dutko it paid $12,500 a month; Wexler got a couple thousand dollars more. Since so much of the lobbying was simply making the case, PacifiCare also spent another $130,000 in 1998 to consulting and accounting firms that compiled the masses of data and research it needed.

Deciding who *not* to hire was the dicey part. PacifiCare's budget was squeezed after a recent merger, so any hope of keeping a full-time staff in the capital was put on hold. The company also decided to drop its two-hundred-thousand-dollar annual membership in the Health Leadership Council, yet another lobbying coalition. In addition, Nick Franklin had had dreams of seeing his boss, CEO Alan Hoops, hobnobbing with the CEOs of the Business Roundtable. But that hope was dashed when the Roundtable tripled its already hefty dues.

So Franklin was forced for the most part to work with what he already had—which turned out to be quite a lot. Both of PacifiCare's lobbying firms were headed by Democrats; Dan Dutko was a former congressional staffer and Ann Wexler worked in Jimmy Carter's White House. Yet their firms had evolved in the age of Gingrich and Republican majorities in Congress. The Dutko Group had turned out to be valuable because one of its partners, Gary Andres, was a mammoth fundraiser and top adviser for House Republicans. The Wexler Group had an expert on health policy, Dale Snape, formerly of the White House's budget office, as well as a lobbyist who was close to the Senate GOP, Cynthia Berry. "Good public-affairs firms in Washington, if they're worth their salt, have the ability to deal with the Republican and Democratic sides of both chambers," Franklin explained.

Such connections came in handy. During the final stretch to the 1998 election, lawmakers rushed to complete legislation and also grabbed for as much campaign cash as they could. PacifiCare had to be vigilant on both fronts—and ready to whip out its checkbook. It did so when it forked over five thousand dollars in soft money to the Republican Party for the chance to meet and greet right there in southern California a cavalcade of GOP stars, including Gingrich and a slew of heavyweights among California's Republican delegation, such as David Drier, who was in line to become the next chairman of the powerful House Rules Committee. For a company as exposed to federal meddling as PacifiCare, that was a command performance.

The hard part was to know when it was safe to stop giving. The Democrats were also pressing for more funds as part of their last-ditch Unity '98 campaign. Republicans had at least two multimillion-dollar fund-raising drives under way—Majority '98 and a clandestine effort called Operation Breakout, which was meant to gather enough scratch to neutralize the AFL-CIO's massive independent expenditure campaign.

Everywhere a corporation turned, there was a group pushing a point of view and soliciting money for campaign-style ads. The trend was a gigantic change in the way Washington worked. "These groups have the capacity to spend considerably more than we do," said Democratic congressman Martin Frost of Texas, who headed the House Democrats' campaign committee. "We advise our candidates to make sure they have enough money in the bank to counter last-minute attacks by them."

PacifiCare also had to keep money in reserve to sate such eleventh-hour urges. It hadn't any choice. "We have a political problem today because we have an image problem," conceded Ben Singer, PacifiCare's vice president for public relations. "In polls, we're right down there with the tobacco companies." At the same time, he said, "You can't throw dollars and make the problems go away."

Obviously, PacifiCare worked very hard not to throw its money around willy-nilly. But the question remained: Did all the care it took with its political portfolio make a difference in the end? Franklin was philosophical. Corporations can't buy outcomes, he said. They can gain access and then, if they're smart, develop relationships and credibility with decision makers who can help them—or at least give them a fair hearing—down the road. "We're in the information business," he liked to say. But then again, the Patients' Bill of Rights, which looked like a sure thing at the beginning of the year, had no chance of passage before the end of that Congress in 1998. That wasn't bad for government work.

Notice this about most of the above: Very little of it had anything to do with presidential politics. And that is often the case with the nation's money men. Yes, it's true that the president and vice president were used as bait to attract cash for various elements of the Democratic Party. At the same time it was clear: There are essentially two kinds of political money raising: congressional and presidential. And rarely do the twain ever meet.

In fact, the various factions of the parties are often at war with each other. That was particularly the case in early 1999, when Vice President Gore was stumbling around as a presidential candidate and the Democrats in the House were soaring, confident as they were that they were all but certain to retake control of their chamber after the 2000 election.

As a result, the DCCC was hot, hot, hot. The Democratic National Committee, on the other hand, was a depressing place to work. The solicitors knew that much of the money that would be raised there would be sent to supplement the finances of the Democratic nominee for president. And that looked to be Al Gore. Frankly, the prospect made fund-raising difficult at best at the DNC early on.

It was worse than that. Congressman Patrick Kennedy of the DCCC turned out to be more than the son of a famous father. He was one of the most aggressive, hyperactive fund-raisers the Democratic Party had yet produced. He was said to be fearless on the telephone, begging for money for his House colleagues. He also was less than discreet in his pitch.

At the February 1999 retreat of House Democrats at the sprawling Wintergreen resort in Virginia, Kennedy urged his colleagues to put his organization first on the list of groups they raise money for besides their own reelection committees. That's pretty standard. But he went further and shocked even the veteran lawmakers in the audience. According to Kennedy's spokesman Erik Smith, the young Rhode Islander said, "We may not win the presidency. We may not win the Senate. We must win the House. We will win the House." In other words, forget about Al Gore. We're the folks who are going to win, so concentrate your efforts here.

When word reached Gore about the insult, the vice president was none too pleased. Aides said he punished Kennedy by keeping him off the stage when Gore made a political appearance in Providence, the heart of Kennedy's own district. But the message was already out.

"Stick with a winner" was the unofficial motto of the DCCC. And, in their typically opportunistic fashion, the money men filled the House Democrats' coffers.

Money flows to the victor. That's one of the cardinal principles of political fund-raising. After the Republicans snared the majority in the House in 1994, the Democrats' treasuries declined and the Republicans' zoomed. Political-action committees and most large corporations are neither dedicated Republicans nor committed Democrats. They are devoted only to themselves and their own best interests. They give to the people in power or to the people who might be in power soon.

That's not a huge surprise. But this fact has created one of the more peculiar and not-so-obvious elements in campaign finance:

the leadership PAC. Lawmakers who have reached the pinnacle of their power in Washington have set up political-action committees that operate separately from their own reelection committees. These are funds from which the lawmaker can make contributions to other lawmakers or candidates for office. A legislator who has such a leadership PAC often is either an elected leader in Congress or someone who aspires to become a leader. Contributing to colleagues is a very good way to make friends down the road.

What's noteworthy about these funds is that they are very rich. The leadership PACs of Senate Majority Leader Trent Lott and House Majority Leader Dick Armey were among the largest PACs in the country. In other words, Lott and Armey collected millions of dollars from all sorts of people and groups, which they in turn distributed to fellow candidates in much the same way that the American Medical Association or the National Rifle Association raised money for candidates. Prominent politicians, by virtue of their being prominent, have become power brokers, thanks to the money they now gather and dispense.

From the perspective of the money men, leadership PACs are controversial ventures. At last count, there were more than one hundred of them. Yet many donors, especially lobbyists, are loath to say no to the likes of Thomas J. Bliley, Jr., of Virginia, the Republican chairman of the House Commerce Committee, and his Fund for a Responsible Future, or to Senate Minority Leader Thomas A. Daschle of South Dakota and his DASH PAC. That often means being hit up for funds from the same person twice. Moreover, money given to a leadership PAC isn't credited to the original giver. The politician who actually hands the money out gets the glory.

At the same time, lawmakers with clout can demand such obeisance, and vulnerable interests have little choice but to comply. For example, dozens of labor unions contributed to both Richard Gephardt's reelection committee and his leadership PAC, the Effective Government Committee, during the 1997–1998 election cycle. Multiple telecommunications companies also doubled up in their donations to such senior Republicans on the House Commerce Committee as Bliley and House Telecommunications Subcommittee chairman W. J. "Billy" Tauzin of Louisiana and Vice Chairman Michael Oxley of Ohio. These are lawmakers who cannot be refused.

At the same time, a leadership PAC also provides an extra chance for interests to say thanks. Republican congressman Mark Foley of Florida, a longtime advocate for sugar growers, helped defeat an effort in 1998 that would have blocked funding to administer the U.S. sugar price-support program. According to the Center for Responsive Politics, two PACs affiliated with sugar producers, Flo-Sun and U.S. Sugar, contributed both to Foley's reelection committee and to his leadership PAC. Surely they would have given to a third entity if they could have.

So much for strict limits on giving to candidates.

In fact, the politicians who use (and abuse) leadership PACs the most are presidential candidates. To be precise, they don't *admit* that they're presidential candidates, because if they did they would be forced to take no more than thousand-dollar contributions. Leadership PACs afford them much more flexibility than that. And that's why they're so helpful in the early stages of a campaign.

Still, known candidates ranging from Lamar Alexander (Campaign for a New American Century) to Dan Quayle (Campaign America) and from John Kasich (Pioneer Political Action Committee) to Al Gore (Leadership '98) raised millions of dollars in each of their leadership PACs and used that money to pay for travel expenses as they stumped the country in 1997 and

1998 to stir support for their nascent presidential bids. They also gave away some of those dollars as a way to make friends among the political establishment.

The leadership PACs also function as training grounds for fund-raisers. Gore utilized his PAC to, in effect, try out the best and brightest among the Democratic volunteers around the nation and to recruit them for the far harder task of raising thousand-dollar checks in the primary election campaign.

George W. Bush kept his eye on his competitors' funds and noticed that a near-certain also-ran, Senator John Ashcroft of Missouri, had managed to gather close to an astounding three million dollars in his Spirit of America leadership PAC. When the Texas governor put together a campaign staff for his presidential run, he chose Jack Oliver as his finance director; Oliver had held the same position at Spirit of America.

Some fund-raising on behalf of politicians has nothing directly to do with politics. My favorite outrage of this type recently is the Trent Lott Leadership Institute at the University of Mississippi. Lott used his name and the hunger of companies and other interests to influence federal legislation to raise millions of dollars for this brand-new academic center on the campus of his alma mater.

The project was meritorious, but the potential for abuse of power was too huge to be overlooked. For instance, million-dollar givers to the institute in 1999 included MCI Worldcom and Lockheed Martin, both of which were in the midst of a legislative battle over Lockheed's planned purchase of a major satellite company.

Making matters worse was a multimillion-dollar fund-raiser, held at Washington's Kennedy Center, that was organized by such superlobbyists as Haley Barbour, former chairman of the

Republican National Committee, and Carroll Campbell, president of the American Council of Life Insurance and a former governor and congressman from South Carolina. The gala event was a who's who of industries and interest groups that have gargantuan stakes in federal law and regulation.

According to *The New York Times, The Washington Post,* and *Roll Call,* contributors to the cause included Leo Mullin, CEO of Delta Air Lines; Charles Heimbold, CEO of Bristol-Myers Squibb; John W. Snow, CEO of CSX; and dozens of other lobbyists and executives involved in gambling, oil and gas, shipbuilding, telecommunications, real estate, financial services, and tobacco. Several million dollars were collected, all told. And why not? No one could afford not to show up.

And this wasn't the first time, nor will it be the last time, that big-name pols shook down the money men to aid their own personal charities. Republican senators Jesse Helms of North Carolina, Mitch McConnell of Kentucky, and Strom Thurmond of South Carolina all staged successful pleas for funds to help academic programs that were named for them. So did former senator John Glenn, the Ohio Democrat and astronaut.

The classic case involved a shakedown by one senator whom no one had ever heard of outside his home state of Montana. Republican Conrad Burns is better known as a former livestock auctioneer than as a congressional legislator. But he did chair the consequential Senate Telecommunications Subcommittee. That made him a key figure to the likes of U S West and the cable giant Tele-Communications International. No doubt that's one reason they happily forked over a half-million dollars each to benefit the Burns Telecommunications Center at Montana State University.

Burns helped raise five million dollars for the center, which promoted the worthy cause of assisting students who live off-campus to commute through modems and computers. Still, that's a lot of federal friends for a no-name senator.

Money men are under constant pressure to give. Some of it is soft sell in the form of printed invitations to receptions. The request is usually light, but the volume is heavy. Hardly a day goes by when professional lobbyists don't receive at least a few of these invites—and then a follow-up phone call, often from the congressperson directly.

A friend of mine is a frequent contributor by virtue of his job; he's a lobbyist. He collected the unused invitations he received and gave them to me quarterly in great big envelopes. I have hundreds of invitations now, and he tells me that they are only a portion of the number he actually received. (He sometimes absentmindedly tossed many away.) He wished he could throw them all away, he said, but that's not how it works.

Their variety is impressive. Some are formal and cardlike. Others are single-sheet flyers that look like strip-joint throwaways that are handed out on street corners. Prices are $250 for relatively new members of Congress or for freshly minted candidates for the House. Others ask the full thousand-dollar maximum for heavyweight senators and senior House members. Most veterans of the House settle for five hundred dollars a seat.

Actually, seats are rarely part of the deal. To save money, most of the fund-raisers are breakfasts or, more usually, receptions. Finger food and cheap booze are most common. The events are held in private rooms at restaurants and hotels all over town, though many are convened just a stone's throw from the congressional office buildings on Capitol Hill in the clubs maintained by the Democrats (the National Democratic Club) and the Republicans (the Capitol Hill Club). Other favorite, close-by venues include a town house owned by the American Trucking

Associations and such private lobbyist redoubts as the office of the Dutko Group.

Two elements are pretty standard on the invitations. First is a drawing of the Capitol dome. A smallish envelope through which you can see the dome is the number-one tipoff of yet another invitation to a fund-raiser. My friend never even bothered to open most of these.

The other similarity among the invites is a strange hierarchy in the listing of hosts. You might think that members of Congress are more than able to sponsor their own fund-raising receptions. In fact, junior members almost invariably get more senior (read: more influential) members to agree to attend the fund-raiser and serve as the chief draw. Remember, fund-raising is target marketing. And Washingtonians want access to big names if they're going to shell out some campaign cash.

That's why a fund-raising reception for a little-known candidate for the House from California named Charles J. Ball featured the names of Majority Leader Dick Armey and Majority Whip Tom DeLay at the top of the bright yellow invitation. The same was true for Congressman Bob Ehrlich, Republican of Maryland. In 1998, his invitation for a five-hundred-dollar PAC-donation lunch noted that he was a member of the budget and the banking committees. But his junior rank on those panels required that he also list several GOP House leaders as the people who were actually doing the inviting. The etiquette is that the people listed as hosts should drop by the event. In fact, the big dogs sometimes don't show up—much to the chagrin of the paying lobbyists.

Congressmen who have been around for a while don't need to reduce themselves to that kind of gimmickry. They use other angles—like having fun, a rare commodity in the dour and serious capital city. A golf outing is one trick. Parties for lawmakers are others. Republican congresswoman Barbara Cubin of

Wyoming held her event at a Washington Mystics basketball game. Democratic congressman Jim Moran of Virginia liked to take donors to the theater. Democratic congressman Sandy Levin of Michigan featured Motown music. And a few lawmakers emphasize the food. Louisiana congressmen push Cajun cuisine; Congressman Neil Abercrombie had a "Hawaiian Breakfast." Democratic congressman John Baldacci of Maine offered a "spaghetti luncheon with Mama Baldacci's secret sauce." I hear it was pretty good.

But the most powerful lawmakers don't need a fancy come-on or even an introduction. Take the simple card sent in 1998 that read, "Please join Fritz and Peatsy Hollings for a Reception." No PAC manager worth his cell phone had to be reminded that Democratic senator Hollings of South Carolina was up for re-election and could use some money. For Hollings, requests for thousand-dollar donations didn't require explanation.

More than that, lobbyists and other people interested in legislation often fight to be named as hosts on certain invitations. It is considered an honor to hold a fund-raiser or to be listed as a member of a "steering committee" (meaning to serve as a solicitor) for the chairperson of any of Congress's money committees, whether ways and means, finance, banking, commerce, or appropriations. An elected leader of either chamber of Congress gets similar attention.

Money men go out of their way to give and to be seen as giving to the real players in Washington, no matter who they are. Money men market themselves to their colleagues and to the powers that be whenever they commit their fund-raising skills. It's all part of buying into the system.

5

A Day on the Phone

Sitting behind his paper-strewn desk, Peter Terpeluk, a blue-eyed salesman on the Bush for President squad, picked up the telephone and zeroed in on another target for his fund-raising operation.

SECRETARY TO MR. BURNHAM: Good afternoon, Chris Burnham's office.

TERPELUK: Hi, Sharon, it's Peter Terpeluk.

SHARON: Hi, Peter.

TERPELUK: Is Chris around?

SHARON: He's not. He should be on his way back from New York.

TERPELUK: Oh, good. So he'll be back in the office this afternoon?

SHARON: He should be.

TERPELUK: Okay. I got his e-mail. I want to go over that and a couple other things.

SHARON: Okay.

TERPELUK: And have him give me a buzz and make sure that he gets me on the phone.

SHARON: All right.
TERPELUK: Thanks.

Chris Burnham was the former treasurer of the State of Connecticut whom Terpeluk had already enlisted as a Pioneer, one of the more than two hundred Bush backers who agreed early in the campaign to raise at lease one hundred thousand dollars in thousand-dollar increments for the Texas governor's presidential campaign. Terpeluk, who dressed like an investment banker but who actually worked as a business consultant and lobbyist on Washington's Pennsylvania Avenue, was one of the earliest recruits to the Bush fund-raising juggernaut. And Burnham, who actually *was* an investment banker, was just one of more than twenty-five people whom Terpeluk had enlisted to raise big bucks.

Terpeluk, age fifty-one, spent most of a sun-drenched afternoon in the spring of 1999 calling people like Burnham to firm up arrangements for what became known as the pilgrimage: a trip to Texas to meet the great man himself. Burnham was scheduled to be part of a gaggle of would-be financial supporters who would fly to Austin to lunch with Governor Bush. The idea of these encounters was for GOP fund-raisers like Burnham to take their measure of the politician. Terpeluk was one of a handful of Bush loyalists who helped prepare the guest lists for such events.

Terpeluk knew that he was selling a sure thing. He had already played Sherpa to a few delegations of pilgrims, and no one—repeat, no one—had come away disappointed. George W. Bush turned out to be an amazingly charming, disarmingly candid, and unquestionably charismatic man. Terpeluk knew this and solicited people to attend such events from around the country with vigor and confidence. He knew that no one, not the haughtiest chief executive or the most independent-minded entrepreneur, would be able to come away unimpressed or unconvinced. Some of the most arrogant, self-assured leaders in the business world walked away from their pilgrimage believing that they had just met the next President of the United States.

Not that Terpeluk had ever lacked confidence when he was engaged in selling something. The son of a salesman, Terpeluk was always certain, even though (as his friends will attest) he also was frequently wrong. Take the time he told everyone not to worry about that unknown governor Bill Clinton; he could *never* become president. Or the time he called around to alert everyone that Dan Quayle was going to be dropped from the presidential ticket for 1992. Well, Terpeluk sometimes had more enthusiasm than facts.

But he also had friends. Many, many friends. He was a schmoozer, a networker, a connector of people and was paid well for his efforts. His small consulting firm, American Continental Group, represented at one time or another entities as diverse as Pepsi, Intel, Bank of America, and a coalition of travel agents who were battling the airlines. What attracted these groups to him? Insiders knew that Terpeluk was a player in politics and a man who knew the other players, at both the state and federal levels. He achieved this status in large part because he was good at raising money and getting others to raise money for big-name Republican candidates.

As a fund-raiser, Terpeluk (and all the other major solicitors talked about in this book) was a volunteer. The Bush campaign, or any other campaign for that matter, never paid him for his work on their behalf. On the contrary, Terpeluk had to put aside his paying clients' business in order to raise money for Bush.

At the same time, many of his clients came to him and his firm because he did all this pro bono money raising. Political fund gathering isn't just one person asking another person to do him a favor, though clearly that's part of the pitch. Terpeluk was also inviting people to become part of something exciting: a winning campaign. And in many ways, he was a gatekeeper for entry into that glamorous realm. If you wanted to become a player in the George W. Bush campaign, Terpeluk could tell you how to do it. Given the momentum that the Bush effort developed from the beginning, givers and fund-raisers recruited by Terpeluk believed that he was doing *them* a favor. Terpeluk was bestowing on them the opportunity to join the Bush bandwagon at a very high level and long before latecomers and opportunists cluttered things up.

Or at least that's what they often came to believe. Now *that's* a salesman!

On this day in late March, Terpeluk double-checked that his upcoming pilgrimage to Austin would come off without a hitch and tried with some notable success to enlist other people to become Pioneers for Bush.

For four hours that afternoon, he teased secretaries and, when he could finally reach them, instructed corporate chieftains about how they could join Team Bush. Most of his attempts ended with a request for a call back. But he also hit pay dirt almost every time he finally got a prospect on the line.

Take his encounter with Dr. Richard Cheng, the president of a high-tech company in Virginia. Terpeluk was pushing Cheng to raise funds for Bush and to get friends of his to do the same. One issue: Could Cheng solicit money from fellow Chinese Americans who are naturalized U.S. citizens and who hold a so-called green card? Terpeluk checked the Bush campaign's cheat sheet on the legalities of giving and answered forcefully in the affirmative.

TERPELUK: No, there's no problem on that check. If he's a green card, that's fine. Yes, he can be writing checks himself if he's a green card. Yes, oh yes. Oh no, no, no. Richard, any green card whatsoever they can all write checks. Okay? Don't worry about that. How much do you think you're going to try to gather?

So Cheng was in the bag. But Terpeluk never stopped after hooking just one fish. He tried to use Cheng's connections to reel in a few more big fund-raisers.

TERPELUK: Well, then, we can get in touch with your friend, too. I'll set him up there with Bush's guy in California. The chairman of the campaign in California's name is Brad Freeman. He's a good friend of mine. And what I will do is have him get directly with you. So if you have him call me, why don't you put that call together and I'll make sure he's dealing right with the guy at the top. Does that make sense? Give me his name again. Give me his phone number. Fax it over to me and what I will do . . . write down this name, Brad Freeman. *B-r-a-d* Freeman.

What's surprising about campaign fund-raising at this, the highest levels, is that the object isn't to corrupt the politician. It's more about trying to sell the idea of the politician to the would-be giver. Terpeluk used every technique at his disposal. He offered access to the candidate—albeit a very brief encounter, sufficient for a photo suitable for hanging and bragging about but not long enough to really make much of an impression on the candidate himself. Terpeluk also used the allure of the candidate's top aides and even his own minor celebrity. After all, he was acting as agent of Mr. Bush himself.

The other necessary element in making the sale is closing. All afternoon, Terpeluk never left a conversation without delineating, in detail, the terms of his arrangement with whichever fish was on the line, and then also sought the names of other fish. More from his conversation with Cheng:

TERPELUK: So, what do you think, you can get to about twenty-five? Fifty [thousand dollars]? I mean, you tell me who you want to go after and whatever you want to put together would be fine.

Is there anybody else you want me to work on? Then you're just going to go ahead and try to sell some other people. Okay. So what I'll do is I will tell the Bush people that you'll try to raise money—perfect. All right. I understand. All right. Perfect. This is a great strategy and I really appreciate it.

Can I ask you this? If I'm up in New York next week, do you want me to try to meet with Henry Tang? Yeah, that's tough to do. Uh-huh. Well, is there anything wrong with you on behalf of George going to everybody in the committee? Okay. Why don't I tell the Bush people that you're going to work the Committee of One Hundred [a group of prominent Chinese-American business leaders]? Is that fair? All right. Perfect. Thanks, Richard.

Such was Terpeluk's opening effort to raise funds from the Chinese-American community. Next, he tried to persuade a former top policy aide from the earlier Bush administration to help George W. Bush financially. The prospect's name was Bob Grady, and he was at the time a highly successful investment banker based in San Francisco.

TERPELUK: Grady, what are you doing, man? You hit the trifecta, man. You're my richest friend. What is this? So you're not quite as rich as I thought you were? Okay. How you doing, man? I'm doing everything, you know, making hundred-thousand-dollar phone calls, fifty thousand.

Grady, what you gotta think about is what you're going to do. This is what I think you ought to do. I was down there [in Austin] three days last week. Just listen to me, please listen.

They're on fire down there. It's unbelievable. It's Reaganesque. It's Reaganesque. They're big-time guys. If I were you, I'd use your network around the country. Raise a hundred grand and become a Pioneer. I'll fax you all the stuff. Just listen to me. I'll get you all the regs and rules. Have clients, friends start sending you checks. I'm going to have Jack Oliver call you.

Listen, Grady, this is what you want to do. Listen, I'm telling you this as a friend, okay? It's going to separate you from everybody else. I think you do the Pioneers. It's one hundred, one hundred fifty thousand.

Terpeluk and Grady talked about arranging a meeting between another would-be solicitor and a senior Bush policy adviser. They also reviewed what in the political fund-raising business amounts to the salability of the candidate in the eyes of would-be contributors: his standing in the public-opinion polls.

TERPELUK: There isn't a poll in the country where he's [Gore's] above thirty-five percent. Did you see the Pew poll this week? Hello? Did you see it? Grady, fifty-two percent of the people won't consider voting for Al Gore. Now, that's a pretty bad hole, isn't it? Well, exactly.

Everybody you're going to get a check from, no matter where in the country it is, gets to go to a Bush event. If you get a thousand-dollar check from a friend in New Jersey, we got an event in New Jersey. They're there, do the photo, and it'll be done.

You want to do this. Trust me. We'll get the paperwork to you. I'll get it all cooked with [Jack] Oliver. I'll have him call you. Does that make sense? You're going to call? I've got some other slots to go down [to Austin for a pilgrimage] in April. So if you've got somebody you want me to take down, let me know.

And thus Bob Grady became a Pioneer.

How did Terpeluk rise to the position of recruiter of Pioneers? It all began with a dinner in Washington late in 1998 with Heinz Prechter, the GOP's number-one fund-raiser from Detroit. Prechter, a short, powerfully built billionaire who made his first fortune by mass-producing auto sunroofs, worked with Terpeluk raising money for Republican governors. Prechter was close to Michigan governor John Engler who, in turn, was the biggest gubernatorial backer of Governor Bush of Texas. Prechter also was a pal of Bush separately; they had come to know each other in part because Prechter, who made one of his later fortunes in cattle, owned a ranch in Texas.

In any case, Prechter had called Terpeluk and his fund-raising buddy and fellow lobbyist, Wayne Berman, who was also active with GOP governors. Terpeluk, Berman, and Prechter also understood that the real juice in the Republican Party came not from Congress but from the many GOP governors. If the GOP had any chance of winning the White House, the candidate and his money would have to come from GOP-led state organizations. All three had been major fund-raisers for George W. Bush's father and knew each other very well. During the dinner in Washington that night, Prechter said, "Don't commit yourself to any candidate for president yet." But they all knew he was really inviting them in on the ground floor of the George W. Bush for President campaign.

Neither man hesitated. Terpeluk and Berman had worked in tandem for Jack Kemp in years gone by. Terpeluk, in particular, would have been one of Kemp's top money men if the former congressman and football quarterback had decided to run for president in 2000. But Terpeluk knew Kemp. The last thing the white-maned pol wanted to do at this stage of his life was raise money. That was tougher work than Kemp cared to take on. As a result, there wasn't any chance he would actually run.

Kemp hungered to be president, but he didn't have the stomach to beg. At sixty-three, Kemp despised the mercenary part of electioneering, and that pretty much took him out of the running.

Kemp told *Fortune* in 1998 that he hadn't ruled out a campaign. And he said he was raising money for his political-action committee, Freedom and Free Enterprise, to help finance his travels just in case he chose to mount a bid. But that was where the similarity between Kemp and a real candidate ended. Asked about fund-raising, Kemp made a sour expression: "It's the worst part of politics—the time it takes, the schmoozing it takes, the places you have to go, the hands you have to shake. . . ." His words trailed off in disgust.

Kemp was just going through the motions on the money front. His backers practically had to drag him to the phone to dial for dollars. And when he finally did make some calls, he did so grudgingly. "I'm terrible at it," he admitted. He preferred to kibitz rather than press for cash. Only half in jest he said, "What I'm talking about is so important that people should call and say they want to give to me. They ought to line up outside my door." Of course, that wasn't about to happen, and Kemp seemed fine with that fact.

His stint as Bob Dole's vice-presidential candidate in 1996 was a detour, mercifully brief, along his postgovernment road to personal prosperity. After eighteen years in Congress and four more as George Bush's secretary of housing and urban development, Kemp was comfortable sitting on corporate boards and giving speeches for thirty-five thousand dollars each. He had a ski house in Vail that he called "my Shangri-la" and said he would prefer to spend his extra time at family get-togethers, not candidate cattle calls. "I like raising ideas," he said. "I don't like raising money." That's why, in 2000, voters can find him on the slopes.

Terpeluk was especially thrilled at the prospect of leading the way for a new generation of political activists—that is, money men. Sure, many of the people he recruited as Bush contributors were blue-chip business executives from conventional places such as Pepsi and Bell Atlantic. But he took special pride in bringing new blood into the ranks of fund-raisers, such as Rich Gelfond, the co-CEO of IMAX, the giant-movie-screen company, and Steve Canton, president of Telco Communications, among many others.

As Terpeluk liked to boast, this was the best time he had ever had in politics. The candidate was right, and the givers were willing, even eager. They saw a winner and wanted to invest. And that propelled Terpeluk to work with more enthusiasm than ever. On that afternoon in March, he even called his brother-in-law in Los Angeles.

TERPELUK: I'm looking for Mike Poland. Sure. It's his brother-in-law, Peter. Thanks. Okay. Poland, what are you doing, buddy? Working your butt off? This is me you're talking to, not your wife. Well, were your ears burning yesterday? I had a two-hour meeting with—actually a half-hour meeting—with Tom DeLay. Yeah, your golfing buddy. And he's going to be one of the real players for Bush in Congress.

I saw Brad [Freeman] down in Austin last week with Bush. I just want to get a feel for what you want to do. You just gotta tell me. I think we can do it all through Brad in L.A. I just think it's going to be a lot better for you obviously to do it that way. I will have Anne Le Gassick [a professional fund-raiser for Bush] call you and get that whole thing kind of moving because I think we're going to have a couple of events out there, you know, and they may need your help in Palm Springs.

I gotta tell you, Mike, it's a fairly easy sell, I mean, easy, easier than we've had in a long while. Yeah. Well, you think through how much you think you can raise, you know, with your networks all over the country. Everybody that writes a thousand-dollar check gets a photo and a dinner somewhere in the country.

What I don't want you to do is overpromise them. So you think through what's realistic, both in L.A. or wherever you want to be able to do it. Does that make sense? Write her name down, Anne Le Gassick. I'll call her. What else is happening?

Fund-raising isn't done only by phone. And it isn't only a matter of chumming the water with cheap souvenirs like photographs with the candidate. Certainly that was true of Terpeluk, who was a Republican to his marrow.

He didn't just dislike Bill Clinton. He reveled in his impeachment. He watched the proceedings like others watch World Series games, rooting loudly for impeachment and then conviction. He stuck the biggest CLINTON IMPEACHED headline he could find on his refrigerator door. He also obtained a rare complete set of tickets to the impeachment trial in the Senate and had them mounted in a very expensive, museum-quality frame in the wood-lined study of his home. The same room, by the way, contained photos of Terpeluk with the pope, as well as others of him alongside the most recent Republican presidents.

The tickets, under their own dedicated light, were among the biggest attractions during the Bush for President "pre-event" that Terpeluk hosted in May 1999. In his beautiful, showcase home in Chevy Chase, Maryland, Terpeluk threw a party for dozens of Washingtonians who had agreed to raise between ten thousand and twenty-five thousand dollars for a Bush fund-raiser scheduled for June 22. The spacious terrace and front grounds were crawling with two kinds of people: former Bush administration officials and people who still insisted on being called "Mr. Ambassador" from that era, and people in their thirties and some in their twenties who had never given political contributions before.

Terpeluk stood on a white, wood-slatted bench and welcomed the Bush brigades. "This," he said, with a broad gesture toward his wife, "is the most exciting thing in our political lives, the most exciting since 1988." That was the year, of course, when George Bush had been elected president. Terpeluk then introduced one of the "Mr. Ambassadors" in attendance to remind everyone that they needed to pick up their fund-raising instructions and tickets so they can sell, sell, sell for the June event. And then Terpeluk introduced the guest of honor: Don Evans, the governor's best friend and finance chairman, the chief volunteer fund-raiser.

Evans had crisscrossed the country pumping up givers at events just like Terpeluk's. He had obviously gotten accustomed to the drill and was an appealing cheerleader. On the reception line earlier in the evening, he smoothly shook everyone's hand and said, "Thank you for helping my friend. He's going to be the next president." And when he took his perch on the bench, he continued along the same theme.

At the time, Bush hadn't yet said for sure that he was running. But as money men (and women), the attendees were treated to the inside story. Evans said that Bush had found "peace in his heart" about the bid around the time of his inauguration as governor earlier that year and that he was "sleeping soundly" with his decision. Why was Bush running? "Duty," he said, but everyone in the crowd heard the word *destiny*.

Evans urged everyone to "execute, execute, execute." People

who raise ten thousand dollars each, he said, were "the back-bone" of the fund-raising operation. Then he introduced young Jack Oliver and announced that the campaign's goal by June 30 was to raise fifteen million dollars, an ambitious amount indeed.

When the June event came, so many people wanted to attend that a few of them showed up waving thousand-dollar checks. Surprised Bush aides had to process the contributions right there at the door. Well-known GOP fund-raiser Julie Finley received checks in her mailbox for George W. Bush, and she wasn't even raising money for him. And, as is now famously known, the Bush campaign didn't raise fifteen million dollars by June 30. It raised a record-shattering thirty-seven million.

Events like the one at Terpeluk's house were pivotal. Nothing beats enthusiasm and perceived momentum when it comes to sales. And that was what was on display at Terpeluk's that evening. The proof: in just four months, from March through June, the Bush campaign received more than 79,500 contributions from more than 74,000 donors. The average contribution was $466.69, which was high for a presidential election. The campaign reported a breathtaking $30 million cash on hand. Thanks to low-budget fund-raising events (peanuts and hot dogs with a cash bar was as fancy as most of them got), the cost of collecting that money was under a dime on the dollar, less than a third of what was considered the optimum proportion.

The Bush campaign *was* the most exciting political event in Terpeluk's political life. For a change, he was hardly exaggerating at all.

This led to another marketing technique: telling people that time was running short for them to get in on the ground floor for a campaign that was about to go through the roof. This, of course, was all before McCain made his big run. Here was Terpeluk's conversation with real-estate developer Robert Monahan, who had just moved from Pennsylvania to Washington, D.C., and who wanted to become a factor in national Republican politics.

TERPELUK: Hello. Bob Monahan. What you doin', buddy? Have you got the school decision made yet? Trey [Terpeluk's three-year-old son] got into three schools, and he's going to National Presbyterian. So leave it to my Catholic wife to find a Protestant school for my Catholic son.

I want to talk to you about what we talked about last week, how you can get involved. The whole purpose is to get you to be a player. Listen, you can do it. If you call a guy in Denver, and he and his wife give you two thousand dollars, they will go to Denver for a Bush event. You follow me?

But you gotta tell me, 'cause what I'll do is if you think you can, I'm going to get Jack Oliver to give you a call, wire it up with these guys. You know what I'm saying? And you're going to do this totally away from Pennsylvania. Does that make sense? All right. Well, Bob, I'm not going to pull the trigger. But I think what I'm telling you is the window's not going to be open tomorrow. I mean, it's not going to be open forever. There's an entertainment group, I think that's going down to Austin on I think the seventeenth of April or something. Yeah, it's in April. It's in there somewhere. Do you want me to try to get you in there?

Bob, all I'm saying to you is I don't want a couple weeks [to] go by and you give me hell. Fine, that's fine. Yes, yes, yes.

Monahan, of course, called soon and tried to become a Pioneer. But Terpeluk did more than make phone calls. Solicitors of Terpeluk's caliber do more than play at the presidential level. They raise money for members of their party for races for the House and Senate and, increasingly, for governor. In a lot of ways, the states were where the money was for people like Terpeluk. If a corporation needed to know who the "governor's man" is in, say, Texas or Pennsylvania or Michigan, Terpeluk knows and can provide the proper introduction, thanks to his long and rewarding association with the candidate, often before he ever got elected.

Terpeluk took his connection making to an extreme by helping to lead the Republican Governors Association. The result: No GOP governor elected in recent years could possibly not know Terpeluk and the organization's other top fund-raisers. And while he was trying to locate solicitors for George W. Bush's campaign, Terpeluk also hosted fund-raising events for several other politicians, including Maryland gubernatorial candidate Ellen Sauerbrey and California senatorial candidate Matt Fong.

The Fong dinner was held in a private room at the rear of an upscale Italian restaurant down the block from Terpeluk's office. Terpeluk himself served as master of ceremonies. Natty as always, he stood before the four dozen or so givers and tossed red-meat rhetoric. "I never thought I would see another person do more for the Republican Party than Ronald Reagan," he said. "And we do now in Bill Clinton." The crowd all but mewed with pleasure.

Terpeluk turned over the proceedings to round-faced U.S. senator Spencer Abraham of Michigan, who effused about Fong and his prospects. He also pitched hard and without euphemism for money. "Having enough money is indispensable to winning," Abraham said. So, he told the Washington lobbyists in the audience, "go to the limit for your PAC" in giving to GOP candidates such as Fong. He said he wanted Republicans to control the Senate with a veto-proof, sixty-vote majority and insisted that "the tide is running in our direction." He concluded: "I implore you to provide those additional dollars."

Then Fong took the floor. He thanked Terpeluk for his energy.

And then he impressed the crowd with his own ambitious fund-raising plans. In the next fifty days, he disclosed, he had scheduled two hundred fund-raising events all across the country. An aide to Fong reported, in fact, that the candidate would sometimes spend ten hours a day on the phone soliciting money, arriving at the office in California at 6 A.M. in order to make calls to the East Coast. Even for the callous money men listening that evening, those were impressive stats. "If we raise the money," Fong asserted, "we will win."

Well, Fong raised the money, but he didn't win. Barbara Boxer did. She also raised a boatload of cash and bested Fong in TV-advertising strategy that year. Ellen Sauerbrey of Maryland also lost her race. "But that's the way it is in politics," Terpeluk said, philosophically. "It's ups and downs."

One reason: Fund-raising is a precarious endeavor. On the same day that Terpeluk signed up almost everyone he had contacted to help George W. Bush, he was rejected by one would-be solicitor, a business executive named Deepak Chopra. Terpeluk and his partners were counting on Chopra, who owned an X ray–equipment manufacturer near Los Angeles (but who was no relation to the bestselling guru), to hold a fund-raising event for Republican congressman Jerry Lewis of California (who himself was no relation to the comedian). As a lobbying firm, American Continental Group needed to stay on good terms with Lewis because he chaired one of Congress's most powerful appropriations subcommittees. But Chopra got cold feet. This was how Terpeluk dealt with the news.

TERPELUK: What are you doing? You know, I swear all you ever do is work. How much do you think you can do? (*Long pause*) I understand exactly. Yeah. I mean, I hear you. How much you think you might be able to raise?

You can come up blank, right? Okay, let me see if we can

raise it. Yeah, then you take credit. Okay? All right. Well, you know, he's going to carry a pretty big load for us out there. Yes. I hear you. Okay. Let me talk to him about that, and then I'll let you know.

What we'll figure out is how you want to do this, whether you want to quietly raise the money or maybe what you might do is schedule an event out there somewhere else. Yeah, I know. Yeah. Well, you're better off just telling them that, you know, you're asking for the money without having a public event. Is it better to do that? Done. See ya. 'Bye.

Terpeluk sounded upbeat throughout the conversation, but he was grim faced when he finished. He called a couple of his partners into his office to explain that Chopra was reneging on their plan to raise money for Lewis. "He's trying to decide whether to have an event at the house," Terpeluk explained. "He has a little fear of failure. So I said, 'Why don't you quietly try to raise the money?'" Yet everyone in the room knew that probably wouldn't work. Terpeluk told his colleagues they would have to explore other means. "We'll have to raise the money ourselves," he said, and his partners went off to plot and plan. A lawmaker as influential as Lewis could not be disappointed.

Terpeluk climbed his way from the bottom to become one of the nation's top money men. He grew up middle-class in Montgomery County outside Philadelphia, the son of a Ukrainian father and an Irish mother. His father was a salesman and his mother a high-school teacher. Young Peter aspired to stay near home. With a master's degree in public administration from LaSalle College, he was proud to have been hired in his twenties as the city manager of Lower Moreland, Pennsylvania, a burg of twenty thousand souls not far from the City of Brotherly Love.

But Terpeluk had a gift that could not be contained. He got along well with people. And one of those people was fellow Pennsylvanian Drew Lewis, a major Republican mover and shaker, who went on to serve as transportation secretary in the Reagan administration. On his way up in the early 1980s, Lewis took along Terpeluk. At thirty-one, Terpeluk was named a regional administrator for the U.S. Small Business Administration. Barely six months later, he was promoted to acting deputy administrator for the entire agency. He moved to Washington and soon was testifying on Capitol Hill and attending meetings at the White House almost weekly. "Okay," he said. "I like this."

Lewis admonished Terpeluk not to like it too much, however. "Peter, when you're good in government, you know when to get out—on top." So he left at the end of the first term of the Reagan administration. He continued to work closely with government, however, first with Pennsylvania friends who needed help in Washington. And his main entry point became campaign fund-raising, in addition to the personal connections he had made in D.C. By 1988, he was a senior fund-raiser for Vice President Bush and was named a cochairman of the presidential inaugural galas after Bush's election.

Terpeluk was welcomed as an insider, even though he continued to work with private clients from outside government. In 1992, he was a cochairman of Bush's reelection committee and learned about the downside of fund-raising. Things were great at the beginning—when Bush was still president—and murder toward the end, when he was clearly on the verge of losing. "Getting people to part with thousand-dollar checks," he recalled, "was very difficult." He and his wife took Bush's defeat hard. Diane Terpeluk had worked for years as an aide to Bush.

But Republicanism is never completely out of fashion, in the same way that Democrats always hover in the wings during bad times for them. In 1994, Terpeluk was considered an elder of the party when Republicans took control of both the House and the Senate. As a result, American Continental Group attracted clients that ranged from Oxford Health and Andersen Consulting to the Los Angeles Metropolitan Transit Authority and Bell Atlantic. A slew of high-tech firms, like Cisco Systems, also sought its counsel.

What service did Terpeluk and his partners provide? Mostly they gave strategic advice to those who needed favors from government, whether state or federal. Who do I talk to in order to persuade New York governor Pataki? Or, who do I need to see and contribute to in the House in order to have a chance with my company's issue of the day? And there was also this: Where should I sit at the dinner party? Or how do I get my CEO close to the chairman without getting him too close? Those were the kinds of questions that Terpeluk's team was constructed to answer. As for Terpeluk himself, he conceded, "I'm the rainmaker, the maker of relationships."

Being a money man brought many of the relationships he needed to build a thriving business. Such was the circular world of asking and giving favors. In exchange for Terpeluk's dedicated work on behalf of candidates, his clients were among the first on the list of people the candidate, and the candidate's retainers, met in the throes of a debate or pending transaction. In exchange for his good advice, Terpeluk could get a client to write a check that, in turn, would help Terpeluk down the road with the candidates.

At the same time, it would be wrong to say that Terpeluk did all this money raising just to make himself richer. Sure, Terpeluk's prolific fund-raising attracted and retained clients. And his pride surely expanded when he was able to present himself as a power broker among the George W. Bush elite. What's more, his cachet would zoom if Bush won the White House in 2000.

But his heart was on the line as well. No one could work with such gusto or emotion for the money alone. Terpeluk and his wife cried together on the phone as they each watched Jeb Bush and his mother on TV on the night in 1998 that Jeb was elected governor of Florida. And in the next election the stakes—and Terpeluk's hopes—were as high as they could be. "The 2000 election is the whole shootin' match," he confided, with only slight hyperbole. "This is the battle of the century." And if the Democrats win? I ask. "Diane and Peter go to Santa Barbara."

That, of course, was mostly overstated. Terpeluk would never want to leave center-stage politics voluntarily. It was too much a part of what he was.

6

The Money Woman

The title of this book doesn't mean that women don't raise funds for politicians, but it does convey a correct sense of how few women are part of that clique. Beth Dozoretz learned the hard way how difficult it was to break in.

She was shunned, undercut, and occasionally yelled at by the men in charge. Still, she eventually made it to the top of the heap: finance chair of the entire Democratic Party, the first woman ever to hold that key position. Her story is, in microcosm, the tale of how insular, petty, and, like so many other walks of life, outright chauvinistic the life of the money men often can be.

Dozoretz was a newcomer to Washington and to politics when the Clinton administration rolled triumphantly into town in 1993. But really, so it seemed, was everyone else. Along with the Clintons came a whole new set of characters and a different worldview. It featured young, baby-boomer heroes and heroines, all with new hopes and new aspirations and filled with the promise of a new start. After all, the Clintons had run and won on the issue of change. The air in the nation's capital was charged with the sense of that possibility.

Dozoretz was young (not yet forty), thin, bright, attractive, and extremely wealthy. Her third husband, Dr. Ron Dozoretz, was the founder and CEO of what was soon to become a billion-dollar network of health-maintenance organizations. And she was much more than a tagalong wife; she helped run the business for a while and, in fact, was instrumental in helping to navigate it through its difficult start-up phase. At the same time, though, the comfort and ease of the wealth that FHC Health Systems provided to the Dozoretzes aided the couple's entry into the upper reaches of Clintonia.

In Washington, Beth Dozoretz quickly became known as a hostess for powerful Democrats as well as a provider of ample campaign contributions. In essence, she was viewed as a less regal version of Pamela Harriman, the longtime party and fund giver deluxe.

Prior to the era of Bill Clinton, Beth Dozoretz didn't care much about politics. As Beth Goodman, she grew up in Worcester, Massachusetts. The daughter of a dentist, she began her work life as a first-grade teacher and occasional fashion model. She also tried her hand at selling clothes, which proved to be what she liked to do best. She had a real sense of people and what they wanted. She supported her first husband, Dick Schwartz, a student, by working as a buyer for a Massachusetts sportswear company.

Her marriage didn't last, but her love of the apparel trade, especially in New York, did. By thirty-one, according to *The Washington Post,* she had worked her way up to president of Clyde's Sportswear of New York, was earning a healthy six-figure salary, and had already begun and ended a second marriage to a fellow garment-industry executive. The paper quoted Irving Sandorf, the former owner of Clyde's Sportswear: "Beth was just driven to success. . . . She knows how to manipulate people. I don't know if you'd call them 'people skills.' It's more like 'I'll use you, you use me' skills."

That seemed a little harsh for Dozoretz, whose manner and tone of voice tended to be understated and relaxed. She was ambitious and hardworking, traits that often gnawed at men who have the same qualities. Still, it wasn't until after she married Ron in 1990 that she discovered where her talents were best applied: political fund-raising.

Ron Dozoretz was active in fund-raising from Norfolk, Virginia, where his company was based. He enjoyed politics, and his burgeoning business made it wise for him to stay on the good side of the people in power. He once toyed with running for the U.S. Senate himself. But mostly he supported others. He backed Ronald Reagan before turning his political affections to Bill Clinton. As the 2000 election approached in 1998, he even spent time hunting with George W. Bush.

In any case, Beth Dozoretz wasn't very political—at first. She didn't even want to go to the 1992 Democratic convention in New York. But her husband prevailed on her, and she went. She used to tell him, "I can't go to any of these political fund-raisers. You go." She was a product of the 1960s and was distrustful of government and politicians. She also thought fund-raising events were boring.

At the convention, that changed. She attended an event that featured an array of Democratic women candidates that included an address by Hillary Clinton. And that was the beginning. Bells sounded. Fireworks went off. She was transformed and transfixed, she said, by this powerful and charismatic woman not much older than herself. From Dozoretz's perspective, Hillary Clinton and the other women she met had a chance to do great things at a high level and in directions that Dozoretz, a prochoice feminist, thought were just so *right*.

The next thing the Dozoretzes knew, she had become the political junkie of the family. After the convention, she was encouraged to get more involved in Democratic politicking by Democratic senator Chuck Robb of Virginia. She began by helping to start the Women's Leadership Forum, which raised money for Democrats from an underassessed category of individuals: women. She later cochaired the DNC's trustees program, which is the branch of the party's fund-raising apparatus that caters to givers of between fifty thousand and one hundred thousand dollars. And there, too, whenever she could, she tried to involve women.

National estimates indicate that only a quarter to a third of the money given to political candidates comes from women. And certainly, women account for far less than a quarter of the people who do the actual soliciting. Dozoretz took on the challenge with gusto and proved to be a formidable fund-raiser. Democratic candidates knew they had a financial friend in Beth Dozoretz.

The Dozoretzes situated themselves in Norfolk and Washington, taking a beautiful apartment near Georgetown that overlooked the Potomac River. They entertained frequently and befriended the Clintons and the people around them, including Cuomos, Kennedys, Dingells, and the like. But Beth Dozoretz wanted to become more than another hostess. She was a believer and wanted to help promote the Democratic cause.

As she moved into the ranks of megasolicitors, however, she ran into resistance from the men who had been doing almost all the work before she got there.

There was the time, for instance, when she was yelled at by a millionaire from New York in the lobby of Washington's Hay-Adams Hotel. "Stay out of New York!" the millionaire warned her. Why the fuss? Dozoretz had persuaded a Manhattanite to donate one hundred thousand dollars to the Democratic National Committee. Unfortunately, the shouting millionaire thought that the donor was his guy (in the fund-raising sense) and that no one else should be talking to him. Indeed, even though the millionaire hadn't even spoken to the donor for two years, he believed that he should get credit for the donation. Credit, of course, was what money men lived for, and raising more money than anyone else is the goal of any die-hard solicitor. In the end, Dozoretz shared credit not with the shouter but with another solicitor who had actually done some recent prospecting with the donor.

As Dozoretz moved up the ladder among fund-raisers, she and her husband bought a grander residence in D.C. They paid $4.2 million for the spacious home of another highly visible couple, Michael and Arianna Huffington, in northwest Washington and proceeded to make it even more elegant and ready for entertaining than it already had been. And in so doing, Beth Dozoretz seemed only to make the community of power-hungry solicitors even more jealous.

During a small get-together at the Dozoretzes' new residence, the wife of a major donor took a shine to Beth Dozoretz, much to the chagrin of one of the other solicitors at the party. You see, the jealous solicitor considered the woman's husband to be his prospect and went to comic lengths to make sure that wouldn't change. At one point, the solicitor physically put himself between Beth and the husband to prevent Dozoretz from even talking to him. The next morning, the wife sheepishly came up to Beth and informed her that she had been told by her husband that they would give their contributions not through Dozoretz but through the solicitor they had always dealt with.

What a peculiar world!

And that was only the half of it. Ego stroking and celebrity gazing are integral to the fund-raising game, but sometimes the pettiness gets out of hand. In the run-up to a Democratic Party gala in Washington, Dozoretz was among a handful of activists who were raising money hand over fist. The question naturally arose of who would sit where.

This wasn't a minor matter, at least among money men. For Democrats, there were only two places of maximum honor: the seat next to the vice president and, better, the seat next to the president. On more than one occasion, money men have admitted to me that they have seen overeager fund givers sneak into a dinner early in order to rearrange the name cards so that they would be seated closer to the principals.

For the gala, Dozoretz asked if she could be seated next to the president. Big mistake. Whether she deserved that position or not is beyond determining. But without question her competitors immediately began to spread word around town that Dozoretz (1) hadn't really raised all the money she claimed, (2) whined if her demand to be seated next to the president was challenged, and (3) obviously wanted to sit near Clinton because you-know-why, wink wink.

Nice bunch.

Dozoretz won the honor of sitting next to the president that evening, but she paid dearly for it—a price well beyond the hours of toil it took to raise thousands upon thousands of dollars for her party.

The level of envy can border on insane. In the wake of the 1996 campaign-finance scandals, Dozoretz felt tired and beaten down. She took some time away from fund-raising to mourn the death of her father and to spend more time with her young son, Josh. Dan Dutko, a fellow solicitor, one night admitted to Dozoretz that he had been bad-mouthing her around town in part because he was upset that she had left the field for a while. "This is hard work, and we needed you," he complained, and Dozoretz understood. But then again, she said, she had other obligations and needs of her own.

And why else was Dutko upset? Because, he said, when Dozoretz had been active, she had gotten so much attention in the press and he had not. That attention included, he said incredibly, that she had been asked to testify in Congress about one of those infamous White House coffees, and he hadn't.

What? So huge a craving for the spotlight is hard for lesser egotists to fathom, but that nonetheless was one of the more perverse and pervasive aspects of being a money man. A money man is not only the person to see but, more likely than not, is a person who likes to be seen.

Jealousies aside, Dozoretz did become someone who was known as a friend of the First Couple, and that had both good and bad aspects. The good part was that she really was a friend of the First Couple and stood by them when others panicked during the Monica Lewinsky horror show. The bad part was that her minor celebrity status created odd and embarrassing moments.

For instance, after a while, she tried to stay in the background at public events with the president. She knew that being seen standing too close to him or to be seen as *wanting* to stand too close to him made her a target for false gossip, spitefulness, and opportunism by others. At a black-tie fund-raiser in New York, for instance, she tried to stay away from Clinton as he worked a rope line—only to be mobbed by an unruly throng of starstruck gazillionaires. During the chaos, Dozoretz was grabbed on the wrist by a bejeweled woman who used her as bait to bring Clinton closer for a photo. Another woman that same night told Dozoretz flatly, "I'll give you [the Democrats] an extra twenty thousand dollars if you can get me in a picture with him."

Such was the fever that Dozoretz had come to expect when people saw the president of the United States. And when he actually looked directly at them, they felt as if they were, at once, the only person in the room and magically on display to the entire world. That kind of intoxication was hard for even the richest people to duplicate some other way.

What's more, the chattering classes couldn't stop chattering, especially after Clinton agreed to be the godfather of the Dozoretzes' second child, a daughter named Melanne. The often staid Washington community was abuzz for a week about the baby-naming ceremony, which featured both Clintons, a rabbi, an Indian swami, and a Japanese nun, all at the Dozoretzes' mansion in Wesley Heights.

Still, upon her return to fund-raising in 1998, Dozoretz was more confident in her abilities and, therefore, more immune to the craziness of her vocation. For example, she began to take the attitude that it was better *not* to fight all the time. She had managed to develop her own, unique set of donors, and, besides, she figured, wasn't everybody supposed to be working for the same cause? At a Democratic Party fund-raising event in New York, a money man approached her with a scowl on his face. "You're stealing my people!" he growled, referring specifically to one of the rich folks whom he regularly tapped for party donations. This time, Dozoretz relented immediately and suggested graciously that the donor at issue should send his check to the scowling solicitor so the credit could go, exclusively, to him.

That's *extremely* mellow for a solicitor.

The mellowness didn't last long. In early 1999, Dozoretz was named finance chair of the entire Democratic National Committee. The men in charge, of course, were surprised and aghast. Mumbles were heard that Dozoretz had been refused entry to the upper reaches of the Gore for President fund-raising machine and was looking for some other route to the top. In fact, Dozoretz had once offered to, in effect, apprentice herself to top Gore fund-raiser Peter Knight, but Knight refused to relinquish any authority.

Her talents were to be harnessed by the party apparatus instead, and she was thrilled at the prospect. She had grand plans. Over the year or two that she expected to keep the job, she would try to do something that no one had ever managed before: get the three different and often competing branches of the DNC—the national party, the DCCC, and the DSCC—to work together. With only so much money to collect from a finite number of donors, the three branches have always fought with each other over contributors. Dozoretz spoke to House Minority Leader Richard Gephardt and Senate Minority Leader Tom Daschle about the need for cooperation rather than confrontation, and they nodded vigorously at everything she said.

In the real world, however, the very notion was absurd. When Dozoretz suggested such cooperation to veteran Democratic fund-raiser and lobbyist Tommy Boggs, he just laughed.

Dozoretz also had run-ins with the established money men of the party, especially in Los Angeles. She was trying to hold a fund-raiser for the DNC near the time that the movie-making partners of DreamWorks SKG—Steven Spielberg, Jeffrey Katzenberg, and David Geffen—were planning an event to benefit the House and Senate campaign committees. DreamWorks's in-house fund-raising professional, Andy Spahn, was furious. He had, however, been misinformed about the kind of money that she wanted to collect.

Spahn thought she intended to charge twenty-five thousand dollars per couple—just like the DreamWorks crew did, and *that* would have been unacceptable. The big-dollar donors, at least that season, belonged to DreamWorks. Period. In fact, Dozoretz's event was five thousand dollars per couple and wouldn't have conflicted. Still, she was privately relieved when it turned out that the DNC fund-raiser had to be canceled due to the outbreak of war in Kosovo.

For the relative neophyte Dozoretz, the barrage of invective was too much to handle. At the end of one particularly taxing day, she found herself in the back of a cab balled into the fetal position.

For all the slanderous whispers about Beth Dozoretz, there was one fact she would have trouble disputing: She was underprepared for the job she took on. A top solicitor for either party had to labor for years to develop a wide enough set of contacts to be a success. While she was advanced for her stage of development, Dozoretz was not as deeply sourced as she should have been to do her task as well as the party needed.

Part of the blame for this deficiency must rest with the Democratic Party itself. After the campaign-funding scandals during the 1996 presidential race, even the most resilient partisan was understandably reluctant to take on the role as the party's top money collector. No one wanted to be hauled before a grand jury to answer for actions of overeager subordinates. All of the top solicitors knew the story of Marvin Rosen, a predecessor to Dozoretz from the 1996 period. He all but disappeared from public view in Washington, his reputation among the elite fundraisers forever tarnished by the way he handled the scandals. Why would anyone want to be another Marvin Rosen?

Very few people did, or do. Dozoretz obviously saw a chance to make her name in the political community by filling a vacuum. Unfortunately for her and for the Democrats, when she stepped into the role, she also was over her head.

Still, she soldiered on. She endured an odd sort of dressing-down from Los Angeles power broker Eli Broad; when they met, he never deigned to turn around in his chair and look her in the eye. (Broad says he doesn't remember such an encounter.) She had to all but beg forgiveness from Lew Wasserman, the former head of Universal Studios, for what he felt was a slight against him when someone else was allowed to host a DNC fund-raising event that he thought he had been asked to chair. She asked for help from more than one of the established fund-raisers of the party and got their assurances that they would come through, only to be left with the problem anyway.

In the meantime, she continued making phone call after phone call from her dingy office, which had scuff marks on the walls, in a corner of the crowded offices of the Democratic National Committee. And amazingly, the money continued to flow. She remained on budget, barely.

But it was never enough. The superexpensive presidential contest demanded that bigger-buck donors be dunned. As a result, Leadership 2000 was invented so that donors could be asked to raise or give $350,000, which was the largest amount solicited in an organized way by either party. Dozoretz asked Dutko and fellow heavy hitter Alan Solomont to conduct the program, and Dozoretz was pleased they accepted. She protested frequently that she was understaffed and asked whenever she could for help from whoever was in earshot. She made no secret of the fact that she needed the help of additional mainstream men to raise more money from other men.

Finally, the party's acknowledged giant among fund-raisers, Terry McAuliffe, came to the rescue. He had raised the money for Clinton's reelection in record time and held most other records for all manner of Democratic causes. He was held in high regard by every Democrat elected in the last decade and more. What did he and Dozoretz come up with? A Tribute to Terry McAuliffe, a benefit for the DNC to be held at chez Dozoretz. It was sheer brilliance. What politician or fund-raiser could possibly say no?

On June 7, 1999, the vanguard of the Democratic establishment showed up after pledging checks that ranged from twenty-five thousand to one hundred thousand dollars. Total take: over three million dollars. Of course, the president and first lady were there, and so were the vice president and Tipper Gore. Remarkably, the top dogs from the House and Senate also came, so that, for that one night at least, Dozoretz got her wish to have all the warring factions of the party under one tent—a white one in her backyard.

But it remained difficult to raise money as Gore's campaign floundered. Morale at the DNC plummeted, and changes were clearly needed. As fall approached, the White House persuaded outgoing Philadelphia mayor Ed Rendell to take over as the new DNC chairman. And Dozoretz took the opportunity to say good-bye.

She had traveled around the country so often that she felt as if she had missed much of her daughter's first year. Besides, Rendell would probably want his own chief fund-raiser. Why not give him the chance? Enough was enough. The vice president asked her to stay, but she knew it was time to go. She had done her job and was proud that she did it well despite unrealistic goals, communications breakdowns, and the handicap of being a woman. Maybe the next woman in the job would have an easier time of it.

"Anybody who's shattering the glass ceiling," she said, "gets a little bit of a headache."

7

The Real Party Bosses

Haley Barbour knew his business when he chaired the Republican National Committee. He presided over the party apparatus in 1994 when the Republicans ended forty years of control by the Democrats in the House. But most of all, he nurtured the groups that bankrolled the party and provided its most loyal partisans.

He also knew who his enemies were. When Barbour heard that the AFL-CIO would pull out all the stops to elect Democrats to the House in the 1996 election, he called an emergency meeting of his high council. In a glass-lined conference room at the Republicans' Eisenhower Center on Capitol Hill, he spoke in grave tones to a dozen or so of his closest advisers. The meeting included representatives of the Christian right, the prolife movement, big business, and small business. Barbour told the group that he thought the labor federation would spend far more than the thirty-five million dollars it publicly proclaimed it would expend on behalf of Democrats—perhaps as much as two hundred million dollars. The GOP would have to fight back with both money and volunteers. He then went around the table, asking each official, "What do you plan to do?"

They each knew they had to do something. For they were as central to the Republican Party as the AFL-CIO, the trial lawyers, and prochoice groups were to the Democratic Party.

What these groups want, their parties work with all their might to get. And when the party is threatened, the groups turn up the heat on the party's behalf. There's nothing subtle or secret about this quid pro quo.

In 1996, for instance, Democrats in Congress pressed hard to raise the minimum wage, just as organized labor wanted them to. And as if according to Hoyle, Republicans blocked the move on behalf of their business backers. A phalanx of Republicans (and a few Democrats) in the House passed a ban on late-term abortions as a way to placate prolife activists. But President Clinton heard from his prochoice supporters and promised to veto it. Just days before that, the Republican-led House had voted to repeal the ban on assault weapons, a top item on the wish list of the National Rifle Association, a GOP stalwart if ever there was one. Clinton, of course, vowed to veto that measure, too.

Through all the posturing and pandering, each party accused the other of being a tool of special interests. They both were right.

Money men shouldn't be viewed narrowly as rich people or as solicitors who beg rich people to contribute to political causes. Money men are also larger, strategic interests that can be counted on to raise and spend oodles on all manner of political enterprises. And more often than not, those enterprises take on a very pointed and easily predictable partisan cast. These kinds of money men are either Democratic or Republican, rarely both.

Take big labor. For years, it was considered a fading force. But Barbour and his Republican allies were stirred up for good reason in 1996. The now sixteen-million-member AFL-CIO had endorsed President Clinton's reelection early and had followed that with a special assessment of union dues to pay for saturation advertising, computer-assisted organizing, and massive telemarketing for the benefit of Democratic candidates. The enterprise amounted to all-out war by organized labor to turn back the Republican tide of 1994. John Sweeney, the AFL-CIO's activist president, told *Time* magazine that he considered the effort "a matter of life and death."

To counterattack, Barbour's GOP hauled out its own trusted warriors. The U.S. Chamber of Commerce took the lead and formed a sprawling coalition called, uninterestingly, the Coalition, to raise money from corporations to take on Sweeney. "Unions have the money and the motivation," said the chamber's Bruce Josten. "Now the business community is going to get more aggressive in return."

Ultimately, the Coalition flopped; it raised only a handful of millions of dollars, and the AFL-CIO's Democratic blitz went on to work well for two election cycles in a row. But that was hardly the end of the saga.

Both sides are now girding for the 2000 election. The AFL-CIO again is planning to spend tens of millions of dollars on TV and radio advertising and on even more effective get-out-the-vote drives. The AFL-CIO also was instrumental in preventing Vice President Gore's candidacy from evaporating. If the federation had failed to back him in 1999, Gore would have collapsed under the pressure from Bill Bradley. That they came through for Gore gave the veep at least the chance to fight on.

By the same token, GOP groups also are raising and spending many millions of dollars, including a group with anonymous donors, an idea inspired by Tom DeLay. The GOP establishment's near-unanimous support of George W. Bush is what gave him such a commanding lead early on, even before a single vote was cast in the primaries.

Most elections are seen as battles between the national parties. And in many ways that's true. But it's often more useful to view electoral and legislative fights as a conflict not between the parties but between the individual interests that undergird those parties. *Time* called these factional disputes a clash between "warring groups that stand outside the parties and, increasingly, all but control them."

In other words, a handful of interest groups are the real party bosses.

So, then, a distinct cluster of organized interests are the real powers behind the throne. Is that a good thing?

One could argue that since the bosses of each party are almost always fighting each other, the whole system of bosses is healthy—as long as a strong two-party system remains in place. As long as one side or the other never stands unchecked or unopposed, a kind of lobbyists' equilibrium is, de facto, protecting us all.

One *could* make such an argument, but I'm not sure that I would be one of those people. As noted, a particular peril of low voter turnout is that any group that commands a bloc of voters has disproportionate sway over the political process. This is true for any group that can get actual voters to the polls directly. It's also true of any group that contributes enough money to get voters to the ballot box indirectly—that is, by financing either a candidate or his party.

Such groups have a much greater ability to dictate the terms of debate in Washington. The issues that they care about— abortion, minimum wage, gun control, et cetera—are the issues that are fought over, almost annually, in Congress. And more often than not, because the partisans each have their own champions in one party or another, these matters are almost always fought to a standstill over time.

What's missing from this scenario is any hope for other issues to come to center stage. If lawmakers spend so much time trying to please their bosses, what happens to the other folks? Probably not as much as should happen. For instance, do we really want the abortion issue to clog up the works on every foreign-aid bill every year? And why must the federal government insist on having union labor on its projects in this country? Wouldn't it be cheaper if there was a little give on that question here and there? The bosses make these kinds of tie-ups perennial events. And time spent on these matters takes time away from potentially more useful endeavors. Money saved by skewering the bosses every once in a while might also become money used to help the rest of us.

And what issues don't come up but should? As we will see later in this chapter, Social Security and Medicare wouldn't be such insoluble problems if the senior citizens' lobby wasn't so insistent on keeping the level of benefits up. What's more, putting more limits on gun ownership surely would be a consensus item were it not for a vigorous progun lobby.

At the same time, it's hard to know with any precision what progress is being stifled by the bosses. After all, the bosses force all sorts of issues off the table by virtue of their claim to debate time. We won't know what we should be talking about in the nation's capital until there's more freedom to conduct conversations.

The power of the national parties has been dwindling since the early 1960s. Individual candidates for office once relied on the parties for their financing, but no longer. They are independent contractors these days, with occasionally shared goals and joint political operations. The Democratic or Republican label is more a marketing tool for office seekers than a badge of a coherent organization tied together by real financial need.

More to the point, the dividing line between the parties barely exists on the level of political philosophy. One of the legacies of the Clinton administration is a blurring of the line between what a Republican and a Democrat stand for on the major issues of the day. Tax cutting, for instance, is no longer the purview of Republicans alone. Nor is reducing the welfare rolls or cracking down on criminals.

On the other hand, Republicans are racing as quickly as they can to protect Social Security, a traditionally Democratic program. The GOP also wants to remake itself into the education party and, if it has the slightest chance, the party that helped save Medicare, another solidly Democratic issue.

When Ross Perot referred to the Democrats and Republicans as Tweedledum and Tweedledee, he wasn't far wrong. But that's true only on the top-line issues—the matters of vast, popular concern about policies that touch the lives of most Americans. Congressional leaders and senior administration officials chat about those subjects endlessly on Sunday talk shows. And their perspectives are often read, incorrectly I believe, as the view from the top—the direction legislation inevitably will take.

To understand how Washington really works, I think a sophisticated observer should take a different angle: the view from the bottom. Washington isn't a place that operates from the top down like most corporations. Instead, policy and politics make their way from the bottom up. Voters—or, more precisely, large blocs of organized voters—dictate the broadest movements of legislation and regulation.

That isn't to say, naively, that the voters always decide. Nor am I trying to diminish the influence that a charismatic or visionary leader can have on certain topics and trends. What I am suggesting is that it's far more instructive to look at the factions that are constantly agitating for action than at the personal druthers of the politicians who hold "positions of power."

The groups that push the hardest and in the greatest numbers to solve what amount to real problems usually end up being the forces that shape the policies that make their way into law. The rhetoric that pours out of the tube on Sunday morning is a consequence of these forces, not the other way around.

These aren't usually ad hoc interests. They've been around throughout our history and have long found a home in one party or the other. In response, the parties have developed positions almost identical to theirs.

I'm not talking about those mega-issues mentioned above but, rather, those second-tier concerns that are more narrowly focused, such as the Democrats' demand to raise the minimum wage on behalf of labor or the Republicans' resistance to gun control for the benefit of the gun lobby.

On issues like these, the parties *do* have differences, which can be traced directly to their backers—their bosses—as seen from the perspective of the bottom up.

The president of the AFL-CIO looks down on the White House—literally. From his eighth-floor office just across Lafayette Square, John Sweeney can look into Bill Clinton's window. But he doesn't have to spy in order to know what's going on there. He already has Clinton's number and the fealty of Clinton's Democratic Party. With only a handful of exceptions, labor unions give almost all their political money to Democratic Party organizations and to Democratic candidates. In return, few Democrats in high office can afford not to be sympathetic to labor's pleadings.

Unions represent just 16 percent of American workers. But in political terms, that's still a lot of folks. Indeed, with voter turnout so low, sixteen million people and their families, properly motivated to get out and vote, represent a massive bloc that can often spell the difference between winning and losing in close contests.

Moreover, the AFL-CIO has been working carefully in concert with other Democratic constituencies to enhance that heft. In particular, Sweeney explained, his labor federation has been working with "our natural allies: civil rights, women, environmentalists." In other words, labor overtly sides with the other real bosses of the Democratic Party to elect Democrats to Congress.

Take the election of Democrat Ron Wyden. The young Oregonian rode to victory in January 1996 in a special election that was called to fill Bob Packwood's vacated Senate seat. Not many experts thought he would win. But environmentalists and labor operatives took up Wyden's cause. They worked hand in glove—meeting regularly and sharing information—and leafleted and phoned his way to victory. The GOP estimated that union money in the Oregon election paid for 230,000 phone calls, 350,000 letters to voters, and thirty-seven full-time political operatives.

After that success, Sweeney started to hire and train bright, young politicos. And then he set them loose in key congressional districts. In the 1996 election cycle, the AFL-CIO budgeted fifteen million dollars for phone banks and get-out-the-vote workers, as well as twenty million for advertising. In 1998, it poured even more money into the foot-soldier operation, which was designed to get Democratic voters to the polls on Election Day.

All this money, which wasn't subject to federal limits, didn't "expressly advocate" the defeat of a candidate. But it came awfully close. And the Republicans cried foul. GOP officials griped that AFL-CIO members were paying for these activities even though 40 percent of them usually voted Republican.

No matter, in 1999 the AFL-CIO executive council voted to

spend forty million dollars on political activities geared to the 2000 election. This was over and above the many millions of both hard and soft money that individual unions already planned to spend on Democrats. But the purpose of the special expenditure was clear: to help Democrats get elected to Congress and to retain the White House. And how does labor plan to make that happen? Andy Stern of the Communications Workers of America told the *National Journal:* "We're trying to create an independent political army."

You might remember the last time that labor asserted itself politically. It wasn't a pretty sight. During the presidential campaign of 1984, Walter Mondale was labor's favorite. But its endorsement of the Minnesotan proved to be an albatross around the candidate's neck. Mondale was labeled a "special-interest" pol and an "old-style" Democrat, liberal to the core. Thanks to Ronald Reagan, *liberal* was already starting to become an epithet.

Mondale never shook the criticism and lost the election. His defeat spawned a rise in "new" Democrats, who weren't as much in the thrall of organized labor. The Democratic Leadership Council and its corporate sponsors rose as an alternative to labor as a potential party boss for the Democrats. The election in 1992 of "New Democrat" Bill Clinton was read by many insiders as the end of labor's political preeminence even with its captive party.

Don't believe it. The Republican romp of '94 proved that the Democrats needed all the help they could get. They also learned that corporate backing is fickle and flees to whichever party is most firmly in power. New, aggressive leadership at the top of the AFL-CIO in the person of Sweeney and his colleagues cemented the value of the "old" party boss.

In many ways, 1996 was labor's trial run. It hit its stride in 1998. With labor's backing, especially in getting voters to the polls,

Democrats gained five seats in the House instead of losing seats to the Republicans, as was widely expected. Newt Gingrich, the symbol of the 1994 insurrection, resigned as Speaker as a result, and Democrats no longer doubted that labor could deliver for them.

"I did learn something in '98," Richard Gephardt told the *National Journal*. "I did not think labor's effort was going to work. I was worried that they were not really going to be able to motivate and educate and inform their members to the extent they did. I was wrong."

Labor also proved able to defend itself. In 1998, it faced the greatest challenge to its political muscle since the defeat of Mondale. Proposition 226 in California was a referendum that would have required union members to give written permission for their union dues to be used for political purposes. Several other states had similar provisions pending. Without question, Prop 226 was the cleverest and potentially most devastating attack on labor's clout that the corporate world had devised in a decade.

But the Republican Party and corporations in general failed to mobilize. Efforts to raise money to pass Prop 226 were half-hearted at best. Labor, on the other hand, saw the provision as a death knell if it became law. As a result, unions organized voter brigades all the way down to the shop-steward level. Some twenty-five thousand rank-and-file workers were recruited to get out the vote. In June, Prop 226 was defeated soundly, which produced a domino effect that toppled the other, similar propositions around the nation. What's more, the network of labor voters that was assembled to beat Prop 226 was energized again later in the year to elect Gray Davis, a Democrat—and a prolabor Democrat at that—to the California governorship.

All of this was accomplished with the help of millions and millions of labor dollars, very few of which were given directly to either candidates or the Democratic Party. Instead, unions largely controlled the flow of their cash, sending it into internal-educational efforts, voter-registration drives, and issue-advocacy advertising.

The result was a huge increase in voting by union sympathizers. So as the overall number of voters shrank, labor's power grew. Ironically, labor has more clout now than it did when "New Democrat" Clinton was first elected nearly eight years ago.

The AFL-CIO's model in many ways was one of its fiercest enemies: the Christian Coalition. And that's odd because the Christian Coalition modeled itself on organized labor and environmental groups. Without apology, the Christian Coalition is part of the bedrock of the GOP, although, unlike the AFL-CIO, its influence appears at the moment to be waning.

The Christian Coalition's decline began in 1996 when the Federal Election Commission filed suit to stop the 1.7 million–member organization from working so closely with the Republicans. The Christian Coalition, which had a budget reported to be about twenty-five million dollars a year, denied the allegations but was already thinking about changing its structure to do completely aboveboard what it had long done covertly: back the GOP.

During negotiations to settle the suit, the Christian Coalition offered to form a political-action committee, something that it had strenuously avoided for years as it defended its tax-exempt "educational" status. It even considered going further and transforming itself into a full-fledged political organization. But that would have hamstrung the group. It would have had to abide by the strict rules that apply to purely political entities, such as disclosure of contributors, prohibition of corporate gifts, and a five-thousand-dollar-per-candidate donation limit. That would have been far too out in the open for the secretive arm of Pat Robertson's empire.

In 1999, it *did* form a PAC, so that it could overtly support its favorite candidates. But it also continued to operate as an "educational" entity under the rubric of a state affiliate. The door was opened for it to coordinate openly with candidates and the GOP. Yet it was not nearly as robust an organization as it once had been.

In May 1995, thirty-three-year-old Ralph Reed, executive director of the Christian Coalition, was pictured—in black and white—on the cover of *Time* magazine. Reed and his coalition were feared, even reviled, and the young politico was well worth the attention. At the time, Reed was traversing the country acting as much as an emissary from the Right as the leader of a single organization based in Chesapeake, Virginia. "I get home as often as I can, even if it's only for a day," said the father of three. Still, that wasn't very often.

That spring, for instance, he addressed the New Hampshire State Senate, a privilege usually reserved for presidential candidates. And his host was no less than the GOP governor of the state, Steve Merrill. "They want to know you don't have two heads, that you don't have horns," Merrill told Reed, who still looked like the Eagle Scout he once was and responded with a laugh too loud by half for his slender frame.

Reed's message in New Hampshire was the key to the Christian Coalition's growing influence in Washington. Conservative Christians, he said, are "too large, too diverse, too significant to be ignored by either major political party." America's Christian right, he asserted, in effect, could not be written off as a group of pasty-faced zealots, led by divisive televangelists such as Jerry Falwell. Rather, thanks to Reed, the religious right was trending toward the mainstream with aims—and tactics—that were decidedly secular.

Reed and his coalition stood for far more than the prolife position on abortion. They were part of the emerging vanguard of the Republican Party and were pressing lawmakers on such broadly appealing issues as tax cuts and budget-deficit reduction. The widening of the Christian activists' worldview had pushed the organization to grow rapidly. In 1995, it boasted 1.6 million active supporters and an annual budget of $25 million, up from 500,000 activists and a $14.8 million budget just two years earlier.

According to *Time,* "Reed's success represents the most thorough penetration of the secular world of American politics by an essentially religious organization in this century." Bill Lacy, a top strategist for Bob Dole's presidential bid, was even more specific: "Without having significant support of the Christian Right, a Republican cannot win the nomination or the general election."

Reed was so hot a commodity that presidential candidate Senator Phil Gramm of Texas offered to hire him as his campaign's political director, the number-two staff job. Reed declined. It would have been a demotion. As executive director of the Christian Coalition, Reed headed a much more powerful and effective machine than almost any presidential campaign.

By mobilizing eager volunteers down to the precinct (and local church) level and handing out thirty-three million voter guides—often in church pews—prior to November's election, the Christian Coalition was credited with providing the winning margin for perhaps half of the Republicans' fifty-two-seat gain in the House in 1994. The Christian Coalition also poured one million dollars into the effort to pass Newt Gingrich's Contract with America, including $250,000 for advertising, direct mail, and phone-bank work on behalf of the balanced-budget amendment, which isn't found anywhere in the Scriptures.

That the religious right could become such a player was inconceivable when the movement began in 1979. Back then, Paul Weyrich and Richard Viguerie helped Jerry Falwell set up the Moral Majority. Their idea was to mobilize white Evangelicals in the South and border states—many of whom had once supported Jimmy Carter—against Washington's intrusiveness. The Moral Majority gained legitimacy during the Reagan administration, but Falwell never bothered to build any grassroots support.

Enter Ralph Reed. After Pat Robertson ran unsuccessfully for the Republican nomination for president in 1988, Robertson converted his huge mailing lists into the Christian Coalition and then turned its operation over to Reed, then twenty-seven. By the mid-1990s, a survey by *Campaigns and Elections* magazine reported that the Christian right exercised considerable control of Republican parties in thirteen states and complete control of the GOP in eighteen others.

These days, the annual meeting of the Christian Coalition in Washington routinely draws major presidential wanna-bes, and Christian Coalition lobbyists sit in on legislative strategy meetings hosted by members of the House and Senate Republican leadership.

Why? Because the Christian Coalition can deliver. It can stir a flurry of telephone calls and letters to lawmakers on almost any subject within a matter of hours. It also gets people to the polls on Election Day. To train its operatives, the group ran leadership schools that instructed supporters how to form rapid-response networks, connected by phone, fax, and modem. At one time, these same operatives attended monthly satellite downlinks of *Christian Coalition Live,* an hour of specific instruction on political organizing. Reed himself played host.

The narrowcasts began with the words, "Let's come together in prayer" and moved quickly to such topics as how to become a

Republican committee member and how to "blitz e-mail" about the latest legislative initiative. Christian Coalition members were a long way from what *The Washington Post* in February 1993 derided as "poor, uneducated and easy to command."

One monthly meeting on the outskirts of Charleston, South Carolina, was attended by several lawyers and physicians—all in business suits. Still, despite its sophistication and secularization, the movement was insular and eager to impose its Bible-based morality on the public. Even within the GOP, its influence was a matter of controversy. A group of money men, mostly New Yorkers, banded together to form the Republican Leadership Council largely to combat what they saw as the Christian Coalition's self-defeating intolerance.

At the same time, a spate of stories appeared after the 1998 election that asserted that the power of the organization was in eclipse. Doubts were raised about the number of members it actually had and the size of its political expenditures. Without question, both its budget and membership were declining. Pat Robertson was forced to infuse the organization with a million dollars from his own pocket in order to keep the group afloat. And worst of all, Reed, the young genius who had brought the organization to national prominence, left the group to start his own political-consulting firm.

Reed's successors proved to be political lightweights by comparison. Robertson hired a former congressman, Randy Tate, and a former interior secretary, Donald Hodel, to succeed Reed. But even taken together they didn't come close to replacing him. They lacked the strategic vision, fund-raising savvy, and charismatic leadership that Reed had possessed even at such a tender age. The organization suffered almost from the moment Reed walked out the door.

In an effort to regain some of its lost footing, the Christian Coalition all but endorsed the presumptive GOP presidential nominee, George W. Bush, in the autumn of 1999. Even though Bush wasn't as socially conservative or as prolife as Christian Coalition members would have preferred, Robertson realized that he had to connect the group with what he thought would be a winner if he was going to recoup the organization's reputation.

Despite its decline, however, the Christian Coalition continued to be thought of as one of the few groups that could actually elect or defeat a candidate for Congress. Along with avid gun owners, prolife Christian-right voters were among the few predictably Republican voters who cared passionately enough about their issues to show up at the polling booth. But could the Christian Coalition still deliver them? The 2000 election was shaping up to be one of its most important tests, with its status as party boss very much on the line.

Here's a boss who's not on the decline and also decidedly not a Republican: Ellen Malcolm, the prochoice activist who founded and heads the nation's largest political-action committee, EMILY's List.

The group's influence has been felt for many years, including and especially 1996. To win a second term, Bill Clinton's campaign needed to attract women's votes. And few people had more to do with corralling them for him than Malcolm and her list.

"EMILY's List," she said with slight hyperbole, "has become the entrepreneurial life force of the Democratic Party." A gadfly and tireless political promoter since her days as an aide in the Carter White House, Malcolm founded EMILY—short for Early Money Is Like Yeast (it makes the dough rise)—in 1985. Back then, she was unhappy with the shortage of women getting elected to office. Her idea was to recruit, train, and endorse prochoice, Democratic women candidates and then induce thousands of other women around the country to contribute to their campaigns.

She did this to tremendous effect. For the 1998 election cycle, EMILY's List had more than fourteen million dollars in receipts. Members of the EMILY's List network choose from a roster of recommended candidates—devised by Malcolm et al.—and then contribute one hundred dollars or more to at least two of them. For 1998, fifty thousand members contributed a record $7.5 million to candidates during the two-year election cycle. To date, the organization has helped elect seven prochoice Democratic women to the Senate, forty-nine to the House, and three to governorships.

EMILY's List also recruits candidates who agree with its positions and then convenes seminars to help teach them, their campaign managers, and their press secretaries the latest campaign techniques. In addition, the group maintains an in-house staff of political, fund-raising, and public-relations professionals.

EMILY's List also launched Women Vote!—a ten-million-dollar multielection campaign aimed at mobilizing Democratic women voters throughout the country. By helping to turn out women voters on Election Day, the organization asserted, "EMILY's List WOMEN VOTE! will counter religious political extremist organizing and help Democratic candidates up and down the ticket." Take *that,* Christian Coalition!

The Women Vote! program was modeled on EMILY's List's 1994 California effort, during which it targeted 902,000 "angry" women voters—Democrats who didn't often vote—and got half of them to the polls. The drive was credited with keeping Senator Dianne Feinstein and Congresswoman Jane Harman in office. For 2000, Malcolm's idea is to help *both* male and female Democrats "from the school board to the White House."

And Democrats hope she's right.

The nation's trial lawyers also maintain a list, and it's big enough to make them a boss as well. Unofficially, it was once called Pam's List, after an ex-president of the Association of Trial Lawyers of America, Pamela Liapakis. No matter what it's called, it isn't a list of potential voters. Rather, it's a list of likely recipients of campaign cash. ATLA, with more than fifty thousand members, showers Democrats with money, but only the Democratic candidates who vote against restrictions on lawsuits. In the expectation that Clinton would be one of those kinds of Democrats, lawyers rained $2.5 million onto Clinton's reelection effort in 1996, more than any other occupational group did.

ATLA has labored to defeat an array of state and federal tort-reform measures for years. Occasionally one slips through, and more are likely to as the titans of the new economy in Silicon Valley heap scorn on the shareholder lawsuits that the trial lawyers love to bring—and that high-tech companies hate to be served.

But the lawyers have a not-so-secret weapon in this battle: mountains of cash. The state-by-state settlement of lawsuits against tobacco companies recently has infused (or will soon infuse) the already wealthy trial-lawyer bar with hundreds of millions of extra dollars. The cash has already emboldened the lawyers to file suits against other industries (notably gun makers). And soon they will step up their political giving as well.

Most of their donations go to the Democratic Party, the longtime protector of the right to sue. Asserted John Coale, a Washington, D.C., trial lawyer, "This is a very partisan issue between the parties. The Democratic Party has sided with us over the years, as we have with them. Our best efforts have always been to help them get elected. The Republicans, the Chamber of Commerce, and that crowd are constantly trying to put us out of business."

In the 2000 elections, Coale said straightforwardly, "If we [the

Democrats] retake the House, tort reform is dead; if we put someone in the White House, it's dead. It's that simple. Political philosophy doesn't have much to do with it."

The Republican bosses agree. "We've got a huge problem with trial lawyers amassing millions and millions and millions of dollars," warned Tom Donohue, president of the U.S. Chamber of Commerce. "If they used a fraction of it, they could buy government at all levels. That worries me greatly."

For their part, the trial lawyers aren't worried. "We're far better organized and better funded than we've ever been," said Richard Scruggs, a prominent trial lawyer from Mississippi. "Taking us on is like taking on Zorro in a sword fight."

To be double sure of victory, trial lawyers are trying to be less partisan in their campaign giving. Utah Republican Orrin Hatch, for instance, was treated to trial-lawyer fund-raisers in New Orleans by dint of his winning personality and the fact that he chairs the Senate Judiciary Committee, an originator of tort-reform legislation. Other Republicans who are willing to be sympathetic—or are in a position to do real damage—also are receiving political benefits.

"If you'll put your ear to the ground right now, you'll find a growing ambivalence about supporting Democrats alone," Scruggs said. "A lot of that was precipitated by [Democratic] Senator [Robert] Torricelli and Senator [Charles] Schumer agreeing to back an asbestos tort-reform measure. They've alienated a lot of trial lawyers." Another reason for Scruggs at least is that his brother-in-law is Senate Majority Leader Trent Lott.

For all this talk, though, the trial lawyers are Democratic Party bosses and are likely to remain that way. The Senate's most recently elected trial lawyer, Democrat John Edwards of North Carolina, was quickly dispatched to talk to Scruggs and a couple of his colleagues at Washington's posh Four Seasons Hotel after

Scruggs made it clear that he wasn't willing to fork over as much soft money due to the asbestos bill.

And at the state level, the trial lawyers are renowned as Democratic partisans. In 1998, trial-lawyer money was instrumental in turning out the Democratic vote in downtown Baltimore that salvaged the reelection of Parris Glendening as governor.

And despite Scruggs's confidence, the trial lawyers will always have to battle to get their way. In 1995, ATLA member Bill Lerach, a San Diego securities litigator whose firm had given more than one million dollars to Democrats since 1990, had dinner at the White House. Four days later, Clinton vetoed the Securities Litigation Reform Act. But Congress voted to override the veto. Even a boss can't win 'em all.

But they do win often enough. In 1999, trial lawyers took a vicious rhetorical pounding but managed to persuade the Republican House to vote overwhelmingly to give patients the right to sue their health-maintenance organizations. Even that half step of a victory showed that the lawyers were a boss not easily messed with.

The lawyers were helped mightily, of course, by the fact that voters *hated* their HMOs. But then again, Republicans are supposed to hate trial lawyers as much as they love businesses. Well, here's a lesson. Being a party boss doesn't guarantee success. It does ensure the right to be a player in the biggest, nastiest fights.

In recent years, presidential candidates have tended to make a fetish of appearing "independent" by denouncing one party boss or another. In 1992, Bill Clinton attacked the politics of Sister Souljah as a way to make himself seem less beholden to minorities. He "triangulated" to separate himself from the congressional win of his own party in 1996. And George W. Bush did the same (using a poverty program) with House Republicans in 1999.

But we shouldn't take these attacks too seriously. They are mostly for show. The preponderance of evidence suggests that once a boss is a boss, a politician has to acquiesce most of the time.

On the surface, the National Rifle Association would appear to be a party boss in big trouble. With its allies divided, its positions against gun control widely condemned, its membership perceived as kooky, and its legislative agenda overturned by the Brady bill and the assault-weapons ban, you might be tempted to believe that it is a force that has been spent.

Think again. I have personally written at least three political obituaries for the NRA in various publications. And the organization is still very much alive and kicking—mostly Democrats.

"We have a political system that rewards intensity," Thomas Mann of the Brookings Institution told *Time* magazine. And the NRA's roughly three million members have nothing if not intensity about their issue, protecting a belief in an unencumbered right to bear arms. "The only way you overcome that," Mann explained, "is to match their intensity with an intensity among those on the other side, and in the gun debate that has not happened."

Where else besides the NRA can you find a former top lobbyist, Tanya Metaksa, who was proud to spell her last name by saying, "It's *ak* as in *AK-47,* and *sa* as in *semiautomatic*"?

For a long time, the NRA *was* in deep decline. In the mid-1990s, its leaders kept pushing the organization toward extreme positions, such as its defense of cop-killer bullets and its denunciation of techniques that could mark explosives for easy identification. No matter what the gun-control proposal, the NRA would reflexively oppose it as an attack on the Second Amendment.

In some ways, this was a successful strategy. The group's largest increases in membership came right after two major legislative defeats: the 1993 Brady bill, which imposed a five-day waiting period on the purchase of handguns, and the 1994 ban on nineteen categories of assault weapons. "The NRA has been predicting imminent doom and practically the elimination of weapons for years," Robert Spitzer, author of *The Politics of Gun Control,* told *Time.* "Now there was a real threat that provided a galvanizing force for opposition, and that helped pump up their membership."

But a zealous lot like the NRA can go too far. It finally was forced to pull back from its wildest positions after, among many other setbacks, President George Bush resigned from the NRA after one of its fund-raising letters called federal officials "jackbooted government thugs." The rash of school shootings in the late 1990s also made an uncompromising position against gun control untenable. Actor Charlton Heston was brought in as the organization's president to smooth over the NRA's rougher edges.

Through the ups and downs, however, the NRA continued to be a Republican "boss" that, Spitzer said, "can make life so unpleasant that key public figures will yield to them because fighting them is more of a hassle than it's worth."

President Clinton once told the Cleveland *Plain Dealer,* "The NRA is the reason the Republicans control the House." And he was far from wrong. In the 1994 election, according to the Center for Responsive Politics, the NRA's PAC funneled nearly $1.9 million directly into campaign coffers and poured another $1.5 million into commercials, direct mailings, and phone banks. The result: thirty-two incumbent House members thought to be supporters of gun control lost their seats.

Oklahoma Democrat Mike Synar was unseated in a primary by what he called a "stealth campaign" by the NRA. The organization sent several political operatives into the congressman's

district to make sure his opponents' campaigns were profession-
ally run and also, Synar charged, trained supporters to "stalk"
him and interrupt his public meetings with rude questions.

"Their idea was to keep the turnout low, then make sure their
vote got out," Synar said. In the end, among the 21 percent voter
turnout, he estimated that half were NRA members or their
friends.

NRA members are so intense that they sometimes can't be
stopped from voting against people that their leaders say are
friends. Texas Democrat Jack Brooks, an NRA supporter and
chairman of the House Judiciary Committee, was perceived by
NRA leaders as a valuable ally. But after he voted for one of
Clinton's crime bills, which included an assault-weapons ban,
NRA members in his district demanded that the NRA endorsement of his reelection be withdrawn. The NRA dispatched
Tanya Metaksa to argue Brooks's case. But he was defeated anyway by Steve Stockman, a Republican who supported both the
NRA and the far more militant militia movement.

With that kind of voter presence, Republicans tend to be very
deferential on gun issues.

For a Republican to win the White House, he or she needs
the support of Democratic voters in the industrial Midwest,
who often are Catholic and oppose abortion. In other words,
Reagan Democrats. That's why Haley Barbour once called
David O'Steen, a former Minnesota mathematics professor, "a
very good man." The fiftyish O'Steen for years oversaw the
antiabortion National Right to Life Committee, which happens
to have many followers among that important group of swing
voters. In Michigan alone, the committee was said to have more
than four hundred thousand active supporters. That's enough to
make them a GOP boss indeed.

The group was so close to the Republicans that it served as a conduit for its extra cash. The Republican National Senatorial Committee gave the NRLC $175,000 in 1994, some of which was for "voter education" in states such as Minnesota, where there was a close senatorial race. The prolife candidate won. The NRLC's real clout, however, is its millions of volunteers.

Another GOP boss with plenty of grassroots clout is Washington's chief advocate of small businesses, the National Federation of Independent Business (NFIB). This isn't what you might expect. When people put a face on the Republican Party, they see fat cats of the corporate kind. In fact, the mainstays of the Republicans increasingly are small-business owners who hate federal red tape and taxes. Appropriately, then, Jack Faris, president of the NFIB, is the son of a gas-station owner. Equally appropriately, he also is a former finance director of the Republican National Committee.

Faris worked hard to find some Democrats who are conservative enough to support, but he didn't tend to find too many. Only two of the thirty-one candidates the small-business lobby pushed hardest in 1994 were Democrats. Its million-dollar PAC is considered a Republican piggy bank.

You would expect nothing less from a boss.

The most fearsome force in American politics is an exception to all the rules. The group isn't partisan. It doesn't contribute money to candidates or to the political parties. And its leader, a man named Horace Deets, is a relative unknown. When I asked Congressman Robert Matsui of California, a veteran lawmaker and a senior member of the House Ways and Means Committee, about Deets, he said: "If you told me he was short and bald, I would have to take your word for it. I don't know what he looks like."

That's a remarkable statement considering that Deets is head honcho of the American Association of Retired Persons (AARP). He is the only person in Washington besides the president who wields a veto pen—at least when it comes to the issues of Medicare and Social Security.

If Congress and the president were to go too far in their efforts to fix either program, the sixty-two-year-old Deets would emerge from the shadows of anonymity to unleash the AARP's more than thirty-three million members, one in every five registered voters.

Both parties can be bossed around by that many people, making Deets a money man—or at least a power broker—of immense proportions. That's the theory anyway. In practice, managing such a force isn't always so easy.

The AARP was formed in 1958 for the two reasons that still motivate it today: service to the elderly and greed. The organization was founded by seventy-two-year-old Ethel Percy Andrus, the first female high-school principal in California, who became, in retirement, an energetic crusader against the stereotype of an enfeebled older class. "To Serve, Not to Be Served" was her motto.

But to create her group required cash. So she turned to a Poughkeepsie, New York, insurance broker fifty years her junior named Leonard Davis. At the time, most insurers refused to sell health policies to anyone over sixty-five, but Davis saw profit in Andrus's vision. He convinced Continental Casualty of Chicago to cover Andrus's group and provided the fifty-thousand-dollar seed money to launch the AARP.

Soon the organization and its insurance sales were soaring. Membership reached 750,000 by 1963, and Davis founded his own insurance company, Colonial Penn, which replaced Continental as the AARP's insurer. A dozen years later, the AARP's membership stood at ten million, and Davis's company was raking in revenues of $445 million, mostly from the AARP.

Then scandal struck. *Consumer Reports* concluded in 1976 that Colonial Penn's Medicare supplementary health insurance offered the least protection of the sixteen policies it surveyed. Two years later, AARP suffered even greater public-relations damage when it fired its executive director, Harriet Miller.

Miller sued Colonial Penn, Davis, and Davis's lawyers for allegedly causing her dismissal. She charged that they dominated the AARP's board and had turned the association into "a convenient and effective cover" for enriching Davis by selling overpriced insurance. In 1980, the case was settled, and Miller got $480,000. Davis disassociated himself from the AARP the next year, and the insurance business was handed to someone else.

Remarkably, the storm of controversy did not blow the AARP off course. Its unique blending of buying and providing social services filled so large a need that it continued to prosper. Today, the AARP is a more than five-hundred-million-dollar-a-year operation with a membership that rivals the Catholic Church. And its anchor remains health insurance (now competitively priced), which a few years ago earned it nearly one hundred million dollars in annual management fees. The AARP also collects fees or royalties from the sales of an association-sponsored mail-order pharmacy (the country's biggest), auto- and home-owner insurance, a growing number of investment funds, and a credit card. For the dirt-cheap price of eight bucks a year, members enjoy discounts for car rentals, hotel stays, and tours.

Anyone who is fifty or older would be nuts not to join.

This money machine underwrites an advocacy organization that would make Dr. Andrus blush. The AARP provides information to the elderly through the nation's largest-circulation magazine,

Modern Maturity, which is published in-house and mailed six times a year to more than twenty-two million households. The association also produces the more politically directed *AARP Bulletin,* a tabloid that is sent to the same readers eleven times a year. *That's* a lot of political power.

Except for his anonymity, Deets is the very personification of his organization's unholy alliance between social work and entrepreneurialism. He began his career in the 1960s as a Catholic priest in his native Charleston, South Carolina. There, he taught high school, uplifted the downtrodden, and protested the Vietnam War. But he was not fulfilled. He pushed in vain for an inner-city parish and a summer camp in the country for underprivileged kids. He was too full of ideas and ambition for the stolid church to contain. "I knew I would be frustrated the longer I stayed," he said. "I had a growing dissatisfaction that I couldn't do all it was possible for me to do."

He left the priesthood in 1972 and went on in the secular world to counsel alcoholics and, later, to work as a trainer for the Equal Employment Opportunity Commission (EEOC) in Washington. When his program at the EEOC was eliminated in 1975, he accepted a three-month contract with the AARP.

That was his lucky break. The person who hired him was Harriet Miller, who was elevated to executive director soon thereafter. Over the next decade, Deets became the AARP's indispensable Mr. Fix-It, serving at one time or another as acting director of almost every department, from personnel to public relations. By 1987, he was the chief operating officer in all but title.

That year, Miller's successor, Cy Brickfield, announced his retirement, and the board fell prey to a common Washington malady: superficiality. In a town obsessed with perceptions, it decided to hire a handsome and familiar face. Jack Carlson was a former fighter pilot who had already headed a major association, the National Association of Realtors. He looked and sounded like an executive director—lots of gray hair and confident bluster.

But he was a free marketeer in an organization that believed deeply in the wisdom of government intervention. He also lacked the discipline and skill required to run such a sprawling and complex operation. He lasted just fifteen weeks before the board turned to Mr. Fix-It.

Deets sees his job as an extension of his priesthood days. "In some way I have not retired from social ministry," he says. But he also is no pushover. His earliest acts included firing the director of the AARP's West Coast office and beginning the arduous process of rousting Colonial Penn's lawyers, who still held sway with the board.

His years as a top executive had converted him into a zealous student of management theory, and, for a while, he published his own management quarterly called *Quest*. But, true to principles, he folded the magazine after coldly concluding that it didn't fit the AARP's mission. He is even tough-minded about religion. He admits he no longer attends church regularly because he wants to provide real service to his fellow man "rather than having a Sunday break."

Indeed, Deets is a man of steel beneath a mild-mannered exterior. He has finished three marathons (the last when he was forty) and has gone as long as twenty-five months without missing a day of running, once resorting to jogging behind a snowplow just to maintain the streak. He gets by on five or five and a half hours of sleep a night and reads four newspapers before 9 A.M.—every day—and at least a book a week.

His father was even more disciplined. Horace senior rose from apprentice to supervisor of the electronics shop of Charleston's naval shipyard and didn't miss a day of work due to illness in forty-one years. Like his son, he took pleasure in winning against the odds. As a poker player, Deets says approvingly of his dad:

"He loved to watch you fold when all he had was an ace or king high."

Few people think of the AARP as battling the odds. Its nicknames in Washington include Darth Vader, the eight-hundred-pound gorilla, and Fortress AARP, so invincible is it considered when it comes to legislation. President Clinton invited the AARP's legislative council to the White House soon after he took office. When he was told by Deets that neither President Reagan nor President Bush had ever bothered to invite them, Clinton was aghast. "Couldn't they count?" he asked.

But it isn't merely numbers that make the AARP so forceful: It is the ingenious way it mobilizes its members. Republican senator Charles Grassley of Iowa said people at his town-hall meetings read the *AARP Bulletin* "as if it were the Bible." The headstrong Newt Gingrich once admitted to the AARP board: "I want you to know that I know I can't do what I want to do on Medicare without you."

The AARP's money fuels a state-of-the-art lobbying juggernaut. This includes a thirty-two-scholar think tank and twenty-two staff lobbyists. It controls a network of more than two thousand volunteers who are trained to ignite a firestorm of protest among thousands of other AARP members whenever headquarters sounds the alarm.

That happened when the Senate was about to vote on a Constitutional amendment to balance the budget. The AARP opposed the measure because it didn't adequately protect Social Security. So AARP lobbyists issued an "alert" that read, "Caution: The Balanced Budget Amendment Could Harm You and Your Family." AARP members were urged to use a toll-free number to connect to a computer that would switch their calls automatically into the offices of their senators or congressmen. All they had to do was punch in their zip or area code. The

AARP also set up volunteer-staffed phone banks in the districts and states of wavering lawmakers and generated letters to augment the calls.

The deluge that ensued did the trick. The amendment was defeated in the Senate even though it had been the Republicans' top priority. To no one's surprise, the number-one reason cited by lawmakers for voting no was the amendment's lack of protection for Social Security. Even senators such as Democrat Tim Johnson of South Dakota, who had made an election issue of his *support* for such an amendment, cited the Social Security argument for their change of mind. Johnson's office received at least four hundred calls and letters on the topic from AARP members in his state.

The AARP also flexes its muscle when it decides *not* to fight. In 1993, senior Democrats begged the AARP not to actively oppose Clinton's deficit-reduction bill, arguing that the presidency was at stake. As a result, the association didn't support the legislation but didn't ask its members to attack it either. It passed by a single vote.

Occasionally, the AARP has made some terrible mistakes. Its most notable failure came in 1989 when it backed a bill that provided health coverage for seniors with catastrophic illnesses. The benefit was welcomed, but the taxes that financed it caused an uproar from the people who had to pay them. That led to a quick repeal. Rather than standing its ground, the AARP compounded its error by reversing its support for the law when it saw how outraged its members had become, a move that left lawmakers without the protection they thought they could count on.

In the years to come, the controversies will only get hotter, particularly when it comes to Social Security and Medicare. In 1960, it took an ample 5.1 taxpaying workers to support one Social Security recipient. Today, it takes about 3.3 workers. By about 2040, when the massive boomer generation will be retired, there will likely be only two or fewer workers to support each retiree.

Put another way, the federal government now takes 17 percent of workers' taxable income to pay for Social Security and Medicare; that percentage will more than double by 2040. In his book *Will America Grow Up Before It Grows Old?* investment banker Peter G. Peterson writes that the "age wave . . . will transform our work lives, our culture, our politics, our ethics, and our society from top to bottom."

Deets's association is ground zero in what is shaping up as the first battle of the new millennium, a war not between countries or companies but between generations. The major engagement will occur a few years hence, when the outsize baby-boom generation begins to retire. A less populous younger generation will be asked to pay the boomers' Medicare and Social Security and probably will refuse.

The conflict has already begun in a smaller way. Boomers are clearly anxious about footing the bill for their elders, which, for Horace Deets, amounts to civil war. The earliest boomers are turning fifty—the age at which they can join the AARP—at the blistering rate of one every eight seconds.

On the one hand, the AARP is the most potent force in American politics, with the potential to grow faster than any other group of its kind. Its membership is ten times that of the National Rifle Association, its budget nearly twenty times larger than the Christian Coalition's. During the next forty years, the number of people fifty and older is expected to almost double, to 129 million. If the AARP continues to sign up half its eligible prospects, it will reach roughly the population of Italy and Greece by midcentury.

On the other hand, it is far from certain that the AARP can maintain its pace. The exploding expense of Social Security and

Medicare has put the organization in a state of siege. And the conflict will only grow worse as AARP struggles to decide which of its members to put first: those who are already retired or the growing number who are still gainfully employed. And then there's the question of whether independent and youth-conscious boomers will want to join an old-persons' lobby at all.

This historic collision of promise and threat has thrown the AARP into a midlife crisis. To deal with it, Deets has instigated a quiet revolution. He has subtly begun to focus more on boomers by shifting the emphasis of AARP's publications and products to its nonretired members. *Modern Maturity* even had sexy Susan Sarandon on its cover.

Deets also is trying to forge a longer view on issues. In contrast to its image as the selfish seeker of ever more benefits for "greedy geezers," the AARP now says it looks ahead to the baby-boom generation whenever it takes a stand. It even acknowledges that Medicare and Social Security will have to change in order to survive and that AARP members will have to sacrifice, at least in the short run.

Given the conflicts ahead, AARP will have to develop some extra flexibility. It can't count on its size—and its vast financial resources—to retain its power. "Size," Deets said, "didn't save the dinosaurs." And it won't be enough the keep the AARP as Washington's money man supreme.

8

Lobbyist Envy

Lawmakers care about three things: getting reelected, getting reelected, and getting reelected.

That's the key to the kingdom in Washington, and the money men know it. Raising money is one of those actions that, when done without too much public notice, definitely aids the cause.

Indeed, fund-raising is absolutely, unequivocally, unabashedly necessary. And that idea isn't heard by voters very often, although it should be. Money may not be the best part of politics, but it is a fundamental one. People aren't elected to office unless they have collected some minimum amount of campaign cash.

One of the few times I heard that fact openly acknowledged by a first-tier politician was at the memorial service for Dan Dutko, the prominent Democratic fund-raiser and lobbyist who died suddenly during the summer of 1999 at a Democratic donors' retreat in Aspen. President Clinton eulogized Dutko as a person of "honor" and "integrity"—words not often used in connection with a lobbyist. Clinton then paused and said that he would not be president if not for Dutko, meaning the lobbyist's diligent—and prodigious—solicitation of funds. It was a brief statement, but the audience stirred as it was uttered. The audience was heavy with lobbyists. They were pleased to hear the president concede a fact they not only knew but had built their businesses on.

The biggest single category of givers in politics is almost always lawyers and lobbyists. The more a lobbyist is able to give—or, more important, raise—the greater his or her ability to work in Washington.

In fact, one of the only *lasting* benefits a lobbyist can give to a member of Congress is campaign cash. That's why many of the most effective lobbyists spend a lot of time calling their fellow lobbyists and directing their clients where to send the next donation. In many ways, the most influential lobbyists are the ones with the most compliant clients—the ones who, when asked to make a political contribution, respond, "How should I make out the check?"

Washington has thousands of lobbyists who raise or give money to lawmakers. A few dozen of them are among the elite. One of those is Fred Graefe of Baker and Hostetler, a Cleveland-based law firm with a large office in Washington where Graefe hangs his hat. His clients are companies that range from health care to telecommunications, and he is ostensibly a Democrat. But he is a Washington lobbyist, which means he plays both sides in order to survive. He lobbies lawmakers of both parties. He also raises money, lots of it, for both sides as well.

"I spend a huge amount of my time fund-raising for members of the Senate Finance Committee, the House Ways and Means Committee, and the leadership of both chambers," he said. "A *huge* amount." Why? Quite simply because it's necessary for him to give in order to get—for his clients. Washington, like the rest of America, is transactional. The only difference is that transactions in the capital are a bit more arcane and much less direct.

"The business of Washington really isn't any different than the business community in general," Graefe asserted. "The kinds of transactions that go on here go on hundreds of millions of times across the country, whether you're selling lumber or whatever. The difference is that I'm trying to sell a legislative issue."

What does he use to grease the deal? Campaign cash, of course. That's what lawmakers need and want, and that's what he can provide in abundance. "Huge amounts of money are required today to run for office, whether you're an incumbent or not," he said. "And races are becoming more expensive, not less expensive." So when lawmakers come to Graefe to ask his help to get the cash they need, he is quick to provide it. After all, in return, they give him what he needs, too.

Of course, Graefe's friends don't automatically grant him special-interest provisions in law in exchange for his fundraising. That would be bribery. Instead, they give him their ears and their time, which are not mediocre commodities. They are, in fact, among the most precious favors in Washington, which is a very hyperactive, busy place. Even junior lawmakers have their schedules blocked out in five- or ten-minute segments from early in the morning until late at night.

So persuading a lawmaker to pick up the phone is a central goal for any lobbyist. Beyond that, the lobbyist every once in a while can also get enough of his friends in the administration or on Capitol Hill to actually provide what he wants by way of legislation. More than one friend is almost always needed to accomplish that. No one person has the power to control outcomes. But by accumulating enough influential advocates, a lobbyist can occasionally manage to win.

That's why, Graefe said, "it matters that you have friends in the Congress rather than people who don't know you." And that's also why "you want your friends to be returned there." So, he continued, "if you want your friends to be there to consider the legislative issues that you're trying to sell, you have to return them to office. And that takes a huge amount of money."

Easy enough. And perfectly understandable. The problem is that money gives lobbyists an advantage that others in society do not have. Money has made Graefe and others like him inside players in a very high stakes game. And insiders in any line of work get a better shake than those who aren't. Graefe analogizes to other types of business, in which "if you like dealing with a guy, you might give him a better deal on price or whatever." The "whatever" in Washington is legislation.

Don't be confused, though, about where those better deals occur. Don't expect to read about them in the morning headlines. The great tides of legislation aren't moved by lobbyists; masses of voters decide those. Will taxes be cut? Will Medicare be fixed? Will education get more money and the military less? Those megamatters aren't manipulated by lobbyists. They're too big. Lawmakers side with their constituents or with their parties on subjects of that scope and size. Why? Because a misstep there can lead to defeat at the polls.

Therefore, it's the obscure and relatively minor issues that produce the most frenetic lobbying. And it is there, on the lucrative edges of legislation, that lobbyists work their ways. Lobbyists constantly obtain special exceptions or extra giveaways for their clients, and few other people ever notice. That makes the margin the place where Graefe and his pals can help the most. A tiny rider to a single bill will rarely threaten the reelection of a member of Congress. Indeed, a lawmaker who extends such a favor could pay back many times over the much-appreciated efforts of a fund-raiser or two.

That's clearly what happened in the battle over one provision pushed by the Federal Communications Commission in a gigantic budget bill a couple years ago. The provision would have stripped NextWave Telecom of New York City, then in bankruptcy proceedings, of one billion dollars' worth of federally auctioned digital wireless-telephone licenses. Graefe, who represented NextWave Telecom, was alerted to this potential catastrophe while he was on a golf course. He left the links to contact some of the friends he had made over the years via fund-raising.

He telephoned Tom Daschle and Bob Kerrey. He also reached White House Chief of Staff Erskine Bowles; Graefe had been a loyal Democratic solicitor for years and was well known to top Democrats such as these. All three men intervened at the eleventh hour on Graefe's behalf, and, with the additional intervention of other lobbyists from the GOP side, the offending provision was crossed out by hand mere moments before the bill went to the printer.

Now that's lobbying, like it or not.

And this is lobbying, too: In 1999, Graefe was thinking ahead about potential changes in the House. And, as ever, he worked the money angle. Not knowing whether Republicans would remain in power after the 2000 election, Graefe was organizing fund-raising events for *all* the potential new chairmen of the House Ways and Means Committee, a powerful fiscal panel that he lobbied frequently. He held events for Charlie Rangel (Democrat, New York), Phil Crane (Republican, Illinois), Bill Thomas (Republican, California), and Clay Shaw (Republican, Florida).

In influence-peddling circles this is known as covering one's bet.

The line between policy and politics is purposely blurred by the money men. And that goes double for money men–lobbyists.

The wall of fund-raiser Wayne Berman's office was papered with photos of himself glad-handing with virtually all of the big-name Republicans of the past two decades. As a longtime lobbyist, Berman knew—and was liked and trusted by—everyone from Ronald Reagan to Newt Gingrich and from George Bush to George W. Bush. They respected him both for his political savvy and for his ability to raise money—as much or more money, in fact, than almost anyone else in town.

It was no surprise, then, that a colleague of his, Scott Reed, interrupted my interview with Berman one day to ask for a favor. Reed was a Washington player in his own right; he had served as campaign manager for the 1996 Dole for President campaign. But Berman had the access that Reed lacked. Reed was pushing a "technical" amendment for a client that needed to be affixed to an appropriations bill that was on the verge of completion in the Senate.

So Berman picked up the telephone and called the chairman of the Senate Appropriations Committee, Ted Stevens of Alaska, one of the crustiest and, at the moment, busiest men in Washington. Then we went on with our interview. A half hour or so later, Stevens called back. I didn't hear everything that was said, but it was obvious that Berman's reminder was all that was needed to insert the amendment into the bill. The money—and time—that Berman had lavished on his GOP brethren was paying off once again.

And yet, lobbyists are not their caricature. They are *not* fat, cigar-smoking men who shove money into the pockets of easily manipulated lawmakers. Nowadays, there are only a few people who fit that description, and they're fun to have lunch with if you have the chance. But they are a tiny—and shrinking—minority.

The new lobbying is more subtle—so subtle that Washington's most powerful interest groups can barely be found inside the Beltway anymore. They still have offices, of course, but they're increasingly inhabited by researchers rather than by traditional kinds of "access" lobbyists. As *Fortune* reported in 1997, "their clout springs from the sincere support they get from actual voters back home, not from their ability to buy the right politicians or to pretend that a last-minute deluge of phone calls constitutes a groundswell." This could be called the Iceberg Principle of legislation: The powerhouses of persuasion aren't too visible above the Washington waterline, but they are very large and menacing nonetheless.

That was one of the surprising conclusions gleaned from *Fortune*'s survey of clout in the capital, which it called Washington's Power 25. This was an authoritative, empirical poll of capital insiders that assessed which trade associations, labor unions, and other interest groups wielded the most influence on the federal government.

To no one's surprise, the AARP placed first. The ever-controversial International Brotherhood of Teamsters was number twenty-five. The calculatedly quiet American Israel Public Affairs Committee (AIPAC), a pro-Israel lobby, was a remarkable second. And the obscure but Republicanly well connected National Restaurant Association was twenty-fourth.

The Power 25 turned out to be as diverse as America itself. It was also a reminder that Alexis de Tocqueville was right more than 150 years ago when he observed that Americans were inveterate joiners who liked to group themselves into quasi-political volunteer organizations. But the survey also rebutted one of the oldest maxims of lobbying: that campaign contributions buy power in Washington. While donations were crucial, they weren't the only paths to power.

Yes, three of the top ten organizations owed their rankings to their substantial campaign donations: ATLA (number five), AIPAC, and the AMA (number eight). But a larger number of the top ten weren't big contributors.

The survey, which polled such Washington players as lawmakers and their senior aides, showed that pressure groups were more valued for the votes they could deliver than for their campaign donations. Most of the Power 25 could boast large numbers of geographically dispersed and politically active members. Money in politics is a mere surrogate for the main target: voters. If lobbyists or lobbying groups can cut out the middleman and provide the votes directly, more power to them—literally.

Half of the top ten groups in the survey in 1997 were propelled there on the strength of their long-established grassroots networks, which are probably better called AstroTurf because of their largely artificial nature. These "kings of the town-hall meeting" were the AARP, the NFIB (number four), the NRA (number six), the Christian Coalition (number seven), and the NRLC (number ten).

Which isn't to say that money doesn't talk at all. The AFL-CIO (number three) garnered high marks in the survey due to both its grassroots organizing *and* its fund giving.

The only investor-related organization that made the Power 25 was the American Bankers Association at number twelve. The other financial-services lobbies were also-rans. The Securities Industry Association was forty-seventh; the National Association of Securities Dealers was eighty-third; the Bond Market Association was eighty-fourth; and the Investment Company Institute, the mutual fund–industry trade association, languished at number 115. Wall Street's stock wasn't too high on K Street.

On the other hand, groups with substantial numbers of members were heavily represented in the Power 25. These included the National Education Association (number nine) and the American Federation of State, County, and Municipal Employees (number fourteen). Both of these groups had deep-seated interests in government, which is another important factor in clout. Two other groups in the top twenty-five were keenly involved in Washington: the Veterans of Foreign Wars (number sixteen) and the American Legion (number twenty-three).

So campaign giving isn't the whole story, but the poll illustrated that there is good reason to give plenty. Donors are wise to have their own team in charge in Congress. The survey showed that it really does matter who holds the majority. For the most part, Republican-leaning groups were rated more highly than Democratic leaners, largely, it appeared, because the GOP was in the majority on Capitol Hill.

Only four of the Power 25 were labor unions. What's more, conservative interest groups outranked their more leftist counterparts. The progun NRA was number six, while its gun-control nemesis, Handgun Control, was number sixty-eight. The antiabortion NRLC was number ten, while NARAL was lost in the weeds at number forty-three.

The same was true of proenvironment groups. The Sierra Club was number 37, the League of Conservation Voters was number 71, the Natural Resources Defense Council was number 79, the Environmental Defense Fund was number 86, and the National Wildlife Federation was down at number 88. So-called good-government groups were even worse off. The Children's Defense Fund was number 40, the League of Women Voters was number 93, Common Cause was number 91, Ralph Nader's Public Citizen was number 111, and the Center for Science in the Public Interest was at the bottom of the list at number 120.

At the same time, some of the most highly ranked groups, including some new and obscure ones, were obviously Republican in their shadings. In fact, the Republican majority in the House worked so closely with a small cluster of trade associations that they became known as the Republican Gang of Five. Their ratings in the poll, as a result, were noticeably high.

The gang included such staple GOP-allied associations as the National Association of Manufacturers (number 13) and the U.S. Chamber of Commerce (number 15). Interestingly, the three others in the group were the National Restaurant Association (number 24), the National Association of Wholesaler-Distributors (number 47 overall, but number 28 among Republicans), and one of the more interesting power brokers of the GOP age, the NFIB (number 4; in 1998, it rose to number 3).

These groups were Republican when being Republican wasn't cool. They provided both campaign funds and electoral ground troops to help their GOP brethren both before and after the Gingrich Revolution in 1994. Their reward was access and influence in Washington. "These groups were with us when we were in the wilderness," said Ohio congressman John Boehner. "And they're still with us now." That made them special interests with very special privileges.

In addition to asking who worked best, the *Fortune* poll asked *what* worked best. According to the poll (and this might be a bit self-serving by the respondents), the most effective method of lobbying was not the giving or raising of campaign donations—that came in the middle range of responses—but the delivering of straight facts to lawmakers. The next two most effective methods involved the intensity with which actual voters believed in those facts and brought them personally to lawmakers' attention.

Lobbyists knew this. So in many ways, lobbying was pretty standard. Almost any campaign involved a slew of actors from the various wings of the influence industry. There are generally access lobbyists inside the Beltway, but also AstroTurf lobbyists back home, publicists for free media, advertisers for paid commercials, and scholars to help shape the arguments. Indeed, there has long been a cookie-cutter sameness to even sophisticated lobbying methods.

But there was always something new. The cutting edge of the new lobbying could be seen in West Palm Beach, Florida. There, Richard Pinsky, an ex-operative for Pat Robertson and Bob Dole, worked as a kind of political detective. His job was to find and bring into the lobbying fold people who were once close to lawmakers whose votes were sought by a lobbying campaign. Pinsky then determined which of these people were willing to make the case to Senator X or Congressman Y. In the argot of the multibillion-dollar influence industry, Pinsky was a grass*tops* expert—as opposed to a grass*roots* expert—since he avoided the hoi polloi and focused on those few people whose opinions the targeted lawmakers trusted.

When Pinsky was hired by the Dewey Square Group, a public-relations and political-consulting firm, to rally support for "fast-track" trade legislation in 1997, he called an old ally, former Republican governor Bob Martinez of Florida. Martinez, in turn, discussed the issue with fellow Tampa resident and Democratic congressman Jim Davis. Davis, a freshman, voted yes on the free-trade measure. Although Davis's spokesman insisted the Martinez talk didn't affect the congressman's vote, the chat couldn't have hurt. Nor did any of the casual but premeditated contacts made on the issue by another Pinsky recruit, former Florida secretary of commerce Charles Dusseau; he wrote to fellow Democratic members of Congress Corrine Brown, Peter Deutsch, and Robert Wexler.

The beauty of the tactic was that the lawmakers usually didn't know they'd been lobbied. The difficulty with it was that it was very expensive. Many, many thousands of dollars had to be expended to make any sort of grasstops effort work. Still, the approach spread rapidly. Dewey Square was just one of several firms, such as Direct Impact and Lunde and Burger, that maintained nationwide networks of politically wired operatives who were willing to reach for their Rolodexes in between their election-year gigs. Campaign professionals such as Susan Swecker of Virginia, Ken Benson of Texas, and Tylynn Gordon of Montana were the new breed of influence peddlers. But they didn't need to register as lobbyists in the nation's capital. They didn't even set foot in the city they affected so deeply. At the same time, they were paid well for their services by the Washington-based influence industry.

And that's the point. Nothing is inexpensive in politics. Everything that's cheap and easy has already been tried. It's the costly stuff that's left.

Take the lobbying done by a Washington-based group called Cause Celebre. Housed at APCO Associates, the lobbying and public-relations arm of Grey Advertising, Cause Celebre puts celebrities together with causes, usually for the benefit of fee-paying corporate clients hungry for publicity.

When MCI wanted to advertise itself to young people, it turned to Cause Celebre, which recruited singer Sheryl Crow to promote voter registration over the Internet. And when Johnson & Johnson, maker of Band-Aids, wanted to find a way to appeal to the parents of young children, Cause Celebre enlisted TV talk-show hostess Leeza Gibbons and David Schwimmer of the sit-com *Friends*. They dutifully reminded lawmakers and the public about the importance of childhood-accident prevention.

Such matchmaking was the brainchild of Cause Celebre's chief, Alma Viator, a showbiz publicist who had worked for theatrical organizations on both coasts and had long made her living inside the Beltway. Viator understood the mutual attraction of Hollywood stars and Washington office holders. Her husband was Ben Jones, better known as Cooter the auto mechanic on the TV series *The Dukes of Hazzard*. Jones also had served two terms as a Democratic congressman from Georgia and had run (unsuccessfully) against Newt Gingrich. In 1998, he contented himself in part by being a member of his wife's stable of celebrities on call.

Why would glitzy stars want anything to do with drab D.C.? "They're looking for their lives to have additional meaning," Margery Kraus, the president of APCO, told *Fortune*. As for why politicians would want to hang out with the stars, Viator suggested that more than just glamour is involved. "When they see each other," she said, "they seem to know each other," because they are both hungry for attention. Like stars, politicians need publicity the way humans need oxygen. "They both feed on that adulation and response," she said. It's commonly said that the most dangerous place to stand on Capitol Hill is between a congressman and a bank of cameras—exactly what a Hollywood celebrity always has in tow.

Corporations and interest groups also crave at times to be the focus of media hype. When the Recording Industry Association of America wanted to sell its version of copyright protection, it (and Viator) staged a concert for lawmakers and their staffs at Washington's Ford's Theater. It featured country-music legend Johnny Cash. Also on the bill was a barbershop quartet of GOP senators that included Trent Lott.

By no coincidence, Cash testified on Capitol Hill the same day as the concert. He was lavished with publicity for both appearances.

Sometimes the linkage didn't work so well. Viator brought a young starlet to Washington to speak in front of a forum on women's health. After the talk, to Viator's horror, the starlet dashed into a bathroom in the Capitol for a quick smoke. Viator said she had to bar the door to prevent anyone from discovering the hypocrisy.

Then there was the time when Cher came to town to attend a benefit for a school that helped learning-disabled children. The singer-actress hadn't realized that the benefit dinner was going to be held not in a hotel ballroom but at a downtown business. When she emerged from her limo, she is reliably reported to have quipped, "What the fuck am I doing at a department store?" She went anyway, smiling.

Most times, though, the cross-cultural stargazing worked well. James Cromwell was well known for his Oscar-nominated role as the farmer in the talking-pig epic, *Babe*. When John McCain spotted Cromwell walking up the steps to the Senate chamber, he stopped to say hello. Cromwell was able to plug his cause: funding for Native American arts education. And McCain got to tell his children that he'd spoken to Farmer Hoggett.

For Viator that was another good day as a modern-day lobbyist—one who is more impresario than actor.

Lobbyists have always been behind-the-scenes players, but not the way they are now. Traditionally, they were secretive and never wanted the public at large to know what they were winning for their clients. Too much sunshine on their efforts, they thought, would melt their victories away.

In many ways, that's still the case. Only today, lobbyists manipulate lawmakers through both secret *and* extremely public means. Public relations and advertising are full-fledged weapons in the lobbyists' arsenal. A Washington lobbyist these days is a manager of all sorts of professionals in the industry of persuasion.

Take advertising. Ever since the "Harry and Louise" commercials paid for by the health-insurance industry helped kill

Clinton's health-care plan in 1994, millions of dollars have poured into TV, radio, and newspaper ads from both sides of virtually every major policy debate. The technique has flourished because it's easy to see and therefore easy to sell to the home office.

The result is that the fastest-growing type of lobbyist doesn't even show up on Capitol Hill and never talks to lawmakers. Some, in fact, maintain their offices on the West Coast, more than 2,500 miles from the Beltway. They are TV-commercial producers, and they work to make the case without ever pressing the flesh.

Two of the most influential ad makers were Carter Eskew of Bozell/Eskew Advertising of Washington and Ben Goddard of Goddard Claussen/First Tuesday of Malibu, California. For an extended stretch in the mid-1990s, they were the go-to guys for so-called issue-advocacy advertising. Eskew, who was in his forties, and Goddard, who was in his fifties, were both former Democratic campaign consultants (Eskew for Al Gore, Goddard for Gary Hart). But their clients were occasionally the sort of companies that made good Democrats cringe.

Eskew created the ad campaign for the tobacco companies that helped kill anticigarette legislation in 1998. He also worked for business groups that wanted to defeat a bill sponsored by trial lawyers, a basic Democratic constituency. Goddard fathered the "Harry and Louise" commercials. In 1997, he wrote ads for a business coalition that opposed the treaty to combat global warming.

Why did these two Democrats switch their allegiances? There can be only one answer: money. "Generally," Goddard said candidly, "issue advocacy is more lucrative." It also is more reliable work. A major race for Senate can cost twenty million dollars, but the client is often volatile and not easy to please. An issue-advocacy campaign can expend double that amount and can occur at any time, not just in an election year. What's more, the client is usually starchily corporate, which means he's less nasty than the average candidate during those late-night phone calls to the media consultant.

At the same time, talent is talent. Goddard's company was bought by yet another firm engaged in the ever-widening lobbying business. And Eskew, beseeched by his old client Gore to invigorate his presidential campaign in 1999, dropped his corporate clients to return to politics—at least for a while. The massive paychecks of video lobbying, though, are likely to lure him back.

Influence merchants are a permanent establishment in Washington. Indeed, the capital's mightiest lobbyists aren't shadowy creatures who shun the spotlight. Many are among the nation's best-known public servants who until recently were Sunday talk-show regulars, and in some cases still are.

It turns out that effective lobbyists spend as much of their time wooing voters as courting members of Congress. The top lobbyists possess both a public persona *and* private access to lawmakers.

We know this thanks to yet another *Fortune* survey conducted by the Mellman Group and Public Opinion Strategies in 1998. On the theory that not every business with a problem with Washington can rely on just its industry's trade association for representation, the magazine asked Washington insiders which lobbying firms had the most clout.

The central conclusion was instructive. Hand-to-hand lobbying is all about access, and the firms that had more of it ranked higher than those with less. And who better to worm their ways into official circles than people who had just been there or who were close to the people who still were? As an added bonus, these also were people who, for the most part, could serve as a credible public face for the interests they served. The top ten of *Fortune*'s list was filled with recently departed leaders of Congress and of the political parties.

The number-one lobbying firm—Verner, Liipfert, Bernhard, McPherson, and Hand—acquired its marquee names over a relatively short stretch in the mid-1990s. They included two former Senate majority leaders, Bob Dole and George Mitchell, and a former treasury secretary, Lloyd Bentsen. The number-two firm, Barbour Griffith and Rogers, was headed by Haley Barbour.

Principals in the other top-ranked firms included such well-known and long-trusted folks as presidential buddy Vernon Jordan and Robert Strauss, the former Democratic Party chairman and former ambassador to the Soviet Union (in a Republican administration), both rainmakers at Akin, Gump, Strauss, Hauer, and Feld, which placed third in the survey. Other household-named lobbyists included ex-Senate majority leader Howard Baker of Baker, Donelson, Bearman, and Caldwell (number eight), ex–White House chief of staff Ken Duberstein of the Duberstein Group (number six), and Tommy Boggs of Patton Boggs (number four), who is the son of ex–House majority leader Hale Boggs and the brother of Cokie Roberts of ABC News.

Judging by this list, it was obviously wrong to suggest that these or other former bigwigs were mere glad-handers or "access men." Rather, they functioned more as generals than infantrymen. Sure, their ability to get a phone call returned was vital in the heat of battle. But many of these former insiders were needed as much for their strategic advice as for their door-opening skills. *That* is a more accurate description of a modern-day lobbyist.

That was why veteran solons found no lack of job offers "downtown." Even though they are prohibited by ethics laws from lobbying their former colleagues for a year after they leave the Hill, ex-lawmakers were still in high demand. The reason: their job was to manage entire persuasion campaigns, not just to beg for favors themselves. They supervised advertisers, fundraisers, telemarketers, and statisticians. They reduced themselves to personal lobbying only part of the time and mostly at critical junctures.

Size didn't matter when it came to lobbying-company clout. Verner Liipfert had 185 lobbyists and lawyers, but Barbour Griffith employed just thirteen. Two of the top ten lobbying companies—the Duberstein Group and O'Brien Calio—were among the smallest of the fifty evaluated. Only four of the top ten were among the ten largest as measured by revenue.

What did matter was political contributions. The survey proved that to be taken seriously, lobbyists had to give campaign cash or, more important, raise it. To be high on the list of clout, they needed to be big-time solicitors. Nearly a third of the top thirty firms had their own PACs. The principals of the firms did their own giving as well. At one time, Tom Boggs and J. D. Williams of Williams and Jensen (number ten) were standouts for their fund-raising. They were among the pioneers of the technique two decades ago.

Now, however, every firm had to have champions on the money circuit. There was no better way to make sure that doors would open when a client needed to get inside.

Clever lobbyists ride the waves of large issues and concentrate on the lucrative margins of major legislation, which largely escape the voters' notice. With the addition of a comma here or a phrase there, they can make or lose big money.

The perfect example of this victory-on-the-margin approach to influence peddling in 1998 was an obscure organization that represents the nation's twelve thousand credit unions. The Credit

Union National Association ranked a mediocre seventieth in *Fortune*'s rankings in 1997. Its leap to eighth place in 1998 was the most pronounced on the entire list. The reason: CUNA persuaded Congress to overturn a Supreme Court decision that would have all but killed credit unions' chance to grow and prosper. In the process, it trounced its archrival, the otherwise far more powerful American Bankers Association, which slipped in the 1998 rankings to number twenty from number twelve the year before.

The dowdy credit-union movement was a sleeping giant. But when the Supreme Court threatened to stop them from expanding to cover larger groups of employees, their very existence was placed in jeopardy. Ex-congressman Dan Mica of Florida, CUNA's new president, had no choice but to try something radical. It turned out he didn't need to look far. While it was a good thing that he knew lots of people on Capitol Hill, those relationships really didn't matter.

The asset that Mica realized he had was located almost entirely outside official Washington. He had real voters whom he would alert to the danger that credit unions faced. He decided to unleash the seventy-four million people who banked at credit unions, more than double the membership of the AARP.

The money men, of course, still played a pivotal role, since such a large number of people needed to be told that their favorite credit union was about to go belly-up. They needed to be instructed on how to contact their representatives in Washington. And that took a considerable amount of money: about seven million dollars a year for a couple of years.

With those millions, Mica hired an all-star cast of lobbying experts, including grassroots organizers (AstroTurf builders) and direct-mail specialists. The latter advised how best to stuff monthly account-statement envelopes with politically charged warnings of imminent doom. Mica also developed a network of a dozen regional coordinators who, in turn, staged dozens upon dozens of members' meetings across the country.

The result was the biggest avalanche of phone calls and letters that many lawmakers could ever recall. Switchboards lit up in offices everywhere on Capitol Hill. Congressional mailbags were stuffed to overflowing with Washington-generated citizen complaints. When Senator Alfonse D'Amato of New York, then the chairman of the Senate Banking Committee, wanted a couple of hundred credit-union members to rally at the Capitol to help him push the credit union's bill, Mica sent out a call for help. Three working days later, some six thousand people showed up from all fifty states. "The credit unions showed they could generate a massive level of grassroots support," said Ed Yingling, chief lobbyist for the American Bankers Association. "There was nothing you could do."

It may not have been pure campaign giving that won the day for the credit unions. But lots of lobbying money, cunningly applied, did produce the sought result.

At the beginning of 1998, almost everyone believed there was nothing the big tobacco companies could do to stop anticigarette legislation. And almost everyone was wrong. In Washington, it's easier to stop something than to make it happen. By the end of the year, the tobacco companies had won the day. And here again, political money, in its broadest definition, was key.

If you recall, a grand compromise was struck between state attorneys general, antismoking activists, and the cigarette companies in 1997. Their plan would force the companies to pay many billions of dollars to the states; in exchange, the companies would be shielded from certain kinds of lawsuits. The problem was that the U.S. Congress, which had to bless the deal, was never brought into the discussions, and it refused to act as a rubber stamp. So, as Congress is wont to do, it kept adding things to the original proposal. In 1998, the tobacco companies began to get cold feet and were itching to walk away from the deal.

But could they? And if so, how? The companies employed a ton of money and a great deal of public opinion–survey data to answer those questions. As the Senate's tobacco legislation grew more elaborate and expensive, tobacco executives noticed a change in public opinion. Their polling and focus groups—both hugely expensive—suggested that they could push voter support for the tobacco bill below 50 percent if they hammered home the notion that the pending legislation was a big-government boondoggle fueled by a huge tax increase. And with forty million dollars in advertising, that's what they did.

Once they lowered esteem for the legislation outside the Beltway, they set to work on insiders. They engaged GOP heavyweights such as Haley Barbour to reassure congressional leaders that they could kill the bill without endangering the reelection of Republicans. They also were helped when tobacco-state senators feuded over how much transition relief to give farmers, a wrangle that deprived the bill's advocates of a few key votes. But most important, the bill's backers were too smug to realize that they needed to fight back against the cigarette companies and also to trim their overambitious proposal. The result was a decisive win for tobacco.

Another come-from-behind win was staged by the HMO industry. President Clinton was determined to gain vindication for the debacle of his original health-care plan by reining in health-maintenance organizations. Like the tobacco bill, the HMO measure seemed a shoo-in. But the American Association of Health Plans, the HMOs' newly beefed-up trade group, put together a multitiered campaign worthy of a presidential-election bid.

Under the guidance of Karen Ignagni, a Democrat, and Mark Merritt, a Republican, the AAHP turned the inevitable into a squabble for another day. All it took was twenty million dollars.

The association arranged to have a pro-HMO message greet lawmakers wherever they went. The group held press conferences from Miami to Manchester. It formed a huge coalition of business groups united by their worry over rising health-care costs. It collected the names of people who, believe it or not, loved their HMOs and were willing to say so whenever they were contacted by fax or e-mail. HMO advertising played on TV, on the radio, and in print. And HMO lobbyists pleaded with lawmakers at home and in the capital. In the end, Congress didn't act.

At the same time, it's facile—and often wrong—to think that big-moneyed interests can simply buy victory in Washington. In at least one case in 1998, the side that spent the most lost in a big way. The issue was a tax break enjoyed by a handful of real-estate firms called paired-share REITs. Some of the most expensive lobbying talent in town was retained to save it. The lobbyists included Dole and Mitchell of Verner Liipfert; Ken Kies of Price Waterhouse; Janet Boyd of Akin, Gump; Katherine Friess of Black, Kelly, Scruggs, and Healey; Rich Belas and Tad Davis of Davis and Harman; John Jonas of Patton Boggs; and Bill Wilkins of Wilmer, Cutler, and Pickering. The other side, which fought to repeal the provision, was much smaller; it was led by Marriott International and included ex-GOP senator Robert Packwood of Oregon.

All the money in the world, however, couldn't save the tax break. The main reason: Barry Sternlicht, CEO of Starwood Hotels and Resorts Worldwide, predicted aloud that the subsidy would survive despite the objections of "one small representative," GOP congressman Mac Collins of Georgia. It's never a good idea to call a member of the Ways and Means Committee "small." To rub it in, the anti–tax break group set up a website that included several other inflammatory comments by Sternlicht. Its address: www.5privilegedreits.com. The benefit was revoked.

Win or lose, though, lobbyists are players in Washington. When President Clinton needed strategic and tactical advice to weather his impeachment fight, he turned to a network of lobbyists that included Tommy Boggs, former White House press secretary Jody Powell, and Tony Podesta, a lobbyist and the brother of Clinton's chief of staff. When the GOP needed foot soldiers to pass their legislative agenda, they convened a group of lobbyists once a week and made them part of a kitchen cabinet called the Thursday Group.

Kevin P. Phillips, author of *Arrogant Capital,* told Jill Abramson of *The New York Times* that Washington had become what the Founding Fathers feared, a "capital so privileged and incestuous in its dealings, that average citizens believe it is no longer accessible to the general public." He added that there was nothing like Washington's "massive, permanent lobbying elite" in other foreign capitals.

In the United States, in fact, it had become common for skilled professionals to leave government to join the ranks of lobbyists. Well over one hundred former members of Congress are now professional lobbyists. Thousands of former congressional staffers are, too. And why not? There's a lot of money to be made "downtown." The most senior lobbyists in Washington make a million dollars or more a year.

Only 3 percent of the lawmakers who retired in the 1970s still work on K Street. But in the 1990s, at least 22 percent of those leaving the Hill became lobbyists—and not just because they had lost their jobs due to voter dissatisfaction. Some, like Oklahoma Democrat Glenn English, left their House seats in the midst of their terms.

Some people actually come to work in Washington with the hope of making lobbying a career. Superlobbyist Robert Strauss told Abramson that lawyers often go to work for the government not because they were ever interested in a career in public service but because "they know that enables them to move on out in a few years and become associated with a lobbying or law firm and their services are in tremendous demand." Service to your country became just another ticket to punch on the way up the corporate ladder.

As of 1987, most of the administrative assistants or top congressional staffers in the House spent five and a half years working in Congress before moving on. As of 1996, the average tenure had dropped to four years, according to a study first reported by the *National Journal.* The length of tenure among senior Senate aides also dropped during the period. According to another study, 58 percent of the departing staffers said they left primarily to earn more money. Lobbying certainly provided that.

That's lobbyist envy. Guy Vander Jagt of Michigan was once a senior Republican on the House Ways and Means Committee. He became a lobbyist and joined Fred Graefe's firm in 1993. At first, business was slow, but when Republicans took control of the House in 1995, Vander Jagt found himself in demand. He could offer the movie industry and other clients a real feel for what Republicans were thinking because, as a former member of Congress, he could attend meetings reserved for his small fraternity. "It's a lobbyist's dream to be sitting there with the committee chairmen and to find out what's going on," Vander Jagt told *The New York Times.* "You have all the benefits of your former life and none of the hardships."

Democrat Tom Downey was crushed when he lost his reelection try in 1992 after nearly eighteen years in the House. But the New Yorker went on to found his own lobbying shop with another former House member, Republican Rod Chandler of Washington. Together, they made millions. And Downey, who was once a lawmaker's lawmaker, told the *Times* he was happy to have been forced to change. And not just because of the extra pay. He said: "I do more interesting things now than I did as a member of Congress."

That's lobbyist envy, too.

Lobbying has become so mainstream, in fact, that American University in Washington offers a course on the subject. Not a course to study lobbying as part of political science but rather as a primer to aid in a future career.

James Thurber, the professor who runs the Lobbying Institute, enlists top-flight lobbyists such as Tommy Boggs to guest lecture. The Workshop on the Art and Craft of Lobbying includes classes on team lobbying, lobbying regulation and reform, lobbying the executive-branch agencies, lobbying on international issues, grassroots technology, lobbying and the Internet, and, of course, an overview of political money.

If they learned their lessons well, the students one day will make a million dollars, too. At least that's their hope.

9

Bang for the Buck

Money in Washington is often automatic. For a lobbyist or a top corporate executive, failing to donate the maximum amount to the chairman of a congressional committee that oversees his industry would be tantamount to malpractice. That was a major reason Senator John McCain's maverick bid for the Republican presidential nomination in 2000 was so relatively well financed, at least initially. His populist appeal later gave him a new burst of support and donations. Indeed, McCain was deeply disliked by most of his GOP colleagues because he pushed so hard for campaign-finance reforms. But his campaign coffers were always brimming. Nothing less would befit the powerful chairman of the Senate Commerce Committee. No trucker, railroad operator, or telephone, cable, or broadcast executive could afford not to give to both McCain's Senate reelection committee and his presidential fund.

McCain collected his early money because it was impolite, as well as impolitic, not to favor the commerce committee's chairman with a token contribution. Was the money that went to his campaign buying special favors? Were campaign contributions in general the best way to purchase influence in the nation's capital? Or is it possible that the donations worked more like protection money in the Mafia days? If you forked over some cash to the organized-crime syndicate, nothing too awful would happen to you. But if you don't give, something awful might.

The longer I stay in Washington, the more I believe the protection-money racket is a good metaphor for what a lot of campaign giving is about.

Political scientists have puzzled for years over what campaign money buys. The results have been largely inconclusive. At the same time, no one disputes that money buys influence in Washington. The only question is what kind of spending buys the most. *Fortune*'s Power 25 survey in 1999 revealed a surprise answer: lobbying expenditures, the most straightforward, unglamorous type of influence peddling, rather than direct giving to candidates or parties. "We couldn't find any direct relationship between campaign donations and clout," said Mark Mellman, one of *Fortune*'s pollsters. "The only place we could find a modest correlation with influence was in spending on lobbying."

The top five lobbying groups spent an average of $3.1 million a year on lobbying versus $900,000 for the bottom five. The amount those groups contributed to candidates or to parties, on the other hand, was all over the lot. Unfortunately, the survey couldn't determine what kinds of lobbying were most effective—whether, say, Washington-based lobbyists were the key to clout or if average voters agitating from the grass roots made the most difference. But clearly there were lots of routes to influence in Washington, and straight-up donations were not, as you might have expected, the obviously best route.

At the same time, campaign contributions, both direct and indirect, were very much in the public consciousness. Donations of both hard and soft money were disclosed and written about constantly in newspapers and magazines. As a result, both kinds of electoral giving were under constant scrutiny and attack.

It has become a consensus that the current campaign-financing system stinks: The givers, the takers, the voters all agree. One very prominent former giver, in fact, started an organization dedicated to changing it all. And for Jerry Kohlberg, this was an accustomed role; he had long been both a pioneer and a pariah. As an investment banker at Bear Stearns in the 1960s, he invented the leveraged buyout and with it became one of the richest men in America. But he cared about more than just making money, which made him an outcast in the industry he helped spawn. In 1987, Kohlberg left the famous firm he cofounded, Kohlberg Kravis Roberts, with a politically incorrect blast that is still remembered on Wall Street. At a meeting in New York, Kohlberg warned KKR investors that his colleagues had fallen prey to an "overweening, overpowering greed" that would surely be their undoing.

A decade later, he repeated the same pattern in another hostile environment: Washington. He committed to spending one million dollars a year to overturn the campaign-finance system in which he was once a major player. He acknowledged that he would probably be "socially ostracized" by business leaders who coveted the access and power that their donations brought them and their companies. But, he said, "it won't bother me too much; I've been there."

Kohlberg wasn't there alone. In one of the most important developments in the decades-old struggle to overhaul federal election laws, he quietly assembled a blue-chip group of corporate elders to stand with him. Longtime advocates of campaign-finance reform hailed his efforts as a breakthrough. Fred Wertheimer, former president of Common Cause, called Kohlberg's Campaign Reform Project the "missing link" that proved the system had become so sordid even beneficiaries were complaining.

Think of these dissenters as Kohlberg's turncoats; several of their companies had been active contributors and satisfied beneficiaries of the money culture in Washington. Members included P. Roy Vagelos, former chairman of Merck; Richard Rosenberg, former chairman of BankAmerica; Thomas Murphy, former chairman of Capital Cities/ABC; Sanford R. Robertson, then chairman of Robertson Stephens; Robert Bernstein, former chairman of Random House; Morton Meyerson, chairman of Perot Systems; Donald Stone, former chairman of Merrill Lynch Specialists; and A. C. Viebranz, former senior vice president of GTE. Kohlberg had gotten each of these people to agree not just to denounce the system but to press with him for its replacement. Superinvestor Warren Buffett soon joined the brigade, as did two highly regarded former senators: Nancy Kassebaum, Republican of Kansas, and Bill Bradley, Democrat of New Jersey. Both had been outspoken critics of campaign spending, but it was Bradley who made it a cause célèbre, including it in his run for the presidency in 2000.

Like his compatriots, Kohlberg knew the ins and outs of political fund-raising firsthand. He began contributing to political campaigns in 1988, when he supported his fellow Swarthmore College graduate Michael Dukakis. Over the next four years, he lavished $275,000 of soft money on the Democratic National Committee. But the more he gave, the less he liked what grubbing for money did to politicians.

Kohlberg's subsequent crusade turned out to be arduous, however, at least partly because of his own actions. Despite his stand on reform, he (and his fellow turncoats) continued to give money to individual candidates. It would have been hard to find a better way to undercut a message. A bigger problem was that while the business members of his group were heavyweights, they also were mostly has-beens. Active executives would have wielded much more clout with Congress, had they joined Kohlberg's bandwagon. But Kohlberg conceded that they were hard to persuade. "They talk about their fiduciary duty to shareholders," Kohlberg said. "They wouldn't be giving all this money unless it was worthwhile."

Precisely. While Kohlberg's small band protested, large numbers of companies, executives, and organizations continued to opt into the system. True, there were a few notable do-gooders: in 1997, General Motors, AlliedSignal, and Monsanto announced that they wouldn't any longer make soft-money contributions. In 1999, Time Warner made the same pledge. But AlliedSignal broke that promise by giving thirty thousand dollars to the Republican Governors Association. And according to *The Wall Street Journal,* seventy-seven other companies made large soft-money donations for the first time during the 1998 election cycle.

Let's face facts. While it might be better for society at large if moneyed interests refrained from making massive contributions to politicians, such restraint probably is not advisable for the companies and groups that have huge financial interests at stake in the nation's capital.

The *Fortune* survey found that there wasn't a correlation between soft-money giving and overall clout. But it didn't prove that giving no money at all was a good idea. In fact, most professional lobbyists would tell any organization with interest in federal legislation that it would be far wiser to donate the money and thus stay in the mix of meetings and information that such money can buy.

From the perspective then of the interested organization, the right thing to do isn't always the best thing.

Putting aside the question of what's right and what's best, soft-money giving and so-called independent expenditures by third-party groups have become gigantic factors in the few competitive elections for national office that still exist.

A 1999 study by seventeen universities in fifteen states showed that the national parties and interest groups were pivotal in congressional elections in 1998 and would probably remain so for years to come. The Brigham Young University–Pew Charitable Trusts study reported that political parties more than doubled their soft-money spending in 1998 compared to the last midterm election. The research also showed spending for so-called issue advertising was on a similar trajectory. "This is a free-for-all," said BYU's David B. Magleby, the project's principal investigator. "I think the parties and the special interests both felt like, 'Hey, all rules are off.' It has made those who give soft money or fund issue ads much more powerful."

The professor expressed a legitimate concern: A lot of money is both undisclosed and unregulated. In addition, so much of it poured into the relatively few competitive congressional races that at times it swamped the money spent by the candidates themselves. According to Magleby, "This constitutes a shift from candidate-centered campaigns to campaigns dominated by interest groups. We have an increasingly unrestrained campaign system that is out of control in terms of accountability."

The study also demonstrated how this money was used. It not only paid for broadcast advertising—the "air war"—but also an extensive and much more clandestine "ground war" of phone banks, mailings, and door-to-door campaigning. And the amounts spent for both types of electioneering were staggering. In the Utah congressional race between Congressman Merrill Cook and Lily Eskelsen, for instance, the study found more than $930,000 in spending from parties and interest groups, including

Americans for Limited Terms, the AFL-CIO, and the National Rifle Association. In Nevada, the AFL-CIO directed thousands of volunteers to oppose the views (and, by inference, the election) of a Republican candidate for the House. Other interest groups that were involved heavily in the 1998 elections included the American Medical Association, the National Right to Life Committee, the League of Conservation Voters, and the Christian Coalition.

Money gushed from these and other sources, making each of them a potent force in Congress. That's what an organization gets by making a difference on Election Day.

Nobody needs to be told that Washington is a peculiar place. But just how peculiar it is sometimes is a shock even for people who have worked there for a long time. For instance, you might expect that the most powerful lobbying groups would also be the most popular ones. After all, elections are fundamentally congeniality contests, and in the capital votes are the coin of the realm.

But it turned out that one of the most consequential lobbies was also one of the least beloved. The standout in the 1999 Power 25 poll was the bad boy of influence peddlers, the National Rifle Association. Despite being under constant attack in the wake of school shootings around the nation, the NRA had managed to rise by two ranks in each of the previous two years until it was tied for second place behind the perennial winner, the AARP. Even more amazing was the fact that the gun lobby was ranked ahead of AARP by lawmakers and congressional staffers, the people who really know who has clout in the capital.

If ever there was a time when the gun lobby should have been vanquished, it was 1999. In that year alone, there were shootings at Columbine High School (fifteen dead, twenty-three wounded), at the Wedgwood Baptist Church in Fort Worth (eight dead, seven wounded), and at the North Valley Jewish Community Center near Los Angeles (five wounded). Then in Atlanta (nine dead, thirteen wounded), Honolulu (seven dead), and Seattle (two dead, two wounded). Yet the NRA not only was alive, it thrived. Despite the shootings—indeed, maybe because of them—the NRA was raising record amounts of political contributions, experiencing rapid growth in membership, and boasting that it was in its strongest financial position in years. "I've been here through good times and bad times," said Wayne LaPierre, the NRA's executive vice president. "We've never been in a better position."

Such was the upside-down world of gun control. The NRA's defenders became most active and effective when the right to bear arms was under assault. The organization itself seemed to get stronger when its issues were in the crosshairs, even if that meant—as it always did—mayhem, destruction, and death.

The NRA's power produced results on Capitol Hill. Despite the spree of mass killings, the NRA bottled up for the year an otherwise popular bill that would have required background checks for buyers at gun shows, banned the importation of high-capacity ammunition clips, and required safety locks on all new guns. How was this possible? Because of its many forms of campaign giving, the NRA was famous for being among the very few lobbying groups that could deliver votes. More lawmakers than were willing to admit it were in Congress in 1999 because the NRA mobilized an extra two thousand or three thousand voters on Election Day, which made the difference between winning and losing.

For much of the rest of this chapter, I will elaborate on why the NRA holds such a powerful position and how it keeps it, at least in the short run, all in the context of how it spends its political money.

The NRA's power was rooted not directly in money but in its three million dedicated members. That was a sizable army of potential voters. But with them also came financial wherewithal. The NRA's annual budget was $137 million, which made it one of the nation's largest and wealthiest cause-oriented groups. Of course, not all that money and those people were political. The NRA used its three magazines—and its Internet portal—to push the sale of equipment and services such as insurance and NRA credit cards, from which it collected a steady stream of royalties.

The association's base was composed of hunters, gun collectors, and outdoorsmen who loved their weapons and the rustic way of life that went with them. Over the years, though, NRA leaders kept an eye on legislation and elections, too, and sifted their membership lists until they had located a die-hard group of 175,000 activists to whom they could turn to stump for a candidate or lobby a congressperson. NRA headquarters in northern Virginia had its own thirty-phone telemarketing center to alert the troops during congressional battles. The association also operated a website that was the envy of the Washington lobbying establishment. Www.nra.org got up to twenty thousand hits on a routine day and several times more than that when gun legislation was under debate. In order to broadcast its message unfiltered by the national press (which the NRA hated), the website had a daily netcast of its own version of the news, called "NRA Live with Wayne LaPierre."

Then there was the straight-up political money. With seven million dollars to disperse, the NRA's political-action committee, the Political Victory Fund, regularly ranked in the top ten of givers to candidates for federal office—mostly, of course, Republicans. Its infamous antigovernment, progun direct-mail solicitations brought in nearly three times as much money by tapping a loyal band of nine hundred thousand donors. Small but regular contributions from this group helped finance nationwide lobbying efforts by the NRA's feared advocacy arm, the NRA Institute for Legislative Action.

But election time was when the NRA really homed in on its targets. In 1998, for example, it spent $150,000 on behalf of pro-gun Jim Bunning of Kentucky. The NRA's PAC also gave the National Baseball Hall of Fame pitcher ten thousand dollars directly, and the NRA's president, Charlton Heston, hosted a fundraiser for Bunning that collected additional funds. At the NRA's direction, two hundred activists fanned out across Kentucky, putting up signs and visiting gun shows to talk up their man. The NRA even mailed out bumper stickers that read SPORTSMEN FOR BUNNING. Every little bit helped; Bunning won by just 6,766 votes out of 1.1 million cast.

Another reason for the NRA's influence was the single-mindedness of its members. Gun-control advocates supported candidates who wanted restrictions on guns, but they rarely cast their votes on that issue alone. NRA members regularly voted one way or the other solely on that issue.

It was not much of a surprise, then, that the NRA played a major role in the Republican takeover of the House of Representatives in 1994. Its victims that year included such powerful Democrats as Speaker Thomas Foley and Jack Brooks, chairman of the House Judiciary Committee. NRA members went after both men because they supported the assault-weapons ban. The result of the GOP takeover was that, finally, the NRA had friends in high places. And that was the problem. The worst thing that can happen to a cause-based group is to get what it wants.

After the 1994 election, NRA membership declined, in part because it raised its annual dues from twenty-five to thirty-five dollars but also because its members didn't feel threatened anymore. The apathy led to the growing influence of right-wing gun zealots known to some internally as the "crazies." Led by Neal Knox, a militant NRA agitator, these zealots forced the group's policy positions to become more strident. The NRA refused to show flexibility, for instance, in its stands against banning various sorts of semiautomatic weapons and "cop-killer" bullets. After the Oklahoma City bombing in 1995, followed by that infamous fund-raising letter that likened federal agents to "jackbooted government thugs," longtime NRA enthusiasts resigned from the organization, and Congressman John Dingell left its board. Even police organizations, once among the NRA's closest allies, abandoned the organization.

But the NRA managed to right itself. The Knox wing eventually fell into disrepute, and the relative moderates began to ascend. In 1998, LaPierre persuaded Heston to become president, giving the organization a friendlier face. Who could be more welcoming than Moses?

In 1999, NRA was on track to have a budget surplus of about five million dollars. By comparison, its chief accuser, Handgun Control, was badly outgunned. Handgun Control was trying to raise bigger sums for its anemic PAC; its ambitious goal was two million dollars, even though it had raised less than one hundred thousand during the previous election. And it was beginning to form a network of activists of the kind that the NRA had long had in place. "We are the ones making progress, not the NRA," asserted Robert Walker, Handgun Control's president. Not really. Despite achieving its highest ranking in three years, Handgun Control still placed sixtieth in the *Fortune* survey, out of 114 groups tested.

But ultimately, the fight over guns was bigger than any single lobbying group, much like the battle over tobacco. The similarities were instructive. Scientists knew the hazards of cigarette smoking for decades before the tobacco companies were finally forced to pay a share of the cost that their product imposed on society. Likewise, gun advocates and manufacturers knew the toll firearms took, especially in cities, and grudgingly gave ground to more and more regulation.

As with tobacco, the defeats and concessions never seemed to satisfy reformers. In 1999, President Clinton was pressing yet another suit against the cigarette industry to collect damages that he said were owed to the Medicare program because of illnesses caused by tobacco use. (The previous settlements had dealt with Medicaid.) Likewise, the suits filed by cities and counties against gun manufacturers were only the first wave, and the Clinton administration, again, was planning other court actions.

Even more telling was the fact that no matter how pro-NRA a lawmaker was, he or she rarely wanted to trumpet that fact. Sure, Republicans and a hearty handful of Democrats were often willing to say that each new gun-control idea went too far. But they mostly said so quietly, and they almost never offered a defense of the organization itself. I contacted several lawmakers whose reelections were greatly aided by the NRA; none would speak for the record.

In addition, even though NRA membership had been growing, overall gun ownership was not. According to the National Opinion Research Center at the University of Chicago, the proportion of men who said they owned a gun dropped from 52 percent in the 1980s to 38 percent in 1998. (Female ownership stayed steady at 11 percent.) The U.S. manufacture and importation of guns, while spiking occasionally, declined by about 20 percent from the late 1970s. What's more, public sentiment overwhelmingly favored more regulation of guns. A poll by *Newsweek* showed in 1999 that 74 percent of the American people supported registration of handguns, 93 percent backed a waiting period for people who wanted to buy handguns, and 50 percent of people who didn't own firearms favored banning handguns completely.

The NRA was an outcast even among some of its friends. One well-known corporate lobbyist who agreed with the association on many issues never invited it to participate in his legislative coalitions. Its political style was simply too aggressive. "The NRA is anathema to business; its game is always to attack," the lobbyist said. "I don't let tobacco join, either, and for the same reason. If they are members, lots of business groups won't join."

To change its image, the NRA would have had to become less fanatical in its devotion to the Second Amendment. But a gentler gun lobby would also have been a less effective one. Blind faith in the cause and proud inflexibility in the face of an arrogant enemy were what bound the rank and file together. The NRA's right flank may have seemed scary to many Americans, but its fervor made it politically potent. With no dearth of opposition, the gun lobby was poised to be dangerous for a long time to come. It got a lot of bang for its many kinds of political spending: direct and indirect campaign giving as well as an active-when-angry membership. But it did not have an endless supply of ammunition.

Which brings us to one last notion. Any purely mechanistic analysis of money and its effect on politics and legislation is sure to fall flat. The outright purchase of power is by its nature a short-run, tactical victory. Over the longer run, more fundamental forces—demographic and economic—will almost certainly prevail.

Lawmakers know that the outlook over the long haul isn't sunny for the gun lobby. As long as guns are available, the NRA is condemned to be in retreat. The organization's best hope is to maintain a holding action against forces that won't rest until guns are regulated more vigorously. Not even the NRA believes that today's restrictions will ever be rolled back. Here's how an NRA supporter on Capitol Hill explained the future to *Fortune:* "We are engaged in a very long, very grim, very hard-fought war. If we are successful, the [gun-control] issue will be plaguing our kids and grandkids. If we aren't successful, they won't be dealing with it because we will have lost."

Money-men groups such as the NRA can often get their way for a while but not forever in the face of fundamental facts. Democracy is too resilient and adaptive for its institutions to do otherwise.

10

High-tech Turnaround

I n 1995, two decades after he and Paul Allen founded Microsoft, Bill Gates decided to open the company's first lobbying office in Washington, D.C. The effort was underwhelming, especially for a firm with annual revenues of six billion dollars. Gates didn't adhere to the standard practice of lodging a slew of high-priced talent in a fancy suite that lent itself to fund-raisers and cozy one-on-ones with wavering lawmakers. There certainly was no view of the Capitol dome out the office window.

Microsoft chose as its sole staffer Jack Krumholtz, a thirty-three-year-old lawyer with no experience to speak of on any congressional or executive-branch staff. Krumholtz didn't rate a secretary. He was placed in a small corner of Microsoft's federal sales office, located across from a shopping mall several miles from downtown. His mandate was confined to software-copyright and data-encrypting laws, and his political war chest was tiny. The company's political-action committee raised and distributed just sixteen thousand dollars.

This studied noninvolvement in national politics sprang

directly from the top. Gates had a deep-seated disgust for the customs of the capital city. He made no secret that the only Washington that mattered to him was Washington State, where Microsoft was based. That other Washington, he said, wasn't "on our radar screen." In 1995, he moaned aloud, "I'm sorry that we have to have a Washington presence."

Gates obviously looked down on mere politicos. And he expressed to his Microsoft colleagues a definite distaste for the entire fund-raising racket. He also was imbued with the cowboy fervor of the burgeoning computer industry, the ethos of which, at least when it came to government, was aloof, even dismissive. It was cool to be indifferent to those lunkheads on the other coast, especially the bureaucrats in D.C. As late as 1998, Krumholtz's lobbying "team" was only three people, including an administrator, and Microsoft was still thumbing its nose at the nation's capital.

That wasn't a good idea. Maybe once upon a time arrogance toward Washington might have seemed amusing. But no one was laughing in mid-1998 when the U.S. Justice Department filed an antitrust suit against Microsoft demanding that it unhitch its Internet browser from its Windows operating system. When that happened, Microsoft had few places it could go for help. Years of neglecting the federal government had left the company without friends in the nation's capital. "They don't want to play the D.C. game, that's clear," said Mark Buse, a senior Republican aide on the Senate Commerce Committee, soon after the suit was filed. "The problem is, in the long run, they won't be able to."

Gates clearly had a lot to learn about dealing with official Washington. He had made a classic mistake. Most corporations, labor unions, or wealthy individuals eventually will have business in the nation's capital. And they have little choice but to act in their own interest by playing the Washington—meaning the money politics—game.

And I'm not just talking about campaign donations. Politicians need to be treated like royalty, and Gates, who was the richest man on earth, had scarcely given them time to snap a photo with him. He deigned to visit the capital only one day a year, and then in the company of other high-tech CEOs such as Intel's Andy Grove, Adobe Systems's John Warnock, and Novell's Eric Schmidt. In fact, "CEO Day" each June had become a metaphor for the misunderstanding that existed between the high-tech world and Washington. The executives scheduled themselves so tightly that they had to race from meeting to meeting in a bus and eat their brown-bag lunches en route.

The executives saw themselves as bold risk takers who should be praised for not riding in limousines and for strictly limiting their visit so they could rush back to run their job-creating businesses. Lawmakers saw the CEOs as arrogant grandstanders who were too busy making billions of dollars to pay the obeisance that other corporate chieftains routinely offered. Nontech corporate leaders thought of visits to Washington as part of their jobs; some even stopped by monthly to meet with key lawmakers and officials in the executive branch.

For years, the gap between most techies and politicos had been a chasm. During one meeting on Capitol Hill between top officials from Silicon Valley and Republican leaders in the Senate, Trent Lott spent a lot of time explaining the duties of Senator Mitch McConnell of Kentucky, who chaired the National Republican Senatorial Committee. After the meeting, one of the more Washington-savvy executives noted aloud how heavy-handed Lott's appeal for campaign contributions had been. Several of the exec's colleagues looked at him quizzically;

they hadn't even realized that they were being dunned for campaign cash.

Gates in particular refused to play by almost any of Washington's rules. In 1997, Microsoft's political-action committee and other sources laid out sixty-one thousand dollars, which was almost nothing for a corporation its size. To the extent Gates did stick his nose into politics, he managed to anger Congress's Republican majority. He gave minor contributions to liberal organizations in Washington State that advocated gun-control measures, and he opposed restrictions on raising taxes. His corporate counsel and his few lobbyists routinely asked Gates to spend more time and money in the nation's capital, but he always refused. Specifically, the lobbyists had begged him to permit the company to commence a long-planned advertising campaign to educate the public on the browser issue—to no avail.

But high-tech leaders, including the recalcitrant Mr. Gates, began to get off their high horses in 1997 and 1998. That was when they finally began to understand that no big business could afford to ignore the country's capital.

Part of the impetus to get involved was spawned by Microsoft's troubles with the Justice Department. Microsoft, of course, had to get going with a full-fledged Washington effort after the suit was filed. But it was not alone. The whole tech community stepped up its efforts. In particular, Microsoft's opponents tried to wring every advantage they could from Microsoft's tussle with the government.

Bob Dole and Jody Powell were retained to put together an anti-Microsoft lobbying coalition. Netscape, Sun Microsystems, and other companies with a stake in slowing Microsoft were among its backers. One reason the anti-Microsoft firms moved so quickly was that they were led by a veteran of Washington battles. Unusual among high-tech leaders, Jim Barksdale, the chief executive of Netscape, had visited Congress frequently and was known for the expert way he buttonholed lawmakers in the hallways. Barksdale had learned his techniques as the chief operating officer of FedEx and as the CEO of AT&T Wireless Services, both highly regulated businesses that couldn't afford to avoid Washington.

He also was unusually well connected. He was an acquaintance of Lott while at the University of Mississippi; their wives had been sorority sisters there. Barksdale also had gotten close to Conrad Burns, chairman of the Senate Communications Subcommittee. In June 1997, Burns wrote a letter to the Federal Trade Commission urging an investigation into possible antitrust violations by Microsoft. Five days later, Barksdale delivered a keynote speech at the opening of the Burns Telecommunications Center at Montana State University.

Now that was a money-man trick if I ever saw one!

Slowly, Microsoft also got off the dime and started to pitch a whole lot more than dimes into the capital's money pit. Starting in that fateful year of 1998, the company quietly began to finance the research of several Washington think tanks, including the Heritage Foundation, the Cato Institute, and the Hudson Institute. Later, those same research institutions would churn out "leave the Web alone" treatises that were exactly what Microsoft wanted lawmakers to hear.

The company also went on a hiring spree. It retained Haley Barbour to mend fences with the GOP majority on Capitol Hill. Microsoft executives also started to act more like the supplicants they really were—at least in Washington. Chief Operating Officer Bob Herbold visited Senate Commerce Committee chairman John McCain, whom many considered the capital's leading Mr. Clean. Herbold asked what Microsoft needed to do to improve its image in the Capitol. McCain reluctantly recommended that Microsoft shed its standoffishness and get its hands dirty with a vigorous lobbying campaign. And that's what it did.

"We want to be a member of this community," Krumholtz told *The Washington Post,* and that's the goal Microsoft pursued, with a vigor rarely matched in the annals of influence buying. In an effort to discourage the Justice Department from seeking overly harsh remedies against it for monopolistic practices, Microsoft beefed up its Washington staff to ten persons and hired almost every gun-for-hire lobbyist in sight.

Since the Republicans were in charge in Congress, Microsoft begged the Republicans hardest of all. In the 1997–1998 election cycle, Microsoft was among the ten largest corporate givers of soft money. Eighty percent of that money went to the Republican Party, according to the nonpartisan Campaign Study Group of Springfield, Virginia, and *The Washington Post.* Hard-money donations by Microsoft's PAC and its employees also rose gigantically, to $1.4 million. The firm also doubled its lobbying expenditures to more than three million dollars a year.

Among its outside consultants were, in addition to Barbour, Carter Eskew, former Ronald Reagan polemicist Michael Deaver, House GOP adviser Grover Norquist, and former Republican congressman Vin Weber of Minnesota, who was close to then-Speaker Newt Gingrich. Among its Democratic lobbyists were former congressmen Vic Fazio of California and Tom Downey of New York, a close friend of the vice president.

Microsoft even hired White House and Gore pollster Mark Penn to help with the overall lobbying strategy. And only in Washington could a key member of that team also be the arch-conservative Ralph Reed. Reed used his grassroots lobbying expertise to organize one hundred thousand of the firm's customers, retailers, and shareholders into a network called "Freedom to Innovate," which could be called on to write, telephone, or e-mail lawmakers to argue against the Justice Department suit.

At the same time, the anti-Microsoft coalition also ramped up its effort. Netscape hired former Federal Trade Commission member Christine Varney and Vice President Gore's onetime domestic-policy adviser, Greg Simon. They worked with the broader anti-Microsoft coalition, which eventually called itself the Project to Promote Competition and Innovation in the Digital Age or ProComp. Much of this was done in coordination with Jody Powell's public-relations firm, Powell Tate, and Bob Dole's firm, Verner Liipfert, according to *The Washington Post*.

The most extensive efforts in this battle, however, were conducted by the late-arriving Microsoft. It even tried to soften its image through advertising. One commercial featured a blind child using a computer for homework. Another presented a story about Melvin and Lola's cows. The text of the commercial read: "He sorts through all his cow statistics on Microsoft Excel spreadsheets. . . . Melvin uses software to manage his herd because his livelihood depends on his cows." The ads ran heaviest in the Washington market and during the Sunday-morning talk shows that are watched most closely by capital politicos.

Some of the maneuvering was more subtle. Microsoft commissioned a poll by Democrat Peter Hart and Republican Robert Teeter that showed that two thirds of Americans believed that Microsoft benefited consumers and that the Justice Department's lawsuit was wrong. It also invited dozens of lawmakers to its Redmond, Washington, campus, including McCain and Bill Bradley, to show them firsthand what a good-hearted, well-intentioned company it really was. Microsoft even wooed and won over Senator Burns. Following Barksdale's lead, the company

donated $184,000 in cash and software to the Burns Telecommu-
nications Center. Ever since, Burns has been mostly silent on the
antitrust issue (though he denies any connection).

While Microsoft was making up for lost time, the rest of the
high-tech community was also shedding its political prissiness—
and not just those companies who wanted to take advantage of
Microsoft's troubles. The entire e-business world, in effect, was
scared smart about Washington by Microsoft's misfortune, and
businesses rushed to become players by becoming potent sources
of money and, eventually, influence.

To be fair, the first glimmerings of an effort to improve relations with politicians had begun before the Microsoft suit. In
1996, Silicon Valley's wealthy business owners provided millions
of dollars to defeat California's Proposition 211, a ballot initiative
that would have made shareholder lawsuits easier to file. That
was the last thing that startup companies needed. And after their
victory on Prop 211, the mildly libertarian tech executives began
to adopt more conventional political labels and to get more involved in politics.

In those years, the common wisdom had been that Silicon
Valley was Democratic, mostly because the energetic Clinton had
made such a show of accepting support from executives there.
In fact, the Valley was largely unaligned—it just had never
paid much attention. But two people who did pay attention at
the presidential level were two partners of the venture-capital
firm Kleiner Perkins Caufield and Byers. John Doerr leaned
Democratic; Floyd Kvamme was Republican. They both decided
to become leaders in the struggle to awaken Silicon Valley from
its political slumber.

Kvamme grew incensed when he read an article in the San Jose
Mercury News on August 21, 1996. Its lead paragraph read: "A
constellation of Silicon Valley executives, including some of the

brightest stars of the high-tech industry and several Republicans, Monday endorsed President Clinton for reelection, declaring him the bridge to the future." The article included a photo of John Doerr on a conference call with Clinton and Gore, who gratefully accepted the endorsement of the fifty Valley luminaries that Doerr had assembled.

In response, Kvamme, his wife, and a family friend holed up in Kvamme's study and began to contact their Republican buddies. Eventually they put together a list and personally stuffed one thousand envelopes with letters seeking the executives' endorsement of the lagging Dole-Kemp ticket. The letter detailed several reasons why Silicon Valley shouldn't support Clinton and Gore, ranging from the tax increases they had backed to their support for trial lawyers on the shareholder-lawsuit issue. The title of the letter was "Silicon Valley for Bob Dole and Jack Kemp: The Winning Team for 21st Century Technology." Each mailing included a blue postcard that the executive could check and return as an easy way to sign up to endorse Dole and Kemp.

Throughout early September, Kvamme kept pushing for more endorsements and began to keep in touch with the growing group by fax. By Monday, September 16, he wrote to each endorser, "Thank you very much for agreeing to endorse the Dole/Kemp ticket. Response has been very good ... over 100 Chairman, CEO and President, or Venture Capital Partner titles in the phone area codes 408, 415 and 510."

Kvamme's last "urgent" fax for support went out on September 23, and the next day he wrote a memo to Dole/Kemp headquarters proudly proclaiming, "On behalf of 195 executives (at last count) here in the Silicon Valley, California, I am very pleased to inform you that we are endorsing your candidacy for President and Vice President of the United States. Most of us have not previously been involved in the political process; however, this year we feel that the characterization of the High

Technology community as a stronghold of the current president is not accurate."

The Dole/Kemp headquarters in Washington was both surprised and pleased. It dispatched Kemp to attend a rally in the Valley the following week, by which time Kvamme had assembled 225 executives for the GOP ticket. And he didn't stop there. On November 1, the Friday before the election, Kvamme was among 245 Silicon Valley execs who bought full-page ads in a handful of newspapers, including *USA Today,* to ballyhoo their support. From a standing start and without the assistance of any Dole/Kemp staffers, that was a remarkable performance.

Unfortunately, it was also too late to do much good. The cause was lost by then.

But the race was on, at least in the high-tech community. Silicon Valley began to organize in earnest for elections to come. Kvamme teamed up with Doerr, in fact, to institutionalize the blossoming power of the Valley. In 1997, they helped found the Technology Network, or Tech Net, a group of 140 executives who convened briefings and fund-raisers for candidates of both parties. One backer called it "The Portal to Silicon Valley" because it was where a politician had to go to learn what was happening in the fast-growing world of e-commerce.

For years, there had been only a handful of places politicians could pan for campaign gold and be sure to fill their saddlebags: New York City, Washington, D.C., Los Angeles, and maybe Chicago, Houston, and Miami. After Tech Net was formed, you could add Silicon Valley to that list. Every presidential wanna-be from Dan Quayle to George W. Bush has peddled his wares to the wizards of high tech there, and most have come away with their coffers brimming.

At first there was more cachet than cash. Despite the hype, the digital geniuses were, initially at least, electoral neophytes who didn't donate on the scale—or think about government with the same sophistication—as the givers in more established fund-raising venues. For a while, when someone mentioned Washington, Palo Altoans thought of Redmond, not D.C. Gradually, however, members of the high-tech community became eager to attend Tech Net breakfasts and to flog their latest pet issues.

Tech Net had to endure some growing pains. Silicon Valley may have been at the heart of economic growth, but it was still on the periphery of politics. According to Doerr a year after Tech Net was created, "We are incredibly naive about all of this."

Kvamme estimated that only half the Valley's business leaders even cared about politics; Doerr said it was less. And that set up both men as teachers of an ignorant class. At first, its efforts were scattershot. "Tech Net is actively bipartisan, which is a good thing," said Bob Grady. "But it is developing a reputation for being willing to host a fund-raiser for basically anybody. They have to develop more discipline."

They also needed to be less starry-eyed. One campaign button seen at Tech Net gatherings read GORE-DOERR IN 2004. That was never going to happen.

For Kvamme, at least, something else was never going to happen: that the rest of the country would be fooled into thinking that the presidential candidate preferred by the technology community was the Democrat, especially Al Gore, who once implausibly claimed to have invented the Internet. Gore again tried to win the P.R. war over the Valley by forming and meeting regularly with a sympathetic group of high-tech executives who called themselves Gore Techs. But Kvamme and other Republicans set out early to prove that there were plenty of prominent executives who leaned Republican, such as Jim

Barksdale of Netscape and John Chambers of Cisco Systems. Gore's high-profile effort to consult with technology entrepreneurs was designed to obscure the fact that most CEOs from other industries distrusted him because of his aggressive environmental views. Indeed, even Gore's top fund-raisers privately admitted that the amount that can be raised from the Valley was relatively small. (Remember, for the presidential race there's a thousand-dollar-per-person limit.)

Kvamme and several other GOP leaders made sure that they invited George W. Bush to a Tech Net meeting in the spring of 1999. They showered him with hundreds of thousands of dollars. What's more, breaking with the group's nonpartisan tradition, Tech Net actually bought an advertisement that year, listing dozens and dozens of high-tech CEOs who backed Bush.

And then something incredible happened. The aloof libertarians of cyberspace became the hottest celebrities inside the Beltway. Once they made themselves—and their campaign contributions—widely available, the members of the e-community became the darlings of official Washington. They got almost everything they wanted in terms of legislation and regulation. Unfortunately, the lawmakers and executive-branch officials who were doling out those goodies knew little and understood less about the high-tech world. And that couldn't be good for the rest of us.

Back in 1999, for instance, Senator Ron Wyden of Oregon was feeling pretty good about himself. A few magazine articles had declared him one of the most Internet-savvy members of Congress, and he was sure that would impress his ten-year-old daughter, Lilly. "How about that?" he told her. "These magazines say I know something about the Internet!" Lilly started to laugh. "If you're one of the best," she snickered, "I want to know more about the other bozos."

The state of knowledge about the Internet in Congress was abysmally low. In many congressional offices, the boss's computer was a prop for photo ops; older lawmakers barely knew the difference between *e-mail* and *female*. "Us old dogs have trouble understanding some of this," acknowledged Senator Burns of Montana, chairman of the Senate's communications subcommittee.

You might think that such widespread ignorance portended trouble for Internet companies in Washington. But congressional stupidity about technology turned out to be the industry's greatest boon. Lawmakers may not have known much about high tech, but what they did know—that it created wealth, jobs, and campaign contributions—was more than enough to compel them to treat the industry and its concerns with deference.

Not since the days of oil barons and railroad tycoons had the nation's capital been so thoroughly in the thrall of a set of corporate executives. The Larry Ellisons, John Chamberses, Michael Dells, and, yes, Bill Gateses of the world had an open door to any lawmaker at any time, which couldn't be said of the leaders of most older, less cutting-edge industries. In fact, Rick White, a former Washington State congressman who advised technology firms about the capital, asserted in the fall of 1999, "The technology community has a window of a year or two in which, if they act together, they can probably get Congress to do anything they like."

That was a great distance from the industries' humble beginnings in Washington. But by 1999, even bad-boy Microsoft had found a soft spot in the hearts of its loudest critics. Utah senator Orrin Hatch didn't have a nice thing to say about Microsoft during congressional hearings in 1998. "They are now a monopoly," Hatch said ominously, "and they will have to learn to live by the rules that govern monopolies." But a year later he said that he was worried that the judge in the antitrust case might impose a "draconian remedy" against the software giant. Hatch, who chaired the Senate's powerful judiciary committee, added: "I don't have anything personal against Microsoft."

Hatch wasn't the only lawmaker who was newly infatuated with everything high tech. They *all* were. The Senate majority created the Republican High Technology Task Force to promote protech legislation. Not to be outdone, House Republicans devised an E-Contract, modeled on their Contract with America, which was a soup-to-nuts compendium of what the tech community would most like Congress to do. Democrats also pandered by forming the pro-Internet New Democrat Network (founded by senators) and New Democrat Coalition (in the House). Both groups spent a lot of time meeting with and issuing press releases with prominent tech execs.

The love fest with e-business reached a crescendo during two weeks in June 1999 when nearly three dozen high-tech CEOs were featured guests at the White House and on Capitol Hill. Andy Grove of Intel and Lew Platt of Hewlett Packard lobbied White House chief of staff John Podesta for looser export controls on high-performance computers, while IBM's Louis Gerstner, Sun Microsystems's Scott McNealy, Novell's Eric Schmidt, and Bill Gates testified during a wide-ranging "high-tech summit" hosted by the Congressional Joint Economic Committee.

The CEOs got more than a handshake and a pat on the back. E-industries posted a string of legislative victories that was unmatched by any other group. In late 1998 and early 1999 alone, President Clinton signed bills that imposed a three-year moratorium on taxes on e-commerce, limited lawsuits against companies affected by Year 2000 computer glitches, increased the number of visas issued for highly skilled high-tech workers, and extended copyright protections to material published on the Internet. The president even signed into law restrictions on class-action shareholder lawsuits.

And the outlook was just as rosy. Washington decision makers were poised to ease export restrictions on encryption software, extend the tax credit for research and development, and loosen export controls on high-performance computers. That was a lot for one industry.

Some of the issues the industry managed to win were immense. Take the tax moratorium. In 1999, most e-commerce—about thirty-six billion dollars of it—was tax free. The nation's governors and mayors said they were losing billions of dollars in sales and use taxes and complained that government services were being starved as a result. But Congress sided with e-industry, which begged for time before any new taxes were imposed. It argued that the fledgling Internet couldn't possibly determine how to pay taxes to each of the country's six thousand jurisdictions and still flourish as robustly as it had. "Overregulating and overtaxing this new industry will stunt its potential growth," said Stephen Altobelli of the Direct Marketing Association. Congress bought that line and nixed any new taxes until at least October 2001.

With that receptive an audience, new tech trade groups seemed to crop up weekly. Internet-related companies in particular poured into the capital. Among the e-related companies that hired full-time federal lobbyists were 3Com, Yahoo!, Apple Computer, and Dell Computer. In addition, nine Internet companies formed the first lobbying group devoted exclusively to Internet issues, such as fighting e-commerce taxes and promoting privacy protection. Called NetCoalition.com, the organization's founding members included Yahoo!, Amazon.com, eBay, Excite@Home, America Online, Theglobe.com, Lycos, DoubleClick, and Inktomi.

Along with all this lobbying came torrents of campaign cash. The late Eben Tisdale, longtime lobbyist for Hewlett Packard, used to say the technology industry had "deep pockets and short arms." No longer. According to the Center for Responsive Politics, the high-tech industry's political donations reached nine million dollars in 1997 and 1998, more than double its federal contributions for the 1993–1994 election cycle. Technology's 1998 lobbying expenditures topped thirty-eight million dollars, making it more active in trying to influence Washington than any industry other than the highly regulated insurance and energy groups.

"In my opinion they've come a long way in just a couple short years," Senator Hatch said of tech companies in general. "They've become much more engaged in the policy process. They are constantly in my office."

Then again, high-tech's dominance in Washington also couldn't last. The only way the tech community could continue winning was to stay united, and that wasn't happening. Everyone knew that the Internet-browser issue had set Microsoft against a slew of its brethren, though that fight was confined safely to the courts and might well remain there.

High-tech's preeminence could also be threatened if lawmakers actually learned something about the industry. There was evidence that was happening. Senator Burns, for example, wasn't the rube he pretended to be. He even auctioned a pair of old spurs over the Internet, he said, and "got a wonderful price." The Senate in general was getting more sophisticated despite the fact that senators were still prohibited from bringing electronic devices, including computers, into the chamber. A few of the younger members have been known to sneak in small computers in the pockets of their suit coats.

But the biggest threat to high-tech's high success rate was its inevitable clash with other, more deeply entrenched, and Washington-wise interests. That described almost everybody. After all, the commercial Internet barely existed prior to 1994, and many industry leaders were still incredibly young. Ken Kay, chairman of Infotech Strategies, was among the first Washington lobbyists to meet Internet pioneer Marc Andreessen of Netscape in 1993—when Andreessen was still in college!

Still, America Online decided to take on one of the capital's most battle-scarred veterans, AT&T, over access to high-speed cable connections into people's homes. AT&T had an exclusive contract with Excite@Home, a company it partly owned, to provide Internet service over cable. America Online argued that the cable lines were so vital a service that they should be considered more like public rights of way even though they had been constructed with private money.

America Online has since changed its strategy. But the fight over the cost and ease of cable access was sure to be one of the bloodiest and most expensive lobbying conflicts ever. And it was not one that lawmakers would be able to duck. Nor would they want to. Controversy always brings campaign cash. "There is a growing number of people in the Senate who have been taking an interest; it's driven in large measure because of the expected donations from this very wealthy high-tech community," Senator Hatch said. "That's a matter of concern to me."

But it was a matter of pride to the high-tech community. More than two hundred federal lawmakers, including nearly every presidential hopeful, made the pilgrimage to Palo Alto's Tech Net. The reason: VIP tours of Silicon Valley and fund-raisers that produced roughly three million dollars in the 1997–1998 election cycle. In the 1999–2000 cycle, they'll produce much, much more.

As a result, Tech Net had more requests for visits from lawmakers than it could handle. "We're thrilled to have the requests," said Roberta Katz, the former general counsel of Netscape who was Tech Net's new CEO. "But we can only accommodate so many of these folks. We don't try to create a queue as it were. We just say, 'Call us at a later date.' "

Now there's a job that probably doesn't exist anywhere else: telling members of Congress no.

Then again, the high-tech community has learned that it can't afford to make a habit of saying no to federal lawmakers. In fact, it was doing everything in its power to say yes more often. Tech Net opened a Texas branch to tell (and sell) its story in the Austin high-tech corridor—and to Texas lawmakers. And just outside Washington, D.C., another group of tech execs, led by America Online, started a rival group called Cap Net. In 1999, it pooled funds from the growing number of technology firms in Washington and its Maryland and Virginia suburbs and began sponsoring visits by lawmakers.

This was a lot more convenient to congressmen. All they had to do was drive for a half hour to near Dulles Airport in order to get their cool tour and to pick up their campaign checks. "Everybody wants to be able to say they've been out to AOL; there is a celebrity status there," said Mark Bisnow, a former congressional aide who was chief of staff to a Virginia software firm called MicroStrategy. Bisnow himself shepherded several groups of top Democrats and Republicans to see the e-business CEOs that worked just outside the Beltway.

And how did the lawmakers react? According to Bisnow: "They were transfixed."

11

The Shakedown

Money men are involved in a serious business. Political candidates need campaign contributions, and the money men, for whatever reasons, are determined to help the candidates obtain them. As a result, there is no end to the innovations in techniques in political fund gathering. There also are almost no lengths to which the solicitors won't go to get some extra scratch. Old methods are pushed to the limit, and new devices are forever being found. No wonder the process appears to be totally out of control.

During the summer of 1999, the Republican National Committee began to worry that its own members of Congress might be lured astray by the siren song of campaign-finance reform. And *that* just wouldn't do. Debates once again were scheduled to take place in the fall on such popular but little-understood proposals as banning soft money. So party officials quietly began to hold a series of seminars for elected Republican officials to explain how indispensable soft-money donations were and how much of an advantage that kind of electoral giving was to the GOP.

A party official gave me a copy of the presentation that was made at each one of them. If anyone was under the illusion that soft money was called soft because it was squishy or amorphous or only vaguely tied to individual candidates, the GOP explanation dispelled that notion completely. In addition, if anyone believed that the excesses of political fund-raising could reach a ceiling beyond which no party would go, that, too, should be discarded. In the world of political fund-raising, there's no such thing as too much.

The first and most remarkable revelation in the GOP presentation was that it made clear how little elected officials knew about soft money. The title of the speech was " 'Soft' Dollars: What It Means for Our Party." And the opening remarks were rudimentary in the extreme: "Soft money is money raised and spent by political parties outside of federal election law contribution limits. This includes corporate, union and personal contributions."

Then the briefing detailed precisely what soft money was used for: issue-advocacy ads, the development of voter lists, voter-registration drives, direct-mail solicitations, phone banking, "RNC overhead," transfers to state parties, and "direct contributions to state and local candidates." In other words, if you thought soft money was indirect support only, think again.

For every one of these purposes, the presentation stressed, Republicans have much more money than Democrats. In fact, during the 1997–1998 cycle, the various arms of the Republican Party had $139.6 million versus the Democrats' $99.7 million. As a result, the Republicans transferred to state parties $8.4 million more than the Democrats did. The GOP's $20.7 million in transfers included $1.8 million that went directly to state and local candidates and $2.7 million that was used to develop and update voter lists or files.

The RNC clearly kept close track of where every penny had gone. During the 1998 election cycle, the presentation asserted, soft money helped to fund "over 32 million phone bank calls, over 27 million get-out-the-vote mail pieces, over 18 million absentee ballots [and] over 4.5 million issue and get-out-the-vote calls." That sounds pretty concrete for something called soft money, don't you think?

The RNC's soft-money transfers to state parties also freed up other state party funds that were used in direct support for federal candidates—things like mailings, yard signs, bumper stickers, and buttons. What would a campaign be without buttons?

And candidates for federal office were big beneficiaries. For example, the presentation said, the Ohio Republican Party "spent $300,000 in direct candidate support, $91,000 for [congressional candidate] Nancy Hollister [for] 300,000 mail pieces. [And] $25,000 for [Congressman] Steve Chabot [for] 100,000 mail pieces."

Soft money also allowed the party to spend more "hard" or direct dollars on virtually any federal candidate who had even a glimmer of a reelection fight on his or her hands. The presentation lists eighty GOP candidates for Congress who received as much as one hundred thousand dollars in a combination of direct contributions and RNC expenditures that were coordinated with the state parties.

Democrats know, of course, that they would be better off without soft money since Republicans raise so much more of it than they do. Democrats ranging from President Clinton to Senator Ted Kennedy and from Congressman Dick Gephardt to Congressman Patrick Kennedy want to eliminate soft money. Republicans, other than a handful of mavericks such as Senator John McCain and Congressman Chris Shays of Connecticut, are firmly committed to keeping soft money alive in some form.

The reason has little to do with principle and mostly to do with winning and losing. In particular, Republicans need soft money to counteract the tens of millions of dollars that organized labor spends each election cycle. In fact, what the Republicans really need, the presentation implored, was much *more* money. In so many words, the briefing asked: "How high is up?" The answer: the moon. "Rutgers University economics professor Leo Troy estimates the value of union activity during the 1996 presidential cycle as $300–$500 million."

In other words, the message was, Don't stop collecting money—ever.

Political fund-raising is spiraling upward, with no end in sight. Everywhere you turn in Washington and increasingly in the states, new, inventive ways are being devised and plumbed to channel more dollars to more and more politicians. And politicians are always finding new ways to shake the money tree. A classic though not well-known case was the House India Caucus.

Indian Americans tend to be highly educated and, therefore, rich compared to other ethnic groups, which makes lawmakers eager to mine their political gold. The easiest way for a lawmaker to show respect for the Indians' views was to join the India Caucus, which was just one of dozens of clusters of House members that advocated topics from alcohol fuels to the army. Many of these caucuses were completely sincere in their advocacy of these issues. And, in fairness, nobody could contend that the members of the India Caucus participated *only* for the campaign contributions. But the organization certainly turned out to be something of a cash cow.

What was the tip-off that money was the biggest draw for members of the India Caucus? Indian Americans account for about 0.5 percent of the U.S. population. In 1999, the India Caucus had 111 members, or more than 25 percent of the House.

What's more, the handful of lawmakers who were most active in the caucus did especially well in the campaign-cash department. And there was one lawmaker in particular who was without peer. Congress's "Mr. India" was Democrat Frank Pallone of New Jersey, one of the founders of the caucus in 1993, who chaired it for nearly six years. He was also considered one of Congress's most reliable supporters of India's point of view.

In 1999, he said publicly that he would back Indian incursion into Pakistani-controlled territory—something that few U.S. lawmakers would be willing to even consider. He authored legislation that would have suspended the sanctions the United States imposed on India after it tested nuclear devices. Another bill of his would have allowed India to establish a memorial to Mahatma Gandhi in D.C., a favor long sought by the Indian embassy there. Pallone even urged that India become a permanent member of the UN Security Council—something that was never going to happen.

In return for these views, he was a favorite among Indian-American political donors. According to a *Fortune* analysis of Pallone's 1997–1998 contributions, 20 percent of his individual donors had apparently Indian surnames. What's more, 68 percent of those individuals lived outside of New Jersey and thus weren't giving in appreciation of his service to the state. Pallone was so popular with Indian Americans that he was put in charge of raising political cash from that community for all House Democrats through the Democratic Congressional Campaign Committee.

Put bluntly, Pallone had figured out how to get Indians to give. "We do a lot of press with Indian-American newspapers," he explained. Indeed, there was hardly an issue that affected India and the United States that his office didn't contact the influential Indian-American press about. And the tactic worked. Although Pallone didn't sit on congressional committees that dealt directly with foreign aid or even foreign issues, no other congressional lawmaker had a higher profile in the Indian community than he.

Sudhir Parikh, a prominent Indian-American physician from New Jersey, said that for years "the Indian community knew him more than anyone else [in Congress]." And that visibility helped Pallone raise money. Was his contrived celebrity little more than a venal and brazen shakedown? Pallone denied that it was. He had a large Indian community in his district, and he professed that he sincerely believed that improving relations with the world's largest democracy was good policy in general and for the U.S. business community in particular. Besides, he said, "It's only natural that people from the Indian-American community would contribute to me. I believe in what they do."

At the same time, the appearance was unsavory—and familiar. Although none would say so publicly, other senior members of the India Caucus whispered to me that Pallone was replaced as caucus cochairman because he had gotten too close to India and was raising too much Indian-American money.

The notion of too much is a relative term when it comes to election lucre. Earlier, I mentioned leadership PACs, which lawmakers use to collect twice from the usual suspects: once to fund their own reelection campaigns and a second time to advance their own ambitions as party leaders by contributing to their colleagues' campaigns as well.

On its face that's not the worst abuse along the banks of the Potomac. After all, what's a Speaker of the House or a majority leader good for unless he can raise a few extra bucks for the rank and file? But the extra outrage in leadership PACs was that a lot of folks besides leaders—or even "leaders in training"—had them, including freshmen! One freshman lawmaker, Republican Doug Ose of California, set up his leadership PAC even before he officially started his first term in 1999.

A spokesman for Ose, Peter DeMarco, was very high-minded in his explanation: "The congressman established the PAC to help Republican candidates with a strong probusiness agenda." Ose was himself a former real-estate executive who had never held elective office before and benefited from leadership PAC contributions. Only in his case, the money came from actual leaders.

It gets worse. Congressman Ose didn't need to raise much money. According to DeMarco, Ose largely financed his own campaign in 1998, spending about $1.3 million of his own money and using only about $500,000 in contributions from others. Imagine being dunned twice by a no-name congressman who doesn't have to raise any money at all!

But Ose wasn't alone among freshmen fishing around for an extra handout. Another was Republican senator Rick Santorum of Pennsylvania. Santorum set up his leadership PAC, Fight PAC, because both of his initial contests for the House (in 1990) and then the Senate (in 1994) were uphill fights. He had been an underdog, and he was determined to raise some money to assist other underdogs.

The only problem: He was still an underdog. His reelection prospects were so precarious that political professionals doubted that it made any sense for the lightly regarded lawmaker to divide his attention with a leadership PAC. Santorum needed all the money he could gather to get himself reelected.

Santorum didn't see it that way. And why should he? He was always able to raise money for Fight PAC because he made the solicitation calls himself. As you might expect, this method almost always worked. People with an interest in legislation would pay plenty to have the chance to bend a senator's ear. According to Santorum's press secretary, Robert Traynham, the senator took a lot of pride in making those calls. And in return, he received thank-you notes from givers for taking the time. But I don't think his constituents should be so grateful. Do you?

There's even less to be grateful about when you look more closely at where the leadership-PAC money actually came from.

Susan Glasser of *The Washington Post* disclosed that at least twenty senior members of Congress not only collected small-dollar contributions for their leadership bank accounts but also gathered sizable and largely undisclosed soft-money contributions for those same PACs.

In a troublingly common twist, congresspeople of both parties were legally able to collect these unlimited corporate and individual contributions by saying that the funds weren't spent directly on congressional or presidential campaigns: They said in other words that they could raise soft, not just hard, money. At the same time, the money *was* used for a variety of political purposes, including donations to state and local candidates, reimbursement for political travel, and funding for political consultants and polling.

The collectors of soft money in leadership PACs ranged from Trent Lott to Thomas Daschle (who, ironically, was a long-time critic of soft money). And some of the donations were huge. In perhaps the largest such contribution, John Ashcroft accepted a four-hundred-thousand-dollar check for his leadership PAC from the House of Lloyd, a Missouri direct-sales marketing firm.

A lot of this type of money was hidden from view because the PACs were registered in states such as Virginia that had lax disclosure requirements and few if any limits on the amount that could be contributed. What this meant, according to Fred Wertheimer, the longtime campaign-finance reformer, was that if lawmakers who have leadership PACs retire, they might be able to take that big money with them and convert it to personal use. Am I wrong to guess that soft-money fund-raising for leadership PACs might soon become a trend?

One of the worst abuses of campaign giving was the unintended consequence of a truly good idea: the crackdown on gift giving to lawmakers. For many years, lawmakers and their staffs could be wined and dined by lobbyists, corporations, and labor unions without limit—and, seemingly, without regard to ethics or propriety. That ended a few years ago with the enactment of an antilobbying law that severely restricted what lawmakers and their staffs could accept as gifts, including meals.

I thought at the time that the reform was petty and probably not wise because members of Congress had enough trouble finding out what was going on in the world without handicapping them even more by restricting who they could have lunch with. Besides, given all the much larger opportunities that existed for corruption, I doubted that lawmakers could be irreparably tainted for the cost of a good dinner.

As it turned out, I was right but for the wrong reason. One of the few times that lobbyists could still play host to lawmakers and not run afoul of the gift limits was on the occasion of a fund-raising event. In other words, a congressman could not allow his lunch to be paid for (above a modest and cumulative limit) if the host simply wanted to chat. But if the host wanted to bring a check and invite other people with checks—all made out to the congressman's reelection committee—*that* was perfectly fine.

The perverse result was that a law that was designed to insulate lawmakers from the influence of money became an incentive for congresspeople to submerge themselves even more deeply in the morass. Jim O'Connor of America's Community Bankers made a name for himself by hosting small breakfasts for members of Congress. He and his association could pay for the meals as long as the other attendees brought (or promised to send) checks for the guests' reelection committee.

But it gets worse here, too. My lobbyist friends tell me that fund-raising events were getting smaller and smaller all the time. Some were merely excuses for taking their favorite congresspeople out for a meal and a drink. More than one lawmaker, they told me, was willing to declare almost any lobbyist-paid meal a fund-raiser as long as the host of the dinner didn't just pick up the check but also provided one as well—eventually.

Lawmakers' power can be wielded subtly or with a sledge-hammer. The Republicans in charge of the House chose the heavier method and occasionally got caught at it. Some of the starkest examples of a shakedown were provided by the law-maker nicknamed "The Hammer," Tom DeLay. Several of his escapades were originally revealed in *Roll Call*.

When the Republicans took control of the House after forty years in the minority, they decided to seek revenge on the Democrats, and not just other members of Congress. The Republicans weren't satisfied with winning a numerical advan-tage in both the House and the Senate: They wanted to take over "downtown" Washington as well. If they were able to place their own people in charge of the major lobbying organizations on K Street, they could gradually bend public policy in their direc-tion *and* divert a great deal more political money into their cof-fers. Democratic sympathizers would no longer be welcome as leaders of interest groups, especially business groups, which the GOP elite believed should rightly be Republican leaning.

This was not a traditional way of operating. It was, in fact, quite harsh and, as it turned out, counterproductive. When they had been in charge in Congress, Democrats had their own favorites among the lobbyists and lobby groups. But the Democratic takeover of downtown had never been forced or con-trived. It was more of an evolution that flowed naturally from the fact that all the chairmen of the committees were Democrats for a very long time. What's more, if an interest group wanted to hire a former staffer or former member of Congress as a lobbyist, there were a lot more Democrats to choose from.

Furthermore, the rhythm of the capital is slow. Very slow. Consensus and change happen glacially. A democracy, especially one with checks and balances, will almost always frustrate reformers who want to do anything quickly. That's why the Gingrich "revolution" was misnamed. Washington is *not* a place for revolution—that's way too fast. Still, newcomers to power always believe that they can do things differently and all at once.

The GOP leaders started their downtown plan with the Business Roundtable, a big-business bastion. The chief executives of roughly two hundred of the largest publicly traded companies in the country belonged to this old-time lobby, and the newly empowered Republicans believed that all of them should have been much more generous to the GOP in their political giving than they had been. In 1996, when a handful of CEOs met with a handful of the new Republican leaders, the Republicans are said to have told the business executives to fork over more. The business executives said they wouldn't and couldn't because the Business Roundtable doesn't donate money on its own.

Later, quietly, a few of the member companies began to tilt their giving more to the GOP. But it was never enough to satisfy the new leadership, who never hid their contempt for the Roundtable's evenhandedness. Said Ed Gillespie, a former top GOP aide, "They're a wasted resource and just plain irrelevant."

The strong-arm tactics did not stop there. Lists were compiled by DeLay's allies that detailed which companies and interest groups were loyal Republican contributors and which were not. Lobbyists reported that they had been warned not so subtly by GOP henchmen that they would be wise to donate more to GOP causes and had better hire additional former GOP staffers in their lobbying firms if they wanted to have access to congressional leaders.

The most outrageous of these shakedowns involved the Electronic Industries Alliance (EIA). According to Jim Vande-Hei and John Bresnahan of *Roll Call,* top GOP House leaders admitted in 1998 that they had held up legislation supported by many of the EIA's largest member companies in order to pressure the alliance to oust its prospective Democratic president, ex-congressman Dave McCurdy of Oklahoma.

Gingrich, DeLay, and other GOP leaders demanded that McCurdy not be hired and that a Republican replace him—preferably Congressman Bill Paxon of New York, who had just retired from Congress and was looking for work on K Street. According to *Roll Call,* Gingrich spread the word that McCurdy wouldn't be welcome in the offices of Republican leaders. DeLay even contracted outgoing EIA president Peter McCloskey to lobby against McCurdy, and aides to Senator Santorum reached members of the EIA board from Pennsylvania-based companies to urge them to reject the Oklahoman.

That wasn't all. To prove that their threat wasn't idle, the GOPers also took another remarkable and abominable step. They bottled up legislation dealing with intellectual-property rights that EIA members were advocating strongly.

In the end, the Hammer didn't get his way. McCurdy was a moderate Democrat with many friends in the Republican Party. They vouched for him, and the EIA board retained McCurdy despite the pressure. Democrats now had an issue, and they hyped it to the hills. "I think there is a serious crime that should be investigated," said Jerry Nadler, a Democratic member of the House Judiciary Committee. "This is far more serious, as far as I am concerned, than lying about sex with an intern."

At the same time, it wasn't long before the EIA also named Republicans to other prominent posts. And nothing changed about the GOP tactics. Republicans continued to circulate a list that outlined the political donations made by employees of Washington's biggest lobbying firms. Compiled by Grover Norquist, head of the heavily Republican Americans for Tax Reform, the 1999 version of the list even made its way into print in *The Washington Post*—just in case anyone thought the Republicans had stopped keeping track.

Still, lobbying groups continued to hire Democrats. And the Republicans didn't always win in Congress. On the contrary, they began to lose frequently. In anticipation of a possible return to Democratic control in the House in 2000, the Democratic Party committees were raising money at record levels—often from lobbyists hedging their bets and secretly yearning for the GOP to get its comeuppance.

For a while, at least, it looked like the system of campaign financing had become so overloaded with money that some of the biggest participants would begin to opt out. Oddly enough, in fact, some major corporations never opted in.

Nearly a quarter of the Fortune 500 firms contributed nothing to either congressional candidates or the parties. During the 1997–1998 election cycle, 138 companies in the Fortune 500 didn't have a PAC. And 191 companies didn't make soft-money contributions to the political parties. Fully 117 companies did neither.

How could this be? Wouldn't it be suicide for a company not to participate at all? Not necessarily. First of all, not all companies have a lot at stake in Washington. Take Gillette. Its consumer-goods business isn't highly regulated like a utility or a railroad is, and therefore it never saw a need to make large donations. All it really needed was to join "appropriate trade associations," a spokesman said, "to the extent we needed information."

But other large firms refused to participate out of principle. They were as disgusted with the way Washington worked as anyone. Alcoa's chief executive, Paul O'Neill, joined with several other CEOs who dropped out of the Business Roundtable after it tripled its dues a few years ago in order to buy more issue-advocacy advertising. O'Neill also eliminated his company's PAC and wouldn't even consider giving corporate cash. "What's going on with campaign financing has reached well beyond a reasonable limit," he said angrily.

O'Neill wasn't alone. As mentioned earlier, a growing number of companies were simply refusing to immerse themselves in the muck of soft money in particular. A group of one hundred corporate and academic leaders who belonged to the business-backed Committee for Economic Development (CED) signed onto a plan that called for the end of soft money.

These leaders included top executives from Mobil, Honeywell, and Sara Lee. Of soft-money givers, the CED wrote: "The public cannot help but believe that these donors enjoy special influence and receive special favors. The suspicion of corruption deepens public cynicism and diminishes public confidence in government. More important, these activities raise the likelihood of actual corruption."

Common Cause could not have written those sentences any better.

In addition, several companies announced in 1997 that they weren't going to give soft money anymore—even after years of giving—so irate were they at the appearance of corruption that such large donations presented. The companies included General Motors, Monsanto, Ameritech, and AlliedSignal.

But not all of the newly pure-at-heart companies were able to kick the soft-money habit completely. According to *The New York Times,* GM's PAC donated forty thousand dollars to the Republican National Committee after the announcement. At least some of that had to be soft since the hard-money limit to parties from PACs is twenty-five thousand dollars. Ameritech, the Midwest telephone company, gave sixty thousand dollars during the 1998 cycle, most of which the company claimed was contributed in error. And AlliedSignal gave fifteen thousand dollars a year to the Republican Party in 1997 and 1998.

Oops.

When it comes to companies that need to do business in Washington, it's much easier to sound altruistic than to actually *be* altruistic. Paul Taylor, executive director of the Alliance for Better Campaigns, a Pew Charitable Trusts–sponsored group, put the issue most clearly into focus: "Soft money is not a loophole," he said. "It's the system now." And who can live outside the system?

Brian Baird is one person who wishes that he could have. The freshman Democrat from Washington State won one of the most hotly contested House races in 1998. The former psychology professor had narrowly lost to the incumbent, Linda Smith, two years earlier but had stepped up again when Smith left the House to run for the Senate. He won in 1998 with 55 percent of the vote, but it was hard fought all the way.

And it wasn't just his opponent that he was fighting. In fact, Baird's biggest rival was a deluge of advertising paid for by interests outside of his sprawling southwest Washington district. According to a study conducted by American University and financed by the Pew Charitable Trusts, Baird spent one third of his time from January 1998 until Election Day making calls for campaign contributions. He raised and spent an awful lot: $1.6 million. And this is what he said it was like gathering that much: "Day after day after day, six to nine hours a day on the telephone asking people who in most cases I had never met before for money, as much as they can possibly afford to contribute. I was locked away in a tiny room with a headset on. The toll was tremendous. If I went to see a movie, that was three hours I didn't stay on the phone raising money. That was a couple thousand dollars."

In the end, Baird was glad he mostly avoided the cinema. His opponent, State Senator Don Benton, spent $755,000, but that was small compared to the more than a million dollars that was spent by outsiders, especially the Republican Party. At the end of the 1998 election, the RNC started Operation Breakout, which targeted close races across the country and poured money into them, mostly for television ads. Baird's was one of the program's top targets. And these were negative ads, also known as attack ads, which branded the Democrat as weak on crime.

"Every week an average of eighty to one hundred thousand dollars of attack ads were mounted against us," Baird recalled. "The night before the primary, [the RNC] bought a thirty-second ad on *Monday Night Football:* twelve thousand dollars! Luckily, it was a rotten game."

In a six-week span, Baird contended, the RNC pumped in more so-called independent-expenditure money—between $1.2 million and $1.5 million—than Baird had raised in nearly a year and a half. And that was hardly the end of the story. Other interest groups also targeted the Baird race because it was one of the very few that was sincerely up for grabs that year. Americans for Limited Terms ran commercials against Baird; the Sierra Club bought ads that attacked his opponent. Voters could not be faulted for wondering who was saying what about whom, since only about half of the money spent in the contest was actually controlled by the candidates themselves.

"If we're not careful, we'll turn our democracy into a cashocracy," Baird said, which would be characterized by "money rule."

We're pretty close to that now.

According to Sheila Krumholz of the Center for Responsive Politics, the 1998 congressional race cost $1.4 billion; it was the first billion-dollar election. In the House, 95 percent of the winners were also the top spenders. In the Senate, 94 percent of the winners spent the most in their own contests. The most expensive race was the D'Amato-Schumer shoot-out in New York, which cost a total of thirty-six million dollars. The top House contest was waged in suburban Atlanta by Speaker Gingrich, with a total cost of $6.5 million.

In almost two thirds of House races, incumbents held a financial advantage of ten to one—or more—over their opponents, and quite often they had no opponent at all. In addition, the soft money raised by the parties was off the charts. Democrats raised 84 percent more soft money than in the previous midterm election, and Republicans collected 144 percent more. That kind of growth continued through 1999 and into 2000.

The most generous givers could be found in the most regulated—and highly compensated—financial-services sector. In 1997 and 1998, financial interests contributed ninety-eight million dollars to federal candidates. And these savvy investors gave mostly to incumbents. In fact, PACs in every sector donated overwhelmingly to incumbents, up from 65 percent in the 1996 election cycle to nearly 80 percent in the 1998 cycle. Ever-wary business PACs gave incumbents 88 percent of their money. And the heart of narrow-interest giving, Washington, D.C., was the richest source of campaign cash: $104 million to federal candidates, more than double the amount that came from all of New York State.

To be more explicit about the source of these funds, lawyers and lobbyists, at forty million dollars, were the most generous vocational category of campaign givers. No surprise there. Most of that money went to the people who already were in office. And much of those funds were contributed very early in the contests, when they would do the most good.

Early is important. The more a candidate has in the bank, the less likely that he or she will have any sort of serious opposition on Election Day. No sane person would run against an incumbent who has a few hundred thousand dollars to spend right from the start.

"Early money makes a huge difference," according to a memo written in 1999 to the National Republican Congressional Committee. And, at least according to the statistics in the memo, the early money was valuable for more than its deterrence.

The memo, written by Gary Andres, a former White House aide, looked at the total receipts and the cash on hand for all five of the Republican incumbents who lost their reelection contests for the House in 1998. He also looked at the same categories for five randomly selected incumbents who were targeted for defeat by the Democrats but who had won in the end.

Andres tracked these categories over time starting in June 1997, which is considered early in the two-year election cycle. The five losers and the five winners all managed to collect roughly the same amount of money by the end of their campaigns, but the winners were consistently ahead of the losers in receipts and cash on hand from June of the first year of the election cycle through June of the second year. In other words, Andres concluded, raising and hoarding campaign cash should be a priority almost from the moment the results of the last election are recorded.

And that's exactly what most lawmakers do—with the complicity of the nation's PACs. As a result, in 1998, 98.4 percent of the incumbents in the House who sought reelection won. That outpaced the House's average incumbent-reelection rate of 94 percent from 1978 to 1998. The Senate's incumbents also did extremely well. The Senate incumbent-reelection rate was 89 percent in 1998, which was about average over the previous decade. But compared to the 75 percent rate from 1978 to 1986, incumbents were finding it much easier to hold their seats in the Senate.

Money had a lot to do with that. As always.

Campaign cash washed in from everywhere, and some of it was suspicious. The Clinton reelection campaign in 1996 featured some of the most spectacular and outrageous examples of improper contributions of all time, and millions of dollars had to be returned. These were mostly donations from Asian and, probably, foreign sources that were filtered through the now infamous Charlie Trie, the DNC's John Huang, and Johnny Chung.

It was Chung who uttered one of the most memorable similes in the annals of campaign fund-raising: "The White House is like a subway. You have to put in coins to open the gates."

It certainly worked for Chung, a steady and reliable giver of campaign cash to the Democrats and, as a result, something of a White House fixture in the latter days of the first Clinton term. He visited the White House forty-nine times in 1994 and 1995, which is more often than some cabinet secretaries. Two days after he handed Margaret Williams, a top White House staffer, a fifty-thousand-dollar check for the DNC, Chung was invited to sit in on one of the president's regular Saturday radio addresses.

Veteran fund-raisers of both parties knew that they always had to be wary of Asian money. It was merely fact that, first, it was illegal for U.S. politicians to accept donations from foreign nationals, and, second, Asians were known to have tried in the past to skirt that law. Why? Because in several cultures on that continent, giving money to politicians in return for favors was an accepted practice. In addition, a much-treasured trophy from such a transaction was a photo of the donor shaking hands with the politician who had accepted his donation. Photos, not favors, were readily available in this country, but Asians proved willing to pay nonetheless.

They had an eager taker in the Democratic Party. In 1995 and 1996, almost any sense of restraint was tossed out the window by the absolutely insatiable Clinton money operation. Behind in the polls due to the disastrous fight over the health-care overhaul,

Clinton and his people were frantic to buy as much popularity through TV advertising as they possibly could. And that meant they needed to raise money in ways that had once been considered off-limits.

Not so long before then, reputable fund-raisers were leery of and on the outlook for foreign and especially Asian contributions. Accepting these was seen, correctly, as a potentially quick way to jail. But the Clinton camp was desperate for cash. So the usually careful program of screening donations was discarded at the DNC in the tacit interest of collecting more.

Specifically, the president wanted in 1995 to launch a forty-four-million-dollar advertising spree, underwritten by the DNC, of "issue ads" that were effectively Vote for Clinton commercials. The president himself helped write those ads, which made their legality dubious at best. But then again, there wasn't much left of federal-election law other than the loopholes. And although the effectiveness of the DNC-ad blitz has since been questioned, it is undeniable that it changed the way that politicians viewed campaign funding.

The thinking went this way: Clinton won that race handily. He beat Bob Dole who, unlike Clinton, didn't have the money (or the chutzpah) to run ads, paid for by his party, nearly a full year before the November election. As a result, no presidential candidate will be left without all the funds he can get in any future election.

That's why George W. Bush collected record amounts of thousand-dollar checks for his nomination battle. It's also why both he and Al Gore, in effect, infiltrated their own parties' national offices and began to raise gigantic sums of soft money early in 1999.

But let's stop a moment and call this what it is: gluttony.

Remember: The presidential election is supposed to be the one pristine contest on the national scene. It's supposed to be completely funded by the federal government after the primaries. And even the primaries are supposed to be constrained by dint of matching funds: Candidates' coffers are supplemented with taxpayer money in exchange for their restraint in spending during the primaries.

Well, like everything else in the realm of campaign finance, the First Amendment to the Constitution and some way-too-clever lawyers conspired to remove any sense of discipline or propriety. Surely that's what Clinton took violent advantage of in 1996.

Now, I don't believe that he or any of his people accepted money that they knew was illegal. They certainly never thought that they were exchanging cash for substantive favors. It wasn't policy that they put up for sale. But what they did was offer access to the office of the president—and to the president himself—in a way that demeaned it and raised all manner of perception problems, all for the sake of reelection.

Don't you think the president should have better things to do than suck up to a bunch of rich guys?

Well, apparently not this president. In the most shameless and famous bit of pandering for bucks (at least of recent vintage), Clinton hosted in the White House 103 coffees in 1995 and 1996 for fifteen hundred people, most of whom either were major Democratic contributors or were about to become such. The going rate, my lobbyist friends tell me, was fifty thousand dollars per—either raised or contributed personally.

The cost of entry was much higher, of course, for the dozens and dozens of overnight stays in the Lincoln Bedroom that also were auctioned away. What does this say about President Clinton? Or, for that matter, what does it say about the people who would clamor to give enough money to attend one of these events?

Terrible things, that's what it says. Of the president, it says he was without scruples. Of the donors, it says they were without sense. They probably got nothing for their money except an hour of reflected glory. You would think smart people would have better things to do with their time and their money.

But apparently they don't.

That's why we have a runaway system. Neither the politicians nor the money men have any sense of proportion. And sometimes it gets downright wild.

One of the wildest spectacles is kiddie politics. The push for cash is so strong that people with a desire to give often evade the thousand-dollar-per-election limit by allowing other members of their family to donate—including the kids.

The *Los Angeles Times* and the Campaign Study Group published data that showed that young contributors—far too young to have the funds to actually donate on their own—were contributing obscene amounts to federal candidates. Between 1991 and 1998, donors who identified themselves as students made 8,876 contributions of two hundred dollars or more to federal candidates. In 163 instances they gave five thousand or more. During the 1996 presidential race, student donors sent in nearly $2.6 million, a 45 percent increase over 1992.

Official disclosures show that children and high-school and college students gave $7.5 million in political donations from 1991 through 1998. The chance that these contributions were anything other than a dodge and a scam is approaching zero. Indeed, many of these generous donors were too young to drive, let alone vote.

According to the *Times*, "student" giving was just one of the growing number of ways that affluent donors circumvented federal-election limits. The *Times* unearthed at least four donors who were ten or younger who gave one thousand dollars or more. In two other cases, the donors were still in diapers. Campaign aides were reported to have told potential big donors that other members of their families could contribute as well.

The families always deny trying to evade the law. Asher Simon, for instance, was a nine-year-old, thousand-dollar contributor to the campaign of Democratic senator Dianne Feinstein of California. Asher's mom told the *Times* that the lad "supports candidates he agrees with." Good for him.

Then again, no one ever bothers to look too closely into this tactic. The Federal Election Commission rarely investigated election-law infractions by minors. Since 1975, it has levied only one fine—for four thousand dollars—against a parent for contributing money through a child.

Sometimes the politicians are the ones who act like children.

Take Operation Breakout during the 1998 election. The Republican National Committee provided the first five million dollars, and another thirty-plus million was supposed to come from loyal Republican lobbyists and GOP lawmakers. Chairmen of House committees were expected to hand over one hundred thousand dollars each; lesser lawmakers were dunned for half that amount.

According to *Roll Call,* Speaker Gingrich and other GOP leaders pressured their colleagues to meet their quotas. And at least one lawmaker chafed at their insistence. Congressman Phil Crane of Illinois, a senior Republican on the Ways and Means Committee, sent a letter to the leaders, complaining about their heavy-handed tactics. Then again, the letter accompanied his twenty-five-thousand-dollar check.

For donors who aren't sure how to get around campaign-finance laws, there are services out there that critics say provide the know-how. Triad Management Services in years past has served, in effect, as a dating service, putting together conservative donors with conservative candidates, both interested in making a mockery of electoral limits.

While not as high profile as Vice President Gore's visit to a Buddhist temple in California, Triad did get some attention during congressional hearings a few years ago. Headed by Oliver North's former campaign fund-raiser and backed by mostly anonymous donors, Triad helped conservative donors to give to like-minded candidates in every way possible: directly to the candidates, through specially created PACs, and by way of "independent" advertising campaigns. The whole enterprise looked a lot like a money-laundering scheme designed to allow a few rich folks to exceed contribution ceilings—something Triad denied.

The Wall Street Journal gave the following example of how it worked: Robert Riley, Jr., contributed five thousand dollars through five different PACs to his father, Robert Riley, Sr., who was elected to Congress in 1996 from Alabama's third congressional district. In each case, the PACs contributed to Riley, Sr., within weeks of receiving money from Riley, Jr. In its defense, Triad said the practice didn't amount to laundering because the PAC didn't guarantee that money from donors would be used to support specific candidates. Still, the connection was pretty clear.

Triad also used two nonprofit groups—Citizens for Reform and Citizens for the Republic Education Fund—to fund multimillion-dollar "issue" campaigns in Kansas, Alabama, Montana, South Dakota, and Pennsylvania. The campaigns, which were obviously tilted to benefit the conservative candidate in each race, were backed by a short list of largely anonymous donors. However, among the reported supporters were Robert Cone, the former head of GRACO Children's Products, and a foundation connected to the ultraconservative family that controls Koch Industries, a private oil-and-gas and book-wholesaling company.

"Donors who want to spend millions of dollars spend a lot of time trying to figure out what's legal and what's not legal," GOP political consultant Dick Dresner told *Roll Call.* "They use three, four, five, or six different ways so they aren't discovered. Even if their names came up once or twice, the extent of their activities . . . is underestimated."

The Center for Responsive Politics found additional examples of party bigwigs steering contributors to organizations sympathetic—but not directly connected—to their candidates. At the suggestion of the RNC, for instance, cigarette maker Philip Morris reportedly gave five hundred thousand dollars to the American Defense Institute, a group promoting voter turnout among military employees. The Democrats did similar things. At a Florida fund-raising dinner two weeks before Election Day 1996, businessman R. Warren Meddoff handed President Clinton a business card with a handwritten note: "My associate has $5 million that he is prepared to donate to the DNC."

Several days later, White House deputy chief of staff Harold Ickes called Meddoff and then faxed, from Air Force One, a memo to him suggesting that money could go to tax-exempt groups whose activities would benefit Democrats. Among the organizations Ickes recommended was Vote Now '96, a Florida-based group that promoted voter turnout in ethnic-minority neighborhoods that tended to vote heavily Democratic.

The Meddoff money didn't materialize, but *The New York Times* reported that the DNC did direct $450,000 from international businessman Gilbert Chagoury to Vote Now '96, as well as $50,000 from Detroit businessman Samir Danou to the National Coalition on Black Voter Participation, a group that helped increase African-American voter registration and turnout.

So many places for money and only so many people to contribute it. Professional lobbyists in particular feel hard-pressed for campaign cash. Every time they turn around, another member of Congress is trying to shake them down for yet another contribution. Nick Calio, a Republican lobbyist, said, "The requests for help pile up, each one begetting another. If you work at it and are successful, you become part of a talent pool from which an ever-expanding group comes to drink. Moreover, if you demonstrate the ability to raise soft money, they come right back during every difficult period because you've shown you can do it."

The shakedown has gotten so bad that, sometimes, lawmakers have their spouses make the solicitation calls. How can a lobbyist insult the wife of a prominent member of Congress? He can't. He also can't stop lawmakers from coming after him every chance they get for more money. For a lobbyist, that's an occupational hazard.

In a 1998 newsletter put out by the National Republican Congressional Committee, David Rehr, the top lobbyist of the National Beer Wholesalers Association, actually gave advice to lawmakers about how to tighten their grips. "At the NBWA, we generally receive ten to thirty invitations for events per week, dozens of telephone calls from professional PAC fund-raisers . . . and requests from other corporate and business association representatives serving on incumbents' PAC steering committee[s]. . . . You need to elevate yourself above your peers to maximize your PAC support. . . . As an incumbent you have tremendous resources to maximize your PAC support from the business community."

Rehr went on to offer "Six Steps to Maximize PAC Receipts." They included: "Make personal contact"; "Develop a cadre of five-to-ten dedicated Washington, D.C.–based supporters who will tout your record and successes"; "Use previous PAC supporters . . . and likely PAC prospects to form the nucleus of your contact list" and then "Work the list."

Several lobbyists in town had the same sarcastic reaction: Thanks a bunch, Dave. They didn't think members of Congress needed more advice on how to shake them down.

12

No-frills Reform

W hen it comes to campaign finance, where you stand
depends on where you sit. Everyone advocates some-
+thing they call "campaign-finance reform." But
the kind of reform they support is determined largely by which
political party they belong to. With rare exceptions, when lawmakers say they favor campaign-finance reform, they usually in-
tend just tinkering with laws and regulations in ways that would
benefit them and hurt their enemies.

Basically, Republicans don't want to alter the current system,
at least not much. They're so much better at raising money than
are the Democrats under the present regime that almost any
change in the way things now work would harm their chances
of reelection. And why do that? In the 1997–1998 election cycle,
the Republican Party raised $405 million, compared to the
Democratic Party's $245 million. Need I say more?

In general, campaign-finance reformers tend to be Democrats—
at least in the traditional way we think about the subject. Yes, I
know, some of the most famous reform proposals have been

authored jointly by Democrats *and* Republicans, like the plan pushed by senators John McCain, the Arizona Republican, and Russ Feingold, Democrat of Wisconsin. McCain went so far as to hook his hopes of winning the GOP nomination for president in 2000 on campaign-finance reform, and he struck a major chord. McCain, however, was a maverick in his own party on this subject. Few Republicans agreed with his prescriptions.

The conventional notion of reform is to try to leach out of the process as much private money as possible. The first target in almost any reform is to eliminate soft money. The second goal often is to substitute as much taxpayer money as possible for privately raised funds. The more the government bankrolls in political campaigns, the less the candidates will need to rely on "special interests." In addition, as a trade-off for the taxpayer subsidy, the government can impose spending limits on candidates. That would keep out of the system even more well-heeled factions and in that way open the field to more challengers to the incumbent class.

In their hearts, then, reformers dream of isolating elections and candidates from the intrusions of outside interests. In their ideal world, having money wouldn't matter. People would be elected based on their ideas and the extent to which they serve, or endeavor to serve, the greatest mass of voters in their own districts. Period.

Unfortunately, laudable as these objectives may be, they aren't workable for two main reasons that go well beyond the narrow, self-interested druthers of the national parties. First, limits on either raising or spending political money, beyond small interventions by the government, run afoul of the First Amendment. Second, inequities in the campaign-finance system reflect the far larger and far more intractable inequities in society as a whole and can't be legislated away.

So let's say it straight: The goal of making everyone equal in the legislative process through campaign-finance reform is admirable but impractical. Certain individuals and interest groups will always have more money—and thus more advantages— than others. Even some of the country's leading campaign-finance crusaders say so. "The inequalities of the system aren't going to be changed by legislation," concedes Kent Cooper, who heads Public Disclosure (now FECInfo) and is one of the most respected and nonpartisan campaign-finance analysts in the country. Adds Charles Lewis, executive director of the Center for Public Integrity: "You'll never eliminate the inordinate importance and presence of wealth in the political system."

There's just too much at stake for moneyed interests not to work their ways, or at least to spend as much as they can to try to get what they want in Washington. On this matter, history keeps repeating itself. Direct corporate contributions were banned in 1907, and direct donations from labor unions were prohibited in 1947. Yet thanks to a long list of legal fictions (enumerated in chapter 2), both groups manage to funnel millions of dollars into the coffers of candidates all the time. Loopholes have become the law.

In short, says American University's James Thurber, "as long as we allow money to be an expression of First Amendment rights, those who have money will have more influence than those who do not." Sad but true.

At the same time, the Supreme Court recently gave hope to campaign reformers that it might be willing to accept new limits on soft money. In *Nixon v. Shrink Missouri Government PAC,* the high court reversed the Eighth Circuit Court of Appeals and upheld a Missouri law that limits campaign contributions to amounts ranging from $275 to $1,075. In an opinion reminiscent of the *Buckley* case twenty-five years earlier, Justice David Souter, writing for the court's 6–3 majority, said that to "leave the perception of impropriety unanswered, and the cynical assumption that large donors call the tune, could jeopardize the willingness of voters to take part in democratic governance." Democracy works, he said, "only if the government has faith in those who govern, and that faith is bound to be shattered when high officials and their appointees engage in activities which arouse suspicion of malfeasance and corruption." To keep that faith, the court decided, reasonable limits on campaign giving were appropriate.

Had the court ruled the other way, "the entire edifice of campaign finance regulation would have collapsed," said Thomas Mann, a leading scholar on the subject at the Brookings Institution. What's more, Mann added, "The current court still believes that the appearance of corruption is enough to justify restricting campaign contributions." The implicit message, reformers say, is that if Congress was to ban or severely limit soft-money giving to the parties, the current Supreme Court could well acquiesce.

And what about publicly funded elections? The Supreme Court said that's all right, and, clearly, it's an idea with merit and some success in practice, too. After all, before the advent of soft money in the 1980s, that's how the general election of presidents worked. Bona fide presidential contenders got the same amount of money for the general election, none of which came from private interests. And that was that.

But let's face facts. Voters would never stand for the hefty new taxes that would be needed to expand the system to include congressional elections as well. Indeed, the presidential fund came close to bankruptcy a few times in the past decade because so few Americans were willing to check the box on their tax returns designating a few dollars to help pay for the general-election campaign. This was so even though the tax form made clear that the contribution wouldn't cost the taxpayer a single penny. It's not going to happen.

Besides, is it really such a good idea to close off our policy makers from the influence of outside groups? The world is a very complicated place, and unless self-interested organizations make their cases in Washington, legislators are likely to make unwitting blunders.

The fundamental problem is bigger than politics. The greater issue is the chasm that persists between the haves and the have-nots of our society. And a solution to that nagging problem is well beyond the ken of this limited discussion. Inequity lies at the very core of politics and cannot be wished away. Politics can be defined, in fact, as the constant struggle to find, and then to refind, equilibrium in a system that's always going out of kilter. The money men necessarily and in perpetuity will remain central to that chaos.

So what to do? The easy answer is nothing. But reformers like McCain and Bradley are correct in their critiques. There *is* too much money in politics. At the same time, there aren't many things that can readily be done to correct the overarching problem. Many of the plans that are debated in such serious tones in the nation's capital might never pass muster with the Supreme Court over First Amendment concerns, even if they were enacted into law. And if they were upheld in the courts, they would probably be circumvented as quickly and as easily as the current campaign-finance rules. Windmill tilting makes for frothy rhetoric and attractive campaign-headline grabbing. But the result has been that voters who hunger for change in this area have been allowed to develop unreasonable expectations. They hear the words *campaign-finance reform,* and they see a magic wand.

Sorry.

Still, many people are legitimately upset. They want to do something *big*. So here is my three-point, let's-go-for-it proposal. Now

I don't suspect it will be able to pass in Congress nor pass muster completely with the Supreme Court. But it's close enough for us to dream. . . . A little later in the chapter I'll give you my we-can-really-do-this version of reform.

1. Restrict active campaigning to the two months prior to Election Day

Plenty of other countries don't have America's permanent campaign. Here, lawmakers start to worry about and raise money for the next election almost before they take the oath of office. In Britain, by contrast, parliamentary campaigns last only three to four weeks. In France, parliamentary and presidential campaigns are limited to between twenty and twenty-five days. And the list goes on. Suffice it to say that elections in some very civilized places are confined, often by law, to a relatively narrow period prior to Election Day.

Why should we be different? The reason, of course, is that our many precious freedoms don't allow anyone to dictate to anyone else when or how they can express themselves, especially in politics.

But wouldn't it be great if we could somehow agree that national campaigns wouldn't start until just eight weeks or so before the first Tuesday in November? That would reduce the amount of money that candidates would need to raise and spend. It also would situate the campaign at the time that voters actually begin to think about casting a ballot. To make this happen would probably take a formal agreement of armistice between the candidates and the parties. It's doubtful that it could be legislated. But wouldn't it be a relief if it could happen somehow? I think we should try.

At the same time, you might ask, wouldn't such a time restriction hurt the chances of challengers? Yes, it probably would, since a shortened campaign would help the better-known contender, who in most cases would be the incumbent. One solution to that problem, though, is the following proposal.

2. Force media outlets to provide free television and radio time to candidates during these limited-duration campaigns

Television and radio stations would hyperventilate over the lost revenue, but it makes sense that broadcast outlets should be forced to give free airtime to major candidates in exchange for their licenses to broadcast, which, after all, are granted to them by the federal government. Candidates would not be prevented from buying time on the air, but major blocks of free time should also be provided so that the candidates could air their views when voters are most receptive to hearing them.

This proposal might have another beneficial side effect: There would be less incentive for candidates to subject us to their drivel and empty rhetoric the rest of the year.

3. Enforce the existing limits for contributions to the national parties

Right now, tons of soft money are donated to both the Republican and Democratic parties. These moneys go for all manner of programs and functions related to elections, though not directly to candidates—legally speaking. That obviously is a ruse, though, and should be stopped. The specter of unlimited gifts from labor unions, corporations, and wealthy individuals has severely undercut what little is left of the credibility of Washington and its lawmakers.

Currently contributions by individuals to the national parties are limited to twenty thousand dollars a year, and that restriction was upheld by the Supreme Court. Corporations and labor unions can also give to the national parties through their political-action committees. These PACs can give up to fifteen thousand dollars a year to each national party and to the fundraising organizations for House and Senate candidates.

Like McCain and Bradley, I propose that corporations and labor unions not be allowed any longer to give so-called soft money from their own treasuries to any element of the national parties. (This would reinstate the bans of 1907 and 1947.) PAC checks only, and in amounts no larger than the current limits. And individuals also must abide by the twenty-thousand-dollar ceiling; no more soft money from them either.

I don't pretend that big money would disappear from politics if these proposals somehow became law. The funds would flow directly to the states, many of which have no limits on giving from corporations. But at least one avenue, much abhorred by the average voter, would be blocked.

So much for the tough stuff. A few experts in the field of campaign finance in recent years have started to take a different tack. They have begun to think small. The combination of the Supreme Court's reluctance to permit vigorous constraints on political spending and the national parties' understandable resistance to various types of change has left sparse territory on which to operate with any hope of success. But there's still room to maneuver. This new breed of outsider experts has been toying with a variety of rifle-shot solutions to the campaign-finance problem.

In the spirit of their carefully targeted practicality, I would like to offer a few modest proposals. They don't purport to solve every point in dispute. I'm convinced, in fact, that no such fix exists. Rather, I would like to suggest a handful of ways that aren't on their face unconstitutional and also would improve the current system in noticeable ways.

Call it the no-frills campaign-finance reform plan.

1. Curtail fund-raising by professional lobbyists

One of the worst parts of the current campaign-finance system is that people and organizations that have a direct interest in legislation raise funds for the lawmakers who write that legislation. If the money were put into the pockets of the lawmakers rather than the coffers of their campaigns, the contributions likely would be called bribes. But since the link between campaign contributions and legislation isn't clear and direct, the practice is considered legitimate. It shouldn't be. The trading of votes for donations is what many citizens most despise about what they think goes on in the capital city.

And even though everyone in America has the right to express his or her views, including by spending money to air commercials, that doesn't mean that limits can't be placed on that right. To the contrary, one little-known but widely used brake on the system is a ban on the ability of professional lobbyists to give or raise money during legislative sessions.

At the moment, twenty-two states prohibit such lobbyist contributions. According to the Brennan Center for Justice at the New York University School of Law, in fact, two states, Kentucky and South Carolina, ban contributions outright from lobbyists. Going that far, however, might provoke a constitutional challenge. "The broader the circle of prohibited actors you draw, the more constitutionally suspect the proposition becomes," warns Joshua Rosenkranz, executive director of the Brennan Center.

The advantage of the narrower proposal is that the many hours that federal lawmakers now spend chatting over cocktails or on golf courses with check-toting lobbyists would be reduced significantly. Congress is usually in session all but two months a year, August and December. Such a restriction would cram a lot of fund-raisers into a short time. Probably there would be fewer of them as a result. No loss there.

Oddly, among those who would be most relieved by this proposal are the lobbyists themselves. Even though many make their living by, in effect, buying their way into the offices if not the hearts of lawmakers by raising money for them, the constant pressure to give, give, give and to lean on their friends and associates to do the same has ruined the lives of many professional lobbyists. They would be just as happy for the break. Or, at least so they say in private.

Additionally, lobbyists would be hard-pressed to argue in court or anywhere else that such a precise and simple plan is either unconstitutional or bad policy. No one knows of a successful challenge to any of the state bans. And lobbyists are not like other citizens; they are paid to influence lawmakers, and the danger of corruption is high.

But if there were any doubters, Congress could choose to bar contributions only to candidates whom the lobbyists have the occasion to lobby. Or, lobbyists could be allowed to contribute only token amounts, say two hundred dollars. The Brennan Center asserts that these would be neither overbroad nor unduly burdensome on their First Amendment rights. George W. Bush proposes a narrower version of this plan. So why not give it a try?

2. Use federal regulation of television and radio to compel candidates to debate each other more and to air attack ads less

The most expensive part of any campaign is its advertising. Some fund-raisers grouse, in fact, that they should make out their checks directly to a campaign's media consultants rather than to the candidate committee. It would cut out the middleman.

Surprisingly, the cost of those commercials would be even higher if the federal government didn't require stations to provide low rates to candidates. Under the Communications Act of 1934, broadcasters must sell commercial airtime to candidates for federal office at the lowest available price, known as the lowest unit broadcast rate. Indeed, the federal government has a lot to say about what goes on the public airwaves because of its extensive licensing authority. Uncle Sam ought to exercise that authority in the cause of campaign reform.

Many reformers believe that the government should require broadcast outlets to donate free time to candidates in exchange for their ability to continue to operate under federal license. Among media companies, however, that's heresy. So, in the interest of getting something done, I suggest that gentle persuasion might be enough. I think stations should agree out of a sense of civic responsibility (and out of a fear that they might be forced to do so if they don't comply voluntarily) to provide time to candidates for major office prior to an election. There are dozens of examples around the country where they are doing just that, and to great kudos from the press, the public, and the politicians alike.

My favorite proposal emerged from the Gore Commission, a diverse group that studied campaign-finance reform during the second Clinton administration. The commission, formally called the Advisory Committee on the Public Interest Obligations of Digital Television Broadcasters, recommended that the country's sixteen hundred television broadcasters agree voluntarily to air five minutes a night of candidate-centered discourse in the thirty nights preceding all elections. This so-called 5/30 plan would have stations open their newscasts, public-affairs programs, or other regularly scheduled shows to minidebates, interviews, or even straightforward statements read on the air by the candidates themselves.

The idea is to foster experimentation in programming that would inform voters about the upcoming election by using the candidates themselves. And that's important. Too often, the candidates hide behind their image makers. "At last, here's a chance to break the grip that sound bites and attack ads have on our political campaigns," said Paul Taylor of the Alliance for Better Campaigns. "If every station in the country brought journalistic creativity and imagination to this five-minute fix, television will go a long way toward fulfilling its promise of informing and engaging the electorate."

Taylor notes that five minutes a night isn't much, but it's a lot more coverage than most stations now provide. A recent survey by the Annenberg School for Communication at the University of Southern California found that California television stations devoted just forty-one seconds a day on average to the governor's race in its final month in 1998. And of those forty-one seconds, Taylor said, "just a small fraction was devoted to candidates discussing issues."

That same year, Minnesota provided a model of how to avoid superficial TV coverage of a campaign. A coalition of groups led by the League of Women Voters of Minnesota arranged, among other things, to have the three candidates for governor debate five times on television prior to the general election. One of those debates was broadcast statewide and received a very large viewership. In addition, TV stations in Duluth and Minneapolis also aired two-minute issue statements by the major candidates.

The result: In the upset of the season, Jesse (The Body) Ventura, a former professional wrestler and the Reform Party candidate, won the governorship. His campaign had raised only six hundred thousand dollars, but in part because he was seen and heard by so many Minnesotans, he decisively beat his two better-known rivals. He did this by attracting thousands of new and younger voters to the polls. In fact, one in six votes were cast by people who registered the very day of the election. (More on this below.)

The Constitution prevents the government from regulating what can or can't be said in a political commercial, but some fiddling around the edges is allowed in the public interest. In that spirit, I recommend a plan authored by two Oregon lawmakers, Democratic senator Ron Wyden and GOP congressman Greg Walden. They would cleverly use economic incentives to reduce the amount of negative advertising that airs.

Wyden and Walden would take away discounted ad rates from any candidate whose commercials mention his opponent's name, unless the candidate himself appears in that ad and delivers the attack himself. The choice would be to take responsibility or to pay the price. That probably would go a long way toward bringing much-needed civility into the public debate.

In addition, from the standpoint of campaign finance, maybe a little less money will need to be raised if attack ads are shunned in this way.

3. Demand faster and more complete disclosure of political contributions

The Republican panacea for the woes of campaign fund-raising is disclosure. Just tell everybody who's giving how much to whom, and the voters will decide. As a reporter, I like that notion. I believe that democracy works better the more citizens know. Complete information, or at least nearly complete information, is a prerequisite to good decision making. So let's disclose as much as possible and right away.

The first reform must be that donations be reported electronically to the Federal Election Committee. The old paper method is too slow and cumbersome. Digitizing these numbers will allow the fullest and most rapid dissemination of information.

At the moment, federal candidates can file their disclosure reports electronically, but they don't have to. *The Hill,* a newspaper that covers Capitol Hill, explained in 1999 that glitches in the Federal Election Committee software made it difficult for some to send in their donor lists digitally. But, the newspaper said, those technical flaws are gradually being worked out, and soon nonpaper transfer of information ought to be a snap.

In addition, disclosure should be made within twenty-four hours of the donation. Why wait? And that information should be published in whatever way the public can best and most easily get to it. This would include press releases and, most important, distribution over the Internet. This is one of the most significant and least controversial reforms of an early McCain-Feingold bill and is an element in many GOP reform measures as well.

Governor George W. Bush (or rather his very able finance director Jack Oliver) put such disclosures right on the Bush website. By the next election, no serious candidate for Congress or certainly for president will be able to function without a campaign website with similar disclosures.

But we shouldn't stop there. The Brennan Center, in its guide to drafting state and local campaign-finance laws, suggests slicing up disclosures into lots of digestible tidbits. For instance, lobbyists should be filed in a separate database and on a separate website. In addition, I would like to see lobbyists disclose not just their own donations but the amount of money they raise and from whom. The Brennan Center (and I) would likewise impose separate reporting requirements on government contractors and on groups that bundle checks to candidates. These disclosures should also be available on the Web, of course.

I would also push as far as the Supreme Court will allow disclosure of so-called independent expenditures. PACs already have to say how much they spend on efforts to elect their favored candidates, even when those expenditures are "independent" of campaigns. I think that these disclosures should come more often, surely within twenty-four hours in the thirty days prior to Election Day. This might reduce the number of sneak attacks that often distort the end of campaigns. What's more, to the extent that the courts will permit truth-in-labeling rules, I would require that the purchasers say exactly who they are, rather than, for example, The Committee for Fairness and Apple Pie. We deserve to know who's intervening in our elections.

4. Require lawmakers to disclose donations they received from groups interested in the votes they cast

Nearly a century ago, Senator Robert M. LaFollette, Sr., the Wisconsin firebrand also known as Fightin' Bob, traveled the country and read aloud the votes cast by his colleagues that favored the powerful business interests of his day: railroads, steel manufacturers, and oil companies. This calling of the roll incited public outrage and was one reason that direct corporate contributions were banned by the Tillman Act in 1907. At the time, the votes cast by senators weren't widely known by their constituents.

These days, voters are much better informed. But they can always learn more. That's why I would commend a variation of the proposal offered by Senator Russ Feingold. Feingold, a Wisconsinite himself who possesses more than a little of LaFollette's flair for the dramatic, advocates "The Calling of the Bankroll." This involves Feingold himself reading into the *Congressional Record* the amount of PAC contributions given to members of the Senate from PACs interested in the legislation that the chamber is debating at the moment. He did this during an emergency appropriations bill, a gun-control bill, and a defense-authorization bill.

This might be enough for Senator Feingold, but as a policy it's rather limited. I suggest that the idea be expanded to embrace a bit of disclosure that government contractors already have to suffer when they testify before congressional committees. Individuals who personally or whose companies get grants or have contracts with the federal government must append their testimony before House committees with a list of the amount and source of those federal funds. That way everyone, both the lawmakers and the public, are put on notice about potential conflicts of interest.

I recommend that the Federal Election Commission be charged with exposing similar conflicts on the part of the lawmakers. How would this work? When the House passes an agriculture appropriations bill, for example, the FEC could gather the contributions from farmer- and agribusiness-interest groups and simply list them in the *Congressional Record* next to the vote tally. After a vote on an increase in the minimum wage, a similar list could be assembled that would detail labor-union giving.

This would amount to little more than a gross reminder that industries and unions that have a major stake in government actions play a big role in the elections of members of Congress. That sort of reminder, however, is well worth having at key junctures in the legislative process. A more telling list would be a breakdown of donations made to members of congressional committees that originate the bills that become law. The information would be even more useful if broken down by party affiliation.

In the turnabout-is-fair-play department, a lobbyist who is a friend of mine, Mike Tiner, believes that journalists should be forced to accept a bit of disclosure themselves. Why pick on lobbyists or other players in the political process, he asks reasonably, and then let the press off the hook? Therefore, I happily pass along the Tiner Proposal: When publications or any other media outlet endorse a candidate prior to an election, their editorials should also include, at the end, disclosures of ownership of those media outlets.

Tiner recommends that newspapers list their top ten advertisers. I would also include an explanation of the ownership of the publication or broadcast station, very much like a proxy statement would include the names of the top shareholders of a corporation. Because, let's face it, media outlets are companies, too.

5. Encourage more people to register and to vote

For all the talk about the best government money can buy, the truth is that Americans can choose the type of government they want to have. If they want the government to be led by narrow interests, they can achieve that by doing what they do now, which is not voting in any meaningful numbers. But if they participate in elections by showing up at the polls more often, they can take their government back—no matter how much is spent by any set of interest groups.

That's why one vital campaign-finance reform has nothing to do with either the collecting or spending of election lucre. Rather, it involves getting citizens to participate in our democratic method of government. More people must be encouraged to register to vote and then show up at the polls. If they don't, they will continue to lose faith in their leaders and, eventually, in themselves as a force for progress and prosperity in the world.

Why are there barriers to voting now? Why, for instance, are there rules that restrict registration for voting to only a certain time period prior to an election? The answer officially involves worries about voter fraud and ballot stuffing. The deeper reason, I think, is hidebound thinking and worry by the national parties that if too many people were given the chance to register and vote more easily, they might decide to loosen the tight hold the two parties now have on the political process. I say, Let the voters decide.

In 1999, Bill Bradley made the case compellingly during a major address about the need for campaign-finance reform to the National Press Club in Washington. "In 1996," he said,

> only fifty-four percent of the eligible voters actually cast their vote for President of the United States. That means roughly twenty-five percent of the voters elected Bill Clinton president. In 1998, participation in congressional elections dropped to thirty-seven percent. Is it any wonder that people don't feel Congress or the government reflects them? But it is a two-way street. Only if citizens vote can they take ownership of their government. Sadly, the citizens who vote least—the young, the poor, and minorities voters—are those who are often ignored by the national government. A philosopher I like once said, "Individual rights are a protection from society, but for those rights to have any meaning requires one to fulfill your obligation to society." Voting is the first obligation. Therefore, the goal of democratic reform must not be limited to shutting down sources of money—the goal must be to open up the process, remove the barriers that limit participation, and, most important, give people substantial reasons why their votes count.

Bradley went on to make a set of suggestions that aren't unique to him but are good ideas from any source. I would like to mix a few of his proposals with some others to offer the following set of recommendations:

1. **Allow people to register to vote on the same day as the election.** In the age of computers, this ought to be easy and safe, and it is already being tried in several places. To prevent people from registering more than once, the election results can be delayed until the system does a quick check to see if someone's name turns up twice or more. If it does, those votes would be automatically voided. Problem repaired. Besides, Bradley asserted, "no one should ever be told that just because they didn't get interested in the election until November, they're not entitled to vote."

2. **Permit people to vote by mail whether or not they will be out of town on Election Day.** This is already done in Oregon and with great success. It does make for a longer election season, but at least it's evenhanded. Since the mail-in system was implemented statewide for federal elections in the mid-nineties, Oregon has elected both a Democrat *and* a Republican to the U.S. Senate. What more proof do you need?

3. **Give employees time off on Election Day in order to vote.** Bradley suggests a voting-leave law that would require employers to give workers at least two hours off so they can vote. The mandate can probably be more flexible than that. But the concept is sound and seems like a small price to pay for democracy.

4. **Test both voting and voter registration via the Internet and institutionalize the method if it works well.** Employees won't even have to leave their offices—or their homes—to vote if Internet balloting proves to be possible. Technically, of course, it is conceivable. At the moment, though, there are all sorts of concerns that range from security to privacy to potential voter fraud. There are also a slew of mechanical problems (best left to others to describe) that involve the digital backwardness of state and local governments. Also, it would

probably be a wise safeguard to allow only registration in person on Election Day itself for a while at least.

Whatever we do in the future—whether retail shopping or keeping in touch with friends—will be able to be done over the Internet or cable or some other instant-communication tool. Hopefully, voting and registering to vote will be among the many things that will be part of that growing cluster of electronic connections. Surely if we can buy and then register a car over the Internet, we can register to vote and then actually cast a ballot. It only makes sense that we should harness the Internet in ways that will open our democracy to more and more people.

The one other element missing from campaign reform is money. Not campaign money but taxpayer funds. The Federal Election Commission will need more money to do its job, especially auditing campaigns and disclosing gifts quickly and correctly. Congress shouldn't continue to starve the agency, as it has long been doing.

What's more, the agency should be permitted to integrate the many sources of information that are now available. Kent Cooper, who worked at the FEC for many years, early on saw value in combining lobbying disclosures with campaign-finance reports. He has done a remarkable job of combining these databases since he left the FEC and formed the nonpartisan FECInfo (www.tray.com on the Internet). Cooper was right when he first saw what could be; government, through the Federal Election Commission, should be willing to make it easy for the average citizen to see who's paying what to whom in Washington.

After all, it *is* our government, isn't it?

Acknowledgments and Sources

This book is a stew of my own peculiar views on the world of campaign fund-raising mixed together with some straightforward explanations of how the system actually works. It concludes with several proposals for changes in law, a few of which you probably haven't seen before. Those views and proposals are my own, so don't blame anybody but me for them.

Some of the facts and anecdotes, however, may seem familiar, especially if you are lucky (and wise) enough to be a reader of *Fortune* magazine. I serve as *Fortune*'s Washington bureau chief and have been allowed—nay, encouraged—by my editors to indulge my taste in this book's topic on their behalf. The conclusions reached as part of *Fortune*'s annual Power 25 surveys and *Fortune*'s analyses of presidential-level fund-raising over the past two years inform many of the book's pages.

For the opportunity to write the original stories and to include them in altered form in this book, I gratefully thank and acknowledge John Huey, *Fortune*'s managing editor; Richard Kirkland, *Fortune*'s deputy managing editor; and Susan Fraker, an assistant managing editor who is my direct boss and a truly wonderful editor. Others at *Fortune* who aided and edited my stories include Robert Norton, Eric Schurenberg, Peter Petre, Rick Tetzeli, and James Aley. Thank you all.

A very special thanks to Norman Pearlstine, editor in chief of Time Inc., who has provided me a place to practice my profession for almost my entire career. Norm has topped the mastheads at *The Wall Street Journal*, *Time*, and *Fortune* when I worked for each of those publications and was a major reason I worked at each place. He's also cleared the way for me to write books, so it is with great pleasure that this is the fourth of my books in which I have acknowledged his help and support.

Thanks also to my colleagues at *Time,* including Walter Isaacson, Jim Kelly, Steve Koepp, Priscilla Painton, Howard Chua-Eoan, Eric Pooley, Nancy Gibbs, Dan Goodgame, and Michael Duffy, for working with me on several of the stories that also appear in these pages, especially chapter 7.

At Random House, my champion and able editor has for years been Jonathan Karp. This book wouldn't exist without him, nor would it be as readable. Thanks also to Fred Wertheimer, Peter Bernstein, and Will Weisser.

I didn't write this book alone. My researchers included Natasha Graves, Michelle McGowan, Dusty Smith, Eileen Gunn, Tyler Maroney, Vornida Seng, and Vathany Say. Also thanks to Time Inc.'s library staff. The diligent and excellent copy editor of the manuscript was Timothy Mennel.

My lawyer and agent, Bob Barnett of Williams and Connolly, was an inspiration as well as a valued counselor. Thanks again, Bob.

I would also like to acknowledge the support lent to this project, both intellectual and emotional, by my many friends and colleagues at Fox News Channel, including Brit Hume, Tony Snow, Marty Ryan, Jim Eldridge, Roger Ailes, Kim Hume, Fred Barnes, Mort Kondracke, Mara Liasson, Juan Williams, Rick

DiBella, Susan Buikema, Andrea DeVito, Michele Remillard, Laurie Luhn, Jacqueline Pham, Mary Harris, Jessica Barrows, Patti Worch, Dianne Brandee, Chet Collier, Doug Rohrbeck, and Maya Zumwalt.

I also thank my colleagues at *Washington Week in Review,* especially Gwen Ifill, Elizabeth Bausch, Christina McHenry, Jeff Bieber, and Dalton Delan. Thanks as well to Ken Bode and Elizabeth Piersol.

I benefited from the work of fellow journalists who share my peculiar taste for money politics. These include Jill Abramson of *The New York Times,* Lloyd Grove, Susan Glasser, and Ruth Marcus of *The Washington Post,* Peter Stone of the *National Journal,* and the many hardworking folks at FECInfo and the Center for Responsive Politics. CRP reports were especially helpful in chapter 2. The AARP profile in chapter 7 was aided by two books, *The AARP* by Charles R. Morris and *Trust Betrayed: Inside the AARP* by Dale Van Atta.

And thank you most of all to my loving and understanding family: Esther Birnbaum, Harold Birnbaum, Rhoda Galembo, and my own branch of Birnbaums—Deborah, Michael, Julia, and Emily. Love, as well, to my father, Earl Birnbaum, may he rest in peace.

I raise my glass to you all.

Index

About the Author

Jeffrey H. Birnbaum is the chief of *Fortune* magazine's Washington bureau, where he specializes in covering the intersection of government and business, with an emphasis on the White House, lobbying, and national politics. He is also a political analyst for Fox News Channel and a regular on PBS's *Washington Week in Review.* He joined *Fortune* in January 1997 after two years as a senior political correspondent for *Fortune*'s sister publication *Time* magazine. Before joining *Time* in 1995, Birnbaum worked for *The Wall Street Journal* for sixteen years. His last job at the *Journal* was as White House correspondent. He lives near Washington, D.C., with his wife and three children.